# MANAGING DIVERSITY—
## The Courage to Lead

ELSIE Y. CROSS

**QUORUM BOOKS**
Westport, Connecticut • London

**Library of Congress Cataloging-in-Publication Data**

Cross, Elsie Y.
    Managing diversity—the courage to lead / Elsie Y. Cross.
        p.   cm.
    Includes bibliographical references and index.
    ISBN 1-56720-269-1 (alk. paper)
        1. Diversity in the workplace.   I. Title.
    HF5549.5.M5   C757   2000
    658.3'008   21—dc21        99-040353

British Library Cataloguing in Publication Data is available.

Library of Congress Catalog Card Number: 99–040353
ISBN: 1–56720–269–1

First published in 2000

Quorum Books, 88 Post Road West, Westport, CT 06881
An imprint of Greenwood Publishing Group, Inc.
www.quorumbooks.com

Printed in the United States of America

The paper used in this book complies with the
Permanent Paper Standard issued by the National
Information Standards Organization (Z39.48–1984).

10 9 8 7 6 5 4 3 2 1

# Contents

Contents

# Acknowledgments

A book that reflects on more than thirty years of work and life experience owes much to many people. While it is not possible to acknowledge the contributions of all those from whom I have learned and with whom I have shared this exciting journey, there are a number whose influence, both on me and on the field, has been exceptional. In this brief statement I can only begin to express my gratitude. Many of their names will appear again and again throughout the text.

In my early work in the school system in Philadelphia, Bob Blackburn was a major influence. Mark Chesler's work on racism and education was very important then, and continues to be so today. The founders and early members of the National Training Laboratories were mentors, colleagues and friends, and their work and thoughts have shaped my own. Among the many who should be named here, I will list just a few: Edie Seashore, an early and important mentor; Dick Beckhard, Ken Benne, Lee Bradford, Bob Chin, Bailey Jackson, Hal Kellner, Eileen Lang, Rod Napier, Micki Ritvo, Irv Robinson, Orion Worden. Oron South belongs to this group as well, and deserves special note because it was Oron who was the intellectual catalyst for our publication, *The Diversity Factor*, which remains an important vehicle for sharing our philosophy.

Others to whom I owe a debt of gratitude are people who were especially important as theorists about race, gender, social change and social justice. Alice Sargent's work on androgyny changed the thinking of a whole generation. Kurt Lewin's seminal work on communities, community organization and action research provided a solid basis. W.E.B.

Du Bois, Kenneth Clark, Bayard Rustin, A. Philip Randolph, Angela Davis, James Baldwin, bell hooks and many, many others led the struggle for black equality, both by teaching people how to organize themselves and in providing a powerful literature of liberation. The wealth of writers who conveyed the concepts of feminism provided an intellectual and activist structure within which women could work together for equality. Paulo Freire, Frantz Fanon, Jean-Paul Sartre and Albert Camus helped me think in an international context. Maggie Kuhn's skillful leadership of the Gray Panthers demonstrated the power both of women and of the elderly. Saul Alinsky's radical thinking on how people with no money could nonetheless become powerful—by joining together with many other powerless but courageous people to challenge the entrenched privilege of the ruling elite—was provocative and practical. Gertrude Ezorsky's work on racism and social justice has no equal.

As I began to work more intensely in the corporate world, I was privileged to have as colleagues some exceptional leaders: Gary Parlan, Bob Croce, James Rose, Steven Reynolds, Ben Markham and Terry Larsen, to name only a few.

I owe a debt beyond expression to those colleagues with whom I have worked most closely: Delyte Frost, Jack Gant, John Leeke, Kate Kirkham, Carol Brantley, Bo Razak, Patricia Wilson, Joseph Potts and many, many more who have worked with us over the years. Much of what I describe in this book is the result of our collaborative thinking. Our efforts and energies have flowed into the same stream; it is no longer always possible to differentiate the contributions of individuals from the collective wisdom of the whole. To all who have participated in this process, I offer this text as a tribute.

Most important of all have been the contributions and support of my family, my parents, my brothers and sisters, and my son, Barry Cross. Like all families, we have shared much of both sorrow and joy, and their steadfast love has given my life and work a firm foundation. My debt for the constant love and support of my best friend, Sam Romans, can never be repaid.

Finally, this book would have died aborning were it not for my friend and colleague—and the editor of our journal, *The Diversity Factor*—Margaret Blackburn White. Her patient prodding, creative writing and openness to our work, as well as her own commitment to social justice, have made it possible to bring to fruition a project I have long dreamed about.

# Introduction

Many fine books have been written to help our business leaders improve their skills in leading their organizations. These texts break the tasks down in various ways and provide specific strategies and techniques aimed at enhancing productivity and improving return on investment.

This book addresses the same audience—the leaders of U.S. and global companies and other organizations—but has a different focus and a different mission. My focus is on the new skills that are needed if our leaders are to be successful in managing their organizations at a time of major demographic change. My mission is both to challenge those leaders to have the courage to take the risks necessary to face these changes, and to provide them with detailed information that will help them understand the dimensions of the challenge and acquire the skills necessary to prevail.

## THE SCHEME OF THE BOOK

At the crux of the dilemma created by the major demographic change that is occurring worldwide is the reality of oppression. If people were simply moving around the globe in increasing numbers, and finding themselves equally welcome wherever they go, we would not need to learn to "manage diversity."

But of course such is not the case. Throughout history, in every time and place, some groups have dominated other groups. Differences that are in reality as inconsequential as the color of one's skin, or one's gender, or one's religion, have been used to justify the most brutal and inhumane treatment of one group of people by another. Wars, holocausts, ethnic cleansing, slavery, genocide, inquisitions—all have been the result of human beings' need to define one's own group as "we" and another's group as "they."

Americans are not comfortable thinking about "oppression" as a fact of our own national life. We can state with equanimity that various groups of people in faraway lands oppress other groups in those lands. But it is much more difficult for us to use that term to describe the hateful history of racism in this country. We hesitate to call sexism or sexual harassment "oppression." Even when a young gay man is brutally murdered specifically and explicitly because his murderers hate him because of his sexual orientation, we don't want to think of the incident as part of an oppressive system.

But the realities of change do not allow us the luxury of equivocation. People of color, white women, gays, lesbians and bisexuals, people with disabilities—from these groups is our work force of today and tomorrow being constituted. Already it is a cliché to point out that the white men who have dominated our society and our institutions from the beginning of our national history are an ever-decreasing minority now, in the society, and tomorrow, in our businesses.

So the white men who continue to be in virtually all the top positions in our organizations, and in most of the second- and third-level positions as well, have no choice but to figure out how to have the courage to lead in a new environment, working with people they have little direct knowledge of, and who, at some level, they fear. Helping these leaders come to terms with this reality requires an approach that is different from the linear, "do-this-first-and-then-do-that" style of the typical management text. To find the courage to lead in this new world means that our leaders must gain both cognitive and affective understanding of tough topics: racism, sexism, heterosexism and all the rest.

I begin with the cognitive level. Chapter 1 provides an overview of the organizational development model we call the "Managing Diversity Intervention." The model describes a process that moves through three phases. In the first, or start-up, stage, we identify the problem, collect and analyze data, and provide a diagnosis. Education and awareness follow, and then the model shows how the process leads to organization and implementation of a strategic plan. In the second stage, capacity building, numerous components are added that help the organization begin to take ownership of the process and define its own strategies. In the third and final stage, the intervention leads to a major shift in the culture of the organization, and a new value system and way of doing business is institutionalized.

If a manager or an organization could take this model and use it as a game plan, the book could end there. But the fact is that no one can use the model unless they understand affectively as well as cognitively what the problem of oppression is and how it functions in organizations and society. In our work with companies we spend a great deal of time providing managers with opportunities to learn at first hand—from their colleagues and subordinates who are people of color, white women, gays, lesbians and bisexuals, and people with disabilities—what oppression feels like on a personal, individual level. Since I cannot convey these opportunities in this printed text, I draw on information that is most readily available to me—my own life experiences. Chapter 2, then, is biographical, not because I think my own life is so important, or my experiences particularly different from those of other people of color or other women—but because they are not. In selecting just a few details of my life, I am illustrating the larger phenomenon: the fact that every person of color, and every woman, has had experiences in life that are very different from those of any white man.

Chapter 3 continues along the affective plane but moves from the personal to the societal level. The work we now call Managing Diversity has antecedents in the great social movements of the 1960s and 1970s, especially the civil-rights and feminist movements. These movements created the social climate that made it possible for our society to begin to reexamine our history of oppression, and to pressure our politicians to pass corrective legislation such as the affirmative-action and equal-opportunity laws.

During roughly the same period, the study of group process and personal growth gave us tools that have proved powerful instruments for the work of change. In addition, the field that became known as organizational development or organizational behavior came into being and provided a theoretical base for our work in organizations and culture change.

Drawing all these concepts together, we began the process that I describe in Chapter 4, which reflects on anti-racism efforts, in the 1970s, in various institutions—educational as well as corporate—as well as strategies to reduce sexism and its impact. Eventually the work was pulled together into our core intervention, which we called "Managing and Working in a Diverse Work Force Environment"—a precursor of today's "Managing Diversity Culture Change" initiatives. We were already hard at work on these issues a decade or more before the publication of the Hudson Institute's study, *Workforce 2000*, which alerted the nation to the facts of demographic change.

By the 1980s, our work had evolved into a complete culture-change theory, which had been tested in dozens of organizations. In Chapter 5 I describe how the work was implemented in various organizations, and the ways in which our ongoing practice continues to interact with and enrich the theory base. I also show how our experiences in organizations continue to demonstrate that it is *oppression*, or the impact of racism, sexism and other forms of discrimination, that is preventing U.S. business and other organizations from moving ahead. In spite of the efforts of some to convince us that we are now "beyond race and gender" or that diversity is about "all kinds of difference," this is not what we hear when we are invited to meet with corporate CEOs.

What we hear is still the same message we heard when we began: "White women and men and women of color are prevented from achieving their full potential, and making their full contribution to this organization, by systems within our company that create barriers for them, and enable white men to move ahead." That is the problem we addressed in the 1970s and 1980s—and continue to address in the new century.

Chapter 6 describes an eight-year intervention at "Jaraco Corporation." Jaraco was led by a forward-looking CEO who was willing to make a significant investment of time and money in the effort of changing the culture of the organization. He understood that by continuing to tolerate discriminatory practices in the company he was not only condoning things he knew were morally wrong but was wasting the company's money as well. He was frustrated because even when he was able to improve the hiring rates for blacks, he was not able to retain them.

With our help, Jaraco made progress. Together we learned a lot, we changed many practices, we educated hundreds of people at all levels in the organization, and we began to see evidence of genuine change in the corporate culture.

For a period of time in the early 1990s, the "angry white man" made front-page news. In Chapter 7 I consider the dilemma of white men in diversity work, and challenge the perception that so many are angry. In my experience, many smart and courageous white men have put themselves on the line and helped diversity efforts make progress. In this chapter I discuss some of the contributions they have made—as well as some of the quandaries they find themselves in.

Chapter 8 constitutes a case study of one organization, Philadelphia-based CoreStates Financial Corp, where we worked for more than eight years. Under the direct leadership of our top project manager, CoreStates undertook a thorough culture-change process, using many of the strategies that have become standard practice for us, but also adding numerous elements that were unique to that situation.

CoreStates also was willing to share its processes, the failures as well as the successes, as it went along. We are able to identify it by name because much of what I discuss here is already part of the published record. For their courage and openness, we are much indebted to our partners at CoreStates—CEO Terry Larsen, Yvette Hyater-Adams and many others.

In Chapter 9 I review what we know now about what is required to "manage diversity" and the kinds of academic preparation and training that are needed for those who have responsibilities as executives, managers, trainers and consultants in this exciting and difficult field. I also take a look at some of the ways the work has gone off course, as people with little preparation have been assigned responsibility for guiding corporate diversity programs, and other people with just as little preparation have hung out shingles as "diversity consultants."

In the final chapter I return to the theme of leadership, and speculate on what the future may hold for us as we become increasingly a nation in which no demographic group is in the majority. Are we prepared to lead our organizations to overcome the differences that have divided us in the past, and work together to create the future that we all desire? Or are we facing a period of increasing racial and ethnic struggle and bitterness, with a consequent loss of forward progress and productivity?

Appendices provide additional information. Appendix 1, by our colleague Nancie Zane, describes the impact of our diversity initiative at one firm on the senior white male managers. Zane, with the permission of the company, participated in a number of awareness and action-planning workshops over a period of several months. She reports on individual participants' reactions, and analyzes the metamorphoses that many white men seemed to undergo.

In Appendix 2, our colleague Joseph Potts describes how metrics can serve to further the efforts of a Managing Diversity Intervention. The first part of the appendix describes a particular instrument, the Diversity Assessment Survey, and reviews what was learned when it was used in two companies. The second part of Appendix 2 suggests how managers can use the data from the survey to "carry the message" of diversity concerns to the company.

Appendix 3 is a bibliography of selected resources and recommended readings. The literature related to this field is vast, incorporating historical and sociological studies of the civil-rights and feminist movements, the theories of organizational dynamics and organizational behavior, concepts of group process, and personal growth—as well as the more recent but still voluminous material related to the field of diversity itself. In this appendix I point the reader to a representative sample of materials that provide a basic understanding.

Finally, in Appendix 4, we provide a guide for learning how to talk about diversity. Most of us are reluctant to talk about issues of oppression, especially race and sexual orientation. Our Language Guide provides a way to begin to build confidence around these touchy topics.

Any text that claims to provide "the answer" to the difficult challenges of overcoming our long and bitter history of racism, sexism and other forms of oppression is not to be believed. My goal here is much more modest—to draw on my own experience, the experience of my colleagues, and the work of many scholars and practitioners, to provide a "way in" for those leaders who are serious about changing the oppressive culture and practices of their organizations. Armed with this information, and with their own courage, they can help us move a long way toward becoming a country in which democracy is a living reality.

# 1

# Leadership for Democracy: The Managing Diversity Intervention

In a 1992 address to the officers of CoreStates Financial Corp, CoreStates Chairman Terrence A. Larsen said bluntly:

> It has been painfully obvious this year that our nation has significant areas of utter failure in interpersonal relationships. There is profound inequity, lack of respect, and even deep hatred among different groups of Americans. We cannot be satisfied with allowing CoreStates to mirror society in these vital relationships. We must do better than that . . . we must be leaders.

He continued:

> In the CoreStates I envision, everyone will be treated with respect and courtesy and caring—whether they work at one of our banks or at the holding company, man or woman, black or white, whether staff or line—everyone will be well-treated.[1]

Larsen came to our consulting firm, Elsie Y. Cross Associates, Inc., for help in turning his vision into reality. We responded by introducing him to our philosophy of change, embodied in an organizational-change strategy we call the "Managing Diversity Intervention."

In this chapter I review briefly the components of the intervention. In subsequent chapters, I look at what in my own life experiences led me to envision this strategy, how the theory and the practice grew, and where we are now, as a society and as organizations, in terms of being able to see a time when "everyone will be treated with respect and courtesy and caring."

## THE MANAGING DIVERSITY INTERVENTION

The organizational intervention we call "Managing Diversity" responds to the calls of business leaders like Terry Larsen for help in coping with the demands of an increasingly diverse work force and marketplace. It reflects their understanding that leadership in these changing times demands the ability to provide vision, direction, and a sense of purpose and meaning to the amelioration of racism, sexism, heterosexism and other forms of oppression. These leaders will need to demonstrate courage and to possess an understanding of these issues for themselves—in their personal lives as well as in their professional responsibilities—and for the organizations they lead.

Most of the people leading America's major institutions have grown up in segregated communities with segregated schools. They have had limited opportunities to interact with people from different cultures—people whose first language may not be English, or whose skin color is not the same as their own. Many of these leaders have internalized all the stereotypes about race, gender, sexual orientation and ethnicity that are built into the structures of our society and our organizations. They are ill prepared for the heterogeneity which exists in most organizations today and will surely exist in all organizations tomorrow. The dramatic changes that are upon us are creating an imperative to consider real *integration* of all workers—not as a matter of social justice or civil rights, but as a necessity for survival.

Our consulting firm has developed a model for strategic change that aims to integrate concepts of fairness and equity with the business goals of organizations. "Integration" in the model has a special meaning: to include all kinds of previously excluded employees, recognizing that members of all groups are equally competent to perform the tasks for which they were hired and that all must be treated with equal respect and given access to the power needed to perform their functions. The model aims to level the playing field and help the organizations eliminate the waste of time and money that results when some employees are prevented from making their full contributions.

The following chart outlines the core ingredients of our change model:

**The Managing Diversity Intervention Overlapping Processes**

| Start-Up | Capacity Building | Institutionalization |
| --- | --- | --- |
| Problem Identification | Day-to-day Application | Culture Shift |

| Start-Up | Capacity Building | Institutionalization |
|---|---|---|
| Analysis, Diagnosis and Feedback | Consultation | |
| Education and Awareness | Development of Internal Capacity | |
| | Metrics | Skills and Systems Shift |
| Organizing and Implementing | Organizational Culture Review | |

Each component has numerous elements, which are discussed below. However, several things must be recognized before the model can be understood. It is not a stand-alone gimmick or technique. Using the model requires a deep familiarity with the ways in which oppression and discrimination operate in our society and our institutions, as well as a strong commitment to change.

Further, the model is a guide, not a recipe. Each organization is different, and a strategy designed to ameliorate racism, sexism, heterosexism and other forms of oppression must be tailored to their specific manifestations in the particular company or agency.

However, we have discovered over the years that there are common patterns of the interplay of leadership and the amelioration of oppression, and the model has been helpful as we work with leaders to strengthen their own skills and begin the long process of creating a more equitable and productive organization.

## START-UP

As in any change strategy, the first step is to define the problem. Although, like Larsen at CoreStates, most CEOs request our assistance because they have a general feeling that "things aren't right here," they usually have little awareness of what is wrong or how to begin to make changes. Our first task, then, is *problem identification*. For this purpose we use the ordinary tools of organizational development: survey instruments, focus groups, interviews, meetings with key leaders and with employees at various levels in the organization. Because we are specifically being asked to address issues related to race, gender, sexual orientation and other kinds of difference, we also review equal-employment opportunity and affirmative-action (EEO/AA) data and turnover rates by race and gender. Our teams of consultants spend several days in the organization, observing day-to-day relationships in the work force. We also begin an initial review of policies, practices and systems, looking to see if these give clues why some groups are more successful—and happier—than others.

The collected data are then subjected to *analysis and diagnosis*, and feedback and interpretation of the data and their significance are provided to senior executives and to any committees that have been established to guide the process.

The data are always both unique to the specific organization and strongly comparable to similar data from other organizations. For example, a high percentage of people of color in every organization feel that race has been and continues to be a block to their progress. Many white women, as well as people of color, express concern about opportunities for advancement, the ability to transfer to another job, the likelihood that they will be able to attain their career objectives, and the availability of role models.

Out of the discussions around the analysis of the data, we (the consultants) and the client (the executives of the corporation) begin to agree on a common language for communicating around the issues. Usually, we agree that "diversity" is an appropriate term to describe the issues. However, we make it clear that diversity, in our lexicon, involves dealing with racism, sexism, heterosexism and other forms of discrimination. It must not be used—as it is in some instances—as an excuse to avoid the difficulties. If the organization is unwilling to deal with the facts of oppression, it becomes impossible to move ahead to try to solve the identified problems. So the discussions about what the data show, and what they mean for our work together, are crucial and cannot be hurried.

In the course of these conversations, it becomes clear that managing diversity must be approached in the same way that other organizational problems are dealt with. This systematic approach to problem solving in relationship to issues of oppression is as much an intervention as are other major organizational change efforts, such as quality, leadership, safety or reengineering. Each has a specific business purpose and is expected to fulfill particular business—bottom-line—goals.

In the case of diversity, however, in contrast to other organizational efforts, the intervention requires new strategies because of the history and perseverance of discrimination against people who are perceived as different and often inferior or inadequate. Since the problem is unique, it is necessary that the processes, communications, required resources, designs and special products also be unique, and that they be tailored specifically to the manifestation of the problem in the individual organization.

Moving beyond problem identification, data collection, analysis and diagnosis requires skilled leadership as well as the development of close alliances between the leadership team and the consulting team. The work of ameliorating oppression is, in fact, an exercise in developing leadership. The requirements for meeting the challenge are courage, the ability to access one's emotional reserves, to go beyond the traditional ways of knowing, and to be able to face up to some very unpleasant truths. In order to persevere in the work, leaders must have the capacity for empathy and caring, as well as clarity of purpose, patience and trust in "diverse people." They must be able to endure criticism from their own group, the "dominant group" (in U.S. corporations, white men), as well as from members of "subordinated groups" (white women, men and women of color, gay and lesbian people, and so forth). Above all, the leaders must be able to deal with the resistance that is bound to surface—and, all the while, keep their eyes on the bottom line.

These are not the skills that most leaders have acquired on their journeys to success. Gaining competency takes time, patience, fortitude, professional guidance and the willingness to learn new concepts (such as "group-level issues"). Acquiring these skills inevitably calls into question a whole host of previously unexamined ideas and beliefs—and the changes that entertaining new ideas and beliefs (such as those dealing with the reality of life for women or for people of color) creates often spill over into personal relationships.

Helping leaders as well as the entire work force come to terms with their attitudes about race, gender and other forms of difference requires intensive *education* and *awareness*. A workshop with these goals is very different from the traditional stand-up lecture format that is typically employed in human-resource training sessions. The process must be interactive. The experience and feelings of the participants are the core of the subject matter, and the leaders are called "facilitators" because their role—in addition to providing information—is to facilitate the interactions between participants that allow change to occur.

Generally, the Managing Diversity model begins with a two- or three-day workshop designed for top leadership and selected employees, often from lower in the organization. Because what we are "teaching" is the reality of life for those who are different from the leaders by race, gender, sexual orientation or other components, each workshop must include men and women of color, and white women who are not in top executive positions. A subsequent three-day workshop is often held, which is attended by the same executives along with numbers of their peers—white men, men and women of color, and white women, all from senior levels.

The goals of the two workshops are similar: to gain an understanding of concepts and information about race and gender dynamics in the workplace; to create a climate of legitimacy and comfort in which to discuss these issues; and to understand that differences can either be viewed as *negative*—and thus the basis for discrimination—or *positive*—leading to valuing the differences employees bring to the workplace. The final goal of the workshops is to help leaders develop the expertise required to move the diversity initiative forward.

These workshops are very carefully designed, each element being selected to carry the work forward. Each workshop is guided by a staff of four people, diverse by race and gender. Each session includes lectures that provide participants with historical and sociological facts about racism, sexism and other forms of oppression, as well as with information about how oppression exists and operates in organizations and in society. Experiential activities, including simulations that deal with organizational structure and power dynamics, are used to enable the participants to understand emotionally, as well as rationally, the ways oppression impacts on the lives of their co-workers. Hearing the stories of the many painful experiences that people of color and white women have had—and continue to have—in the organization and in society is a unique and powerful experience for many executives, and often provides the direct motivation for making a deeper commitment to the work. Workshops usually close with planning for next steps and for "back home" relationships.

An important part of the educational process is enabling participants to understand the difference among bias and prejudice, which are negative attitudes between *individuals*; discrimination, which is the ability of one *group* to create barriers for members of other groups based on race, gender or other differences; and systemic or institutional oppression, which is the embodiment of negative practices in the *systems* of our organizations and our society.

The process of education and awareness, begun in the leadership workshops, is ongoing throughout the life of the intervention in many different settings and formats. Eventually, if the intervention is successful, the workshops are "cascaded" throughout the organization and continue to be offered on an ongoing basis to new employees, as well as in refresher courses from time to time for all employees. Further education and training are provided throughout the intervention, in advanced seminars that aim to give participants the specific skills required to work competently in the new, integrated culture.

The final stage of the start-up process is *organizing and implementing* the strategies. In most organizations, a task force or advisory committee is formed to guide the intervention, and a staff is employed to carry out its day-to-day work. It is important that the individuals appointed to head the task force or advisory committee be executives or managers who are recognized throughout the organization as being people in positions of power, whose opinions are important to the chief executive, and whose participation thus signals that management is serious about this effort and expects that it will be treated with equal seriousness throughout the organization. In nearly all U.S. organizations these people are white men.

The task force or advisory committee, assisted by the consulting team, resumes the review of policies, practices and systems, considering them now with the new understandings gained in the education and awareness sessions. Certain policies are apt to be selected for close scrutiny—those related to work and family, for example, or pay equity, hiring and promotions, retention and so forth—since these are the most apt to have a negative impact on members of subordinated groups.

## CAPACITY BUILDING

Before moving on to a discussion of what is presented here as a second phase of the intervention, it is important to point out that these processes are overlapping and recurring. Education and awareness don't just "happen" and that's the end of it. The more people learn, the more they need to know. Policies and practices cannot just be reviewed once and "fixed"—there must be ongoing review, amendment, testing and further adjustment.

However, there is a spiral or additive effect to the intervention as it begins to gather steam. Gradually, as a critical mass develops of people who have been involved in the intervention and have begun to understand the issues, it is possible to move from concept to *day-to-day application*. Managers and employees begin to have the capacity to make critical decisions about how the intervention itself should proceed. As individuals, people begin to develop new observational, managerial and communications skills. With the assistance of the consulting team, managerial teams in various functions or businesses learn how to review the specific systems in their organizations to identify where they may have an impact that is different for some groups than for others.

As this is developing, it is possible for the outside team to provide more advanced *consultation* to the organization. The specifics of the consultation required vary from company to company, but are apt to include team building with departments and advisory committees or task forces. The consulting team may make recommendations for ways to improve or correct policies and procedures. They can begin to teach advanced skills for dialoguing across race, gender and other issues. Further, as managers develop basic awareness of the issues—on both an intellectual and an emotional level—consultants can begin to work with them to identify and acquire the management skills necessary to begin to manage diversity effectively.

As a consulting firm, Elsie Y. Cross Associates, Inc., has one overarching goal—to enable each organization to acquire the skills, systems and processes necessary to fulfill the goals it has established for the Managing Diversity intervention, without our help. Thus at an early stage we begin to work with managers and internal consultants to bring them up to speed on the competencies required for this task—that is, to *develop internal capacity* to carry out the work. To this end we provide train-the-trainer seminars—sometimes over a period of several months—as well as skill-based behavioral training in specific areas such as giving and receiving feedback, coaching senior executives, mentoring, conducting appraisals and so forth.

Another major component of the capacity-building phase is the creation of *metrics* that the company can use to track and assess the impact of the intervention. The use of our standardized instruments allows the organization to benchmark its own progress, along well-defined parameters, in comparison with the same parameters for other organizations included in our extensive data base. Specific measurement instruments are also available to assess progress toward meeting goals, achieving equity in pay scales, and related matters. (For further discussion of metrics, see Appendix 2.)

Finally, in this stage, we assist management in conducting an *organizational culture review*. Our experience has led us to understand that even though it is important to work to achieve continual growth in the awareness of individuals around issues of discrimination and oppression, and to constantly review formal policies, procedures, and practices, it is just as crucial to scrutinize all the other components of the corporate culture. Formal rewards and recognition systems are often places where bias and discrimination lurk. Informal relationships and communication patterns nearly always have the inadvertent result of excluding members of "subordinated groups" while enabling members of the dominant group to thrive—with no recognition that chance conversations at the golf course or family excursions with other dominant-group members create an environment in which their own needs are met and others' are overlooked.

There are innumerable other components of corporate culture that disguise racist or sexist attitudes or procedures. Some are familiar, such as the tendency of certain male work groups to display pornographic art in a laboratory or other work site, thus creating an atmosphere that is uncomfortable if not downright hostile for women. Others are less well recognized—for example, the ease with which a heterosexual man may display pictures of his wife and children in his office, compared with the fact that similar displays by gay men or lesbians of their partners will lead to frowns or even openly hostile acts on the part of co-workers.

Even processes right at the heart of the business operations of the company are subject to racist or sexist attitudes and behaviors. The ways corporate managers make decisions derive from their own experiences—that is, generally a white, male, heterosexual perception of the universe that often takes for granted that competitiveness, aggression and narrow focus are the ideal criteria for carrying out business deals. This perception is not only counterproductive in many U.S. situations, it is quite apt to be *strongly* counterproductive in business negotiations with executives and managers from other cultures.

Even what constitutes success, for the company as well as for individual managers, is based on a white male norm. The unspoken value placed on arriving at work early and leaving late; the status awarded a man because he carries home a briefcase bulging with work; the career risk a parent who puts family before job may take—all are the result not of actual necessity or even positive business value, but of the myth that the single-minded upwardly striving employee is the most useful and meritorious employee.

The most remarkable thing about the investigation of the unspoken and informal norms of the corporate culture is that analysis of them often generates near unanimity *across all identity groups* about which norms benefit or "enable" members of the dominant group and create barriers for members of subordinated groups. Once they have been identified, rationalized and labeled they can begin to be reordered. As long as they remain in the realm of "things we never talk about," they are immoveable—and change cannot occur.

As these formal and informal norms, values and assumptions are identified, a process is introduced by which a new culture, based on different norms, values and assumptions, can be envisioned and implemented. The components of the new culture must be clearly articulated and easily and frequently communicated—just as any new business practices must be. Workshops to teach and reinforce the new ways of working are held at the department and division level. Simultaneously, the review of official policies, procedures and systems continues, and adjustments are made where necessary.

The importance of the continuous interactive process of changing the informal culture while working on altering the formal structures cannot be overemphasized. Many companies have wonderful policies on paper, but lack the support in the informal culture to turn those policies into practice. A good example of this gap between policy and actual behavior is in the area of sexual harassment. Since the law is fairly clear about what constitutes sexual harassment and what employers should do to prevent it, nearly all companies have clearly written anti-harassment policies that are widely distributed to all employees. Nonetheless, these very same companies continue to pay out millions of dollars as the result of successful lawsuits brought by employees who have been harassed. A locker-room mentality does not give way easily.

Over time, however, if the organization's leaders have the courage and ability to stay the course, a *systems shift* begins to occur. Now there must be additional, intensive training for employees in the new skills needed for the new culture. These skills, although initially viewed as relevant only to the diversity initiative, are quickly seen as beneficial in all spheres of management. Often the recognition that the organization has failed to deal with diversity challenges reveals that there is a failure of leadership and "managership" in general. When a manager learns how to create and support a team that is diverse by race and gender—the task of team building in a diversity initiative—she or he becomes better at creating and supporting *any* team. When groups consisting of white women, people of color, white men, gays and lesbians, people with disabilities and so forth are helped to develop collaborative work techniques, the managers who have learned how to accomplish this are better managers— in general. When some employees are empowered, all benefit.

As the new culture grows and the old systems begin to be transformed, it is crucial that the organization continue to monitor the new norms. New leaders must be identified—people who are committed to the culture being created and are willing to undertake the ongoing struggle to understand their own biases and prejudices as well as recognizing oppression wherever it appears in the organization.

And finally, people must be held accountable for the success of the initiative. Every organization knows how to set business goals, and every manager expects to be rewarded or admonished for success or failure in meeting them. When diversity is viewed as a business imperative, the organization will set goals and establish criteria for determining if they have been met—and will make it clear to its managerial staff that they will be held accountable for success in this area, just as in any other.

As the new culture takes hold, it is important that opportunities be created in which individual and group success is recognized and rewarded symbolically as well as monetarily. Just as "employees of the year" are brought to the attention of the entire organization if they meet or exceed sales goals or production quotas, similar symbolic recognition must be awarded to employees who have enthusiastically supported the diversity initiative.

The characteristics of the new culture grow out of the strengths of the old culture, and cannot be prescribed or predicted. However, the following list, developed by one of our clients, is typical and provides a useful glimpse into what such a culture might be like:

- Change is anticipated and created.
- Oppressive behaviors and practices are eliminated.
- Employee involvement is pervasive.
- Empowerment is expected.
- Best human capital is a reality.
- Learning opportunities are requested.
- Leader's importance is de-emphasized.
- Self-managed work teams operate successfully.
- True customer focus is achieved.
- The company gains a distinct competitive advantage.

- The company is regularly benchmarked by other organizations considering beginning a Managing Diversity initiative.
- The company has become a "supplier of choice."
- The company is an "employer of choice" for members of subordinated as well as dominant groups.

In the following chapters, I review in more detail the experiences, philosophy, concepts and methodology that led to the development of this model. Before moving on, however, it is important to stress one additional crucial component—the client-consultant relationship.

Because the Managing Diversity model aims at changing organizational practices that derive from a combination of bias and prejudice at the individual level, discrimination at the group level, and oppression at the systems level, the relationship of the client with the consultant is quite different from that in other organizational-change interventions. The client—the senior executives and managers, who are nearly all white men—will have to undertake tasks that are unfamiliar. These men, by and large, have succeeded by playing by rules that they understand and with other players who are much like themselves, who understand the same rules in the same way. If they defeat or are beaten by other white men, the contest feels fair.

In a new, more heterogenous workplace, the group of people who are involved in the undertaking is expanded and includes members of groups who seem very different from the dominant group. The rules no longer seem clear, and the old strategies for success are called into question. Hearing about how the actions of members of the dominant group have negatively impacted the lives of people they are working with can be painful and disturbing.

It is the role of the consultant to partner with the client to come to terms with these feelings and reactions, as well as with the hard facts of what discrimination and oppression have done and are doing to prevent the organization from being as productive and profitable as it could be. When the consultant is different from the client by race and/or gender, the partnership itself creates both new tensions and new opportunities for growth. When I, a small black woman consultant, occupy a position of equal power with that of the CEO, he may lose his bearings. He doesn't know how to talk to me, how to behave around me, how to lead in accordance with the principles he has asked me to help him develop.

Our task is to come to the partnership with compassion, respect, patience and firmness. The client's task is also to come with respect and patience—and the courage to persevere.

## NOTE

1. Quoted in Margaret Blackburn White, "Leadership for Workforce 2000: The CoreStates Experience," *The Diversity Factor* 1, no. 4 (Summer 1993): 26–31.

# 2

## Behind the Model

The organizational intervention we call Managing Diversity appears, on paper, to be similar to other organizational development strategies. Like quality, leadership, team building, reengineering and so forth, the concepts of Managing Diversity can be neatly organized into charts and graphs that suggest a logical linear progression toward a predictable outcome.

At one level, this is true. Our years of experience in the field have taught us that the reality of oppression in U.S. organizations is very similar from company to company, and the Managing Diversity model provides useful mechanisms for analyzing that reality and helping to change it.

However, at a more basic level, the very rationality of the model is deceptive. No one can understand the "problem" of oppression—which is the problem the model is designed to address—without some first-hand experience of it. The unbelievable pain that racism, sexism, homophobia and other forms of bigotry cause cannot be conveyed by charts and graphs.

But the "problem" *cannot* be ameliorated unless the people responsible for change have some experience of the powerful impact the pain of oppression has, and of its costs for individuals and organizations. As the model indicates, much time and effort must be expended in providing workshop opportunities in which participants who are members of "dominant" groups (whites, men, the able-bodied and heterosexuals) hear the stories of the lives of members of "subordinated" groups and begin to have some awareness of what oppression means in the daily, ongoing lives of those around them.

For that reason, this book must take a different tack than that most commonly adopted for management texts. Since we cannot recreate the workshop experience on paper, we must find other ways to expose the reader to the personal realities of racism, sexism and other forms of oppression.

I have chosen to share the story I know best—my own. My own life journey, as a black woman, is not unique. I have had much good fortune as well as plenty of heartache. My experiences of oppression are in no way completely representative of the range of experiences of racism, sexism and other forms of oppression that exist in society. I share them not because they are so horrendous, or have limited my opportunities for success in defining ways, or made my life miserable. I have been, perhaps, victimized by society—but I am not a victim.

I share my story because it is out of these life experiences that my understanding of the work of Managing Diversity comes. I can conceptualize what is required to help whites and men have the courage to lead—because I know from the inside what the failures of our leaders have cost me, those I love, and all those who are relegated to subordinated status in our society. I also know, because I have been paying close attention, what these failures have cost our organizations and our society.

This is, of course, not the whole story of my life. I have chosen to share those incidents that relate most closely to the philosophy, methodology, and purpose of the Managing Diversity intervention.

## BEGINNINGS

I have always believed passionately in the democratic ideal on which our society is supposedly based. In spite of all its shortcomings, I find the idea that all citizens have equal rights to be the best vision that humankind has come up with. Democracy means to me that all citizens have the right to have equal access to jobs, equal access to the ballot box, equal choice in where to live, equal opportunity to attend any school.

Democracy means that all citizens have the right—and the responsibility—to participate fully in society. We all have the right to be educated for citizenship and the ability to influence the development of the public policy that shapes our lives. We all share equally in the right to seek redress of our grievances and to participate in that "eternal vigilance" that Patrick Henry said was the price of liberty.

These are the inalienable rights spelled out in our Constitution and Bill of Rights. Democracy means that no group has the first claim on them. All citizens—whether people of color or women or people with handicaps or gays or lesbians—are guaranteed these rights by the very principles on which our life together is founded.

What is exceptional is not that citizens demand their rights. What is exceptional—that is, contrary to the democratic process—is that some people have claimed those rights for themselves and denied them to others. What is exceptional is that some people—those who are white or male or straight—have been able to gain access to those rights, whereas others—those who are African-American or Hispanic-American or Asian-American or Native-American, or female, or gay or lesbian—are still barred from full access.

In addition to this belief in democracy, I have always had two other unshakable notions: one, that we are all more alike than different; and two, that I could do and had the right to do anything I chose.

Of course, this belief has come hard up against the fact that other people believe differently. White people have believed that black people (myself included) are not their equals, and have demonized and scapegoated us. And men have believed that women (myself again included) are not equal to them—in spite of all the evidence to the contrary.

Much of my life has been devoted to two tasks: following my own sure knowledge that I could do and had the right to do anything, and challenging other people's insistence that I could not do certain things, and that I had no right to persist in my efforts. These competing forces have been difficult to reconcile and have caused me a great deal of anguish. Both my determination to prove that I could do anything I chose, and the anguish of coming to terms with others' negative views of me, have been crucial in the life choices I have made and have led, ultimately, to the concepts embodied in the Managing Diversity model.

To white people, my history might seem to indicate that I could not think of myself as equal and competent. My father's mother and father, and my mother's grandmother, were slaves at the time of emancipation. They certainly experienced the brutality of that terrible institution, and my grandmother and great-grandmother also bore the brunt of the double degradation that was inflicted on women who were imprisoned in slavery.

But the misery of slavery did not define their lives. They were all quite remarkable people, and the women who were my ancestors, especially, achieved successes that I admire to this day and have influenced my own life.

My father's parents, who had been in slavery on the same plantation, had thirteen children together, many of whom went to college and one to nursing school. They became pillars of the Philadelphia community and an integral part of its intelligentsia.

My father was the youngest of this large family, so by the time we were growing up the family was well established in the community. The members of the extended family were also very influential in the lives of my brothers and sisters and me. I was especially close to one aunt, a schoolteacher, who made sure I was properly educated and also had cultural opportunities, as well as an understanding of social justice and civic responsibility. She was on the board of the YWCA and a trustee of the Presbyterian Church. These aunts and uncles were very active both in the church and in the intellectual life of the community; they sang "on the choir," as we always said, and went to discussion groups and cultural events. My grandmother owned two houses in Philadelphia—and this was before 1900, long before the major migrations of blacks from the South to the North.

My other grandmother, my mother's mother, was a high-school teacher. She was very light-skinned—light enough to "pass" for white, which enabled her to get employment where she would have been excluded had she been seen as black.

Our family life was alive with discussions of ideas, business opportunities, culture, sports. Members of the family played tennis—a game I continue to enjoy—and belonged to black tennis clubs. I remember my father refereeing tournaments in my earliest years.

We often went to visit the grandparents and aunts and uncles on Sunday afternoons, and I remember hours of vigorous discussions of current events. They talked about important black leaders like Marcus Garvey, Frederick Douglass and W.E.B. Du Bois, and followed the various freedom movements closely.

They also talked about the horrible lynchings that were continuing in the South, and recalled the anti-lynching movement that had been organized by Ida B. Wells-Barnett at the end of the nineteenth century. We thoroughly agreed with her statement that "we have come to a point in our race history where we must do something for ourselves and do it now. *We must educate the white people out of their 250 years of slave history.*"[1] That goal—educating white people in order for people of color to realize full citizenship—has remained with me as the organizing principle of my own work, ever since.

So during my childhood racism was always part of the surround, but in my early years, I seldom experienced it directly. What I did experience was community. We lived in a neighborhood in which race—at least for us children—was much less important than how we interacted with our neighbors, whether they were black or Italian or Polish, Jewish or Christian, or whatever. In those days there were many places where people could meet and interact, easily and naturally, and then come back to a family that was there and stable and supportive. Church was one such place; the drugstore another—not just because it sold candy and Cokes and other basic necessities, but because it had a telephone.

Most people in our neighborhood didn't have telephones in the 1930s (our family did, because my father was a successful undertaker), so the drugstore became the message center of the community. We kids would hang around, and when the druggist took a call for a neighborhood resident, he would ask one of us to run to get that person—for which service we would get a nickel. The nickel was important. But more important was the fact that we all got to know each other and each other's families. We respected each other, regardless of race. We knew well enough who was smart, who could play baseball or wall-ball well—but basically we saw one another as equals, equally deserving of a fair shake.

That early experience of community has shaped my dream of democracy. Integration never meant to me that you had to be close friends, or marry each other. It meant that you lived together and took responsibility for each other. Integration in my youth meant equal power—not necessarily equal from top to bottom, but equally meritorious, equally deserving of human consideration and respect. There was always a hierarchy of class, but it seemed to me then that the hierarchy was based on effort and merit. I grew up thinking that if you worked hard and got good grades and did all the things you were supposed to do, you would automatically rise in the world. You didn't succeed just because your daddy was richer than somebody else's daddy, or your mama was white and mine was black. No doubt it was a naive notion, but I believe in it still. That experience of *knowing* that we could live together, with all our differences, and still respect each other and look out for each other, continues to make it clear to me that all the other ways of evaluating one another and treating one another are artificial, undemocratic and just plain wrong.

Now I knew well enough, even then, that distinctions were made on the basis of things that had nothing to do with individual effort. We were far from immune from the prejudice against dark skin that permeates American society. My light-skinned grandmother had her biases. There were certain children we were not allowed to play with, because, in her euphemism, "We don't know their parents." It was obvious to me that all the children whose parents we didn't know, whom we weren't to associate with, were very dark-skinned. And I resented it, too, and often would sneak around and play with those children. I also knew that I was smarter than my friends because my family sent me to a different school—a "better" school—than the one in our neighborhood.

I learned some other things from that grandmother. She was not only fair-skinned, she had brown flowing hair and hazel eyes. Even though she always defined herself as a Negro and lived with us as a member of the family, her ability to pass for white often came in handy. She could apply for a job and be hired without question. She was once hired to run the employee cafeteria of a large department store—a job no Negro would ever have been offered. When she came home we would laugh about it; it was a way of "getting over," of using the system against itself, and we treated it as a kind of joke.

The possibility of passing, the way society treats you when they think you are white as opposed to the treatment you receive when society designates you as black, is a phenomenon that very few whites understand at all—or are willing to admit. To me, the whole idea of passing demonstrates that we really are all the same. It is the perfect illustration of the sordid and insane practice of creating the concept of "race" in order to subordinate other people. It is white people's reaction to the color of our skin—or their imagination of the color of our skin!—and the impact that reaction has had on history, that makes the difference— not our abilities or our intrinsic worth. The ability to pass—not to be perceived by whites as African-American—points out the hypocrisy of white-created racial discrimination. After all, if a person who is in some genetic sense "African-American" can attain the same standards, the same educational levels, the same degree of expertise as anyone else, shouldn't she or he be treated in just the same way? Conversely, why should whites of lesser ability and merit be valued more highly? To heighten the irony, recent studies indicate that a high percentage of those who consider themselves "white"—and participate in white-skin privilege—have African genes. Some historians suggest that the figures may be as high as 75 percent!

Here's an example of how passing operates. I had a first cousin who looked totally white. When he turned eighteen, he decided to go to Boston and live as a white man. We couldn't visit him there—it would blow his cover. And we just accepted that as the way things were. When he came to Philadelphia, however, he always visited us, and was very close to my mother and to the whole family. But he had so internalized his identity as a white person that he, a black man, actually spoke disparagingly to us, his family, about black people, even referring to them as "those people." Ironically, when my cousin developed cancer, it was his Philadelphia family that he turned to for help. When we went to Boston to care for him, his friends were shocked to find out that he was "actually" a black man.

And the same prejudices were demonstrated in regard to me, as well. We went to white schools, and of course from time to time we might be called "nigger." But my mother would go to school and say, "Please don't say those kinds of things to my children. It isn't nice, it isn't proper." My mother placed a high value on good manners and proper behavior, and she was offended by such rudeness.

My firm belief that individual merit would win out carried me through elementary school. I thought school was wonderful and gave it 100 percent effort. However, when we completed sixth grade, a white boy whose marks were not as good as mine was awarded the top prize for

academics, attendance and service. The teacher took me aside and confided in me that the prize had to be given to him because he was a boy—
and, although she didn't say it, I knew it was also because he was white.
I had to settle for second place.

From this point on, my belief in fair play was shaken. I think that was
my first immediate experience of both racism and sexism—and I never
forgot it. It didn't make me doubt that I could succeed in whatever I
tried; but it did let me know that there were others who would try to
stand in my way. It also helped me see that this injustice was not a matter
just of two individuals—it was an entire *system* that conspired to favor
the white child and to put me at a disadvantage, even though the official
representative of the system, the teacher, knew she was participating in
a lie.

Such experiences have made it impossible for me not to see how all
kinds of systems in our society operate in the same way. When I see a
woman in a business meeting being ignored, even when her information
is crucial to the success of the discussion; or a man of color being passed
by on the street as the taxi pulls up in front of a white man; or a lesbian
having to keep her family photos in the drawer while her co-workers
display theirs on their desktops—it is immediately obvious to me that
*systemic oppression* is at work.

During my junior and senior high school years there was a lot going
on that led up to the later civil-rights movements, and we were all tuned
in. By threatening to organize a mass march on Washington in 1941, A.
Philip Randolph, president of the Brotherhood of Sleeping Car Porters,
was instrumental in pressuring Franklin Roosevelt to outlaw discrimination in hiring practices in defense industries and to establish the Fair
Employment Practices Commission. The creation of the commission,
along with the fact that there were labor shortages, began to have some
results in expanding job opportunities for blacks.

Paul Robeson, the great black singer, athlete, lawyer and actor, was
challenging the powers-that-be on government's tolerance of racism and
lynching—for which effort he was rewarded by being investigated by
the House Un-American Activities Committee and blacklisted.

Closer to home, there were groups like the Fellowship of Reconcilia-
tion and the Quakers. Although we were never Quakers, one of my aunts
was very much involved in their anti-war efforts, and she included me
in her activities. I remember being very active in a drama group that
they organized, which had a peace theme—this in a period when a pac-
ifist philosophy was not only unpopular, but suspect.

After the Second World War, many of the black veterans came back
full of anger. They had been forced to fight—and many of them to die—
for a country that continued to discriminate against them. None could
escape the irony of being drafted into a military that thought them quite

good enough to give their lives for their country, but not good enough to serve as officers. Segregation resulted in the organization of whole black divisions, some of which became famous—the Buffalo Division, for example, and the highly regarded Tuskegee Airmen. One of my brothers was an MP in Texas, in an "integrated" division—but the black soldiers lived in segregated barracks. The black MPs were prevented from doing the duty to which they were assigned—when they tried to discipline white soldiers they were threatened or forbidden to act.

When they came home, nothing had changed. Many of these men and women who had served their country were unable to get jobs—or if they did, white workers often protested. The hostility in white communities toward these returning black soldiers was palpable.

I remember one particular drawn-out episode involving trolley car drivers. When blacks were hired for those jobs, there was a white riot. The Pennsylvania National Guard had to put soldiers in the trolley cars to protect both the black drivers and black riders. There was violence and death—white citizens attacking black citizens who were only attempting to claim the rights of any citizen to have a decent job.

Some of the returning black veterans, including my brother, began to organize. I remember spending many a Saturday marching in demonstrations or handing out leaflets in North Philadelphia, protesting the discrimination in employment, housing and so forth.

This was a scary and challenging but also exciting time—and the visionary ideals I was exposed to then have stayed with me all my life. It became powerfully clear to me that, as a group, white people do not really believe in democracy—do not understand or support the founding principles of our society. From the days of chattel slavery to today, white people do not concede to those of us who are people of color the basic fact of our citizenship. If we were thought of as just that—citizens—there would have to be different ways of working and living and relating. There would have to be real attention paid to the meaning of democracy—to the importance of education for all citizens, the necessity of both conflict and consensus, the obligation of all citizens to struggle for their freedom, and the right to organize.

Our leaders, too, if they took their oaths of office and their pledges to uphold the Constitution seriously, would have to completely revise their attitudes and practices. All during my teenage years and early twenties, the presidents of our country were not only not taking positive, proactive stances to uphold and protect the rights of all citizens—black as well as white—they were constantly and consistently using anti-black slogans and racist practices as mechanisms to garner support among white voters.[2]

I was thus very much involved in the struggle for equality, but I was far from radical. I participated in the 1963 March on Washington and found it very exciting and energizing. It gave me a sense of being part of a movement. Like many people, I thought naively that we were on the brink of a sea change—that this vast gathering of people of all kinds was going to bring about the end to discrimination and injustice. I believed that when white people saw this their lives would be changed— they would stop rioting against us and lynching us, and would join forces with us to help the democratic dream become reality.

But it was not to be. One of the reasons we have to spend so much time doing "education and awareness" in our work is that white people have "forgotten" what happened in the 1960s. Now, when I discuss the civil-rights movement—especially as it was portrayed on television— most white people don't have any idea what I'm talking about. They don't remember—or don't want to remember—that it was white people who were creating the problems. It was the white police commissioner Bull Connor of Birmingham who turned the high-pressure water hoses on black school children. It was whites who murdered the civil-rights workers—both black and white workers. It was white governors who refused to obey the law of the land. And it was the white-led Federal Bureau of Investigation (FBI) that entered into complicitous cooperation with these lawbreakers.

The March on Washington, which meant so much to me and to so many people who thought that now—*now*—at long last this country would live up to its ideals and recognize the rights of all its citizens—is barely remembered, or misremembered and romanticized. And its promise remains to be fulfilled.

When we talk about the history of the struggles that women and people of color have gone through just to try to claim what is rightfully theirs, we are often described—critically—as "feminists" or "activists." Our work in corporations has nothing to do with trying to win special privileges for subordinated groups. The work is simply about helping those corporations recognize how special privileges for members of dominant groups—whites, men, straights and so on—are built into the systems of society and organizations. And how, if we learn to recognize them and remove them, we can *all* lead happier, healthier and more productive lives.

## RACISM, SEXISM AND OTHER DISASTERS

After high school there was no money for me to go to college, so I took a job at Sears, working a twelve-hour shift, six days a week. Although our family was middle class, it was a status based as much on position in the community and values as on money.

It's hard for white people to realize how difficult it was for black people to get into and stay in the middle class, financially, just fifty years ago. College education was out of reach of most. And even with a degree, African-American people, especially men, were prevented by overt, deliberate racism and discrimination from moving into the professions. I remember that a close friend of mine dropped out of law school because his class was told very explicitly that only three black men would be allowed to pass the bar that year.[3] Most of the men we knew, professionals with various kinds of degrees, worked at the post office or—like my father—became entrepreneurs in businesses serving the black community. Black women fared no better. Women with degrees often had to take jobs as chambermaids or waitresses, or hire out as servants cleaning white people's houses, or set up businesses of their own.[4] And the situation wasn't entirely different for white women. Even those who had had careers during the Second World War—the Rosie-the-Riveters—had been displaced by the returning (male) vets, and in the 1950s most were only able to work as secretaries and in clerical positions.

I worked hard in that job and tried to save enough money for college. After two years I realized that was almost impossible. My doctor knew that I was determined to get a college education and suggested that I talk to the registrar at Temple University, who was a personal friend. I requested that I be allowed to pay my tuition on a monthly basis, and to my surprise the registrar agreed.

I enrolled in Temple's Business School and earned my degree in two and a half years by taking eighteen credits each semester and attending all summer sessions. To meet the monthly tuition payments I took a full-time job as a file clerk for the Army Signal Corps, working weekdays from 4 P.M. until 1 A.M. The pace was grueling, but I achieved my goal and was confident that my business education degree would open doors for me in the corporate world.

For most women, however, white or black, the career path took second place to the marriage-and-family track, and I was no exception, marrying during my last semester of college. My husband was in the military, and I recall one weekend, before we were married, visiting him at Fort Bragg, North Carolina—my first trip into the South since I had been a small child. When the train stopped in Washington, D.C., the conductor came through and told all the Negroes to move into the front coach—it was the front, not the back, because this was still the day of coal engines, and the front coach got all the soot. I argued and fussed with him, but he—a black man—was matter of fact about it: "It's the law, you have no choice. They're not going to move this train until every Negro's in that front car." That trip to North Carolina was my first real experience of segregation in the southern style—where you couldn't go to restaurants and you had to ride in the back of the buses.

Once we were married we were stationed in Oklahoma, which was just as rigidly segregated. I remember that we used to eat in the drive-in restaurants because we couldn't go to the regular ones—until the owners found out that too many black people were driving up, and closed them. There were two incidents during that time that stand out as especially outrageous. I recall that we went once by bus to Texas to visit my husband's father. Of course there were no bathrooms on the bus, and we weren't allowed to use the bathrooms in the terminals. I remember walking a long way to some kind of barn just to use the toilet. This was a really shocking and humiliating experience.

But the other was downright terrifying. When people from the military base took the post bus into town, the custom was that the blacks got on first and filled up the back of the bus, and then the whites filled up the front. I was on the bus one day, sitting quietly in the back, when a black soldier got on and sat down in the front. The driver started out, but then pulled over out in the middle of nowhere and said, "Nigger, move to the back of the bus." The man said, "I'm not moving anywhere. I'm a soldier and I'm going to sit right here." The driver said, "Nigger, I'm a deputy, and I have a gun. If you don't get up and move to the back of the bus, I'm going to blow your head off." I was scared to death. I pleaded with the soldier to move back, and he did, much to my relief—and shame.

I tell these stories not because my lot was so terrible or any worse than many other people's, but because they were my own experiences, and they weren't so very long ago. When people today tell me that managing diversity is about "all kinds of difference" I just look at them with amazement. Obviously, all difference is not treated the same.

## ORGANIZING FOR CHANGE

When I came back to Philadelphia, my degree in business education didn't open any doors for me. The best jobs I could get were low-level, dead-end positions. For awhile I was the manager of a private Negro business and professional men's club. Other positions I held during this period were as a statistician at a nutrition research laboratory, a social worker for Temple University hospital, an account executive and business manager for a public relations firm, and a secretary for a division of the Presbyterian Church U.S.A. In addition, I enrolled in graduate school and eventually earned two masters' degrees and became a Ford Fellow at the University of Pennsylvania.

Never during all those years—before the passage of EEO and AA legislation—was I able to secure an interview in the corporate world, even though my college record was excellent. When I hear people today imply that EEO and AA provide "special privilege" for people of color (or for

women), I wonder how so many have forgotten that the intent and function of the legislation was remedial—to prevent employers from denying
opportunities to people because of their race or gender.

A friend suggested I take the National Teachers Examination, and I
did and passed easily. I got hired as a substitute teacher in, of all things,
special education—which of course I knew absolutely nothing about.

After one year in that position I was hired as a permanent teacher in
business education, and also became a member of the Philadelphia Fed-
eration of Teachers, the teachers' union. That was the real beginning of
my career. I became an organizer, organizing not only teachers, but hospital workers and other groups. Those were optimistic and exciting days
for the unions; we were all activists and really believed in the power of
organized groups of people.

In the course of time I became the student-government sponsor in the
girls' high school where I taught. This was an integrated but poor urban
school—primarily black, but about one-third white and Puerto Rican—
with an excellent academic program. Somehow the girls knew that I was
really sympathetic to them and cared about what happened.

One incident from this period is especially memorable. The girls were
constantly complaining about the food in the lunchroom, and began to
bring me their plates and say, "Look, Mrs. Cross, there's a roach in my
food." At first I just gave the girls some money and told them to buy
another lunch. But I soon realized that that wasn't productive, so I told
them to show the roaches to the vice-principal instead.

Now the vice-principal was a difficult woman, and this made her very,
very angry. She told the girls just to go back and eat and stop bothering
her, and also told them I was just doing this to upset her.

Well, that did it. We had a meeting with all the student-government
representatives, and the girls decided to boycott the lunchroom. I told
them they had to discuss the plan with their parents and bring notes
with their parents' permission to take this action.

The boycott worked beautifully. By the second day, not one student
bought food in the lunchroom. They all came in and sat down, and were
very, very quiet and well behaved. Some had brought food from home
and shared it with those who didn't have anything to eat. It was a moving and beautiful scene—all these girls quietly and respectfully refusing
to eat filthy food.

So what happened? The principal and the vice-principals went into
the lunchroom and told the girls that if they didn't buy lunch, they
would be suspended, they wouldn't get their diplomas, they wouldn't
be allowed to graduate. But the girls wouldn't back down.

I went and asked the principal if he had informed the superintendent
of what was going on—as he was required to do. And of course he
hadn't. Somehow the television stations and the newspapers found out,

and they were on the scene in five minutes. This was during a period when the media were creating an image that there was lots of student dissent and disruption—though I never saw much evidence of it—so the news organizations were always on the alert for incidents.

The next morning, a large team of people from the superintendent's office came and inspected the lunchroom. When they discovered that it had never been cleaned in the 110-year history of the school, they closed it and refurbished it completely, and six months later the girls had clean food to eat in a sanitary environment.

That incident and others like it eventually led to my being invited to become a member of a team working in the Office of Integration and Intergroup Education for the school district. Eleven field agents were appointed—all chosen because they were committed to equality, social change and excellent education.

It is important to note here that the city of Philadelphia at that time was led by a remarkable white man, Mayor Richardson Dilworth. He was one of the first of a number of white men I have worked with and for throughout my career who have helped me understand that even though they may be the recipients of the *benefits* of racist and sexist discrimination, white men also have the power to confront discrimination—they have the courage to lead, in the face of overwhelming opposition. Many white men who head up our major institutions, in my personal experience, understand clearly how the systems they lead perpetuate these injustices, and they have committed themselves to trying to resolve the problems.

Mayor Dilworth was one of these men. He was a patrician, a member of an old and wealthy family, but he had wonderful, humanistic instincts. He was a Democrat in the Roosevelt tradition—maybe even more genuine in his caring than Roosevelt. He understood racism, and he knew that dismantling it would require risk and effort and time. He hired Mark Shedd, a real progressive, as superintendent of schools. And Mark hired a man named Bob Blackburn to start the Office of Integration and Intergroup Education, to begin a process of eliminating racism in the school system.

When I hear people today talking about "starting" dialogues on race I just shake my head. The Office of Integration and Intergroup Education was running dialogues, and a whole lot more, *thirty years ago!* It's hard not to be cynical when there has been so little progress in so much time.

Part of the training that the field agents received for that position was taken at the National Training Laboratories (NTL). The exposure I received there to the work of Kurt Lewin on communities and community organization, force-field analysis and systems theory, as well as to the laboratory method and the T-group, provided the basis for the strategies that would eventually become our theories of diversity culture-change.

(The theories are outlined in the following chapter.) I also attended a summer institute at Cornell University's School of Labor and Industrial Relations, where I met Saul Alinsky, the famous organizer, who was also a major influence on my thinking. Another important influence was my participation in the A. K. Rice Institute at Tavistock. "Tavi" work, which focuses on issues of power and authority, has provided me and many of my colleagues with a sound conceptual basis for our analysis of the structures of organizations and society.

Eventually, the efforts of the Office of Integration and Intergroup Education and its progressive superintendent, Mark Shedd, became too threatening to the power structure. Mayor Dilworth was no longer in office. The superintendent was fired. The two men at the head of the office, Marcus Foster and Bob Blackburn, resigned (Marcus was later murdered by the Symbionese Liberation Army; Bob was shot, in Oakland, California, but not killed), and it was clear that this was no longer a healthy place to work. I, too, resigned, and went back to graduate school on a Ford Fellowship in Educational Administration.

My experiences during these years taught me some sobering lessons. I recognized that oppression is neither random nor unintentional. Whenever an effort gets too close to changing the balance of power in society (or in organizations), the forces in support of the status quo circle the wagons and the enterprise is eliminated. This is a difficult lesson for the leaders of organizations who are committed to managing diversity and opening closed corporate cultures. They are nearly always unprepared for the resistance their efforts engender. The Old Boys' Club, when slighted or threatened, often turns even on one of its own—openly, if the balance of power permits; or by subterfuge, if necessary.

During the next few years, I was doing a lot of things simultaneously: graduate school; training at NTL; a brief stint as a member of the faculty of a graduate program. For about two years I consulted in Europe, for the International Institute for the Management of Technology, in Milan; and also consulted to organizations in Barbados and Jamaica.

I began to realize that what I had been learning, in life, in school, and especially at NTL and other training programs, was coming together around a common theme—how to help other people gain the courage and the expertise that would enable them to break down the barriers of racism and sexism and begin to create more equitable and integrated organizations.

## LIFE IN CORPORATE AMERICA, CIRCA 1970

While I was working overseas, I suddenly realized that there were many ways to apply what we were doing there to situations that happened every day in the United States. It's important to remember what was going on in companies in the 1960s and 1970s.

As a result of the civil-rights movements and the ensuing affirmative action and equal employment opportunity laws, white women and people of color had begun to be hired in larger numbers. Affirmative action had pried open the doors of some of the graduate schools, and for the first time significant numbers of women and people of color were graduating from engineering and business schools and presenting themselves to corporate America, which could no longer simply refuse to consider them.

A number were hired—some as tokens, and these failed; and some as "onlys," and many of these, too, did not succeed. The companies that took any positive steps at all attempted to assimilate the new workers into the workplace, to teach them how to act like and—as much as possible—look like white men. There were actually courses that taught "etiquette" to blacks. Having been raised by a mother who was a stickler for proper manners—who had no qualms about lecturing bigoted people on their rudeness—I always found this as much amusing as degrading.

One of my first consulting positions was with a prestigious research laboratory. A few women, mostly white, had somehow managed to get hired into this bastion of male science. The harassment these women received was brutal. It got to the point that, just to protect the women's physical safety, the company resorted to cutting windows in the doors to the laboratories and offices, so that the behavior taking place inside would be visible to people passing by. Another firm, an international oil company with a large refinery, hired a few women supervisors and assigned them to work out in the refinery yards. When the women went up the ladders that surrounded the oil tanks, the men in the crews would remove the ladders, leaving the women stranded—and then heckle them from the ground. They would disable their emergency telephones so they couldn't call for help. Women were often physically abused and even raped out in those lonely areas.

Another situation was even more egregious. We were working with a governmental authority where women had to go through the union hall to be hired for shift work. It was common knowledge in that agency that just to have a chance at a job—to get the first interview and to be hired—a woman had to have sex with the men. And once hired, in at least one area, it became standard operating procedure for these women to "service" the men on the night shift. They didn't have to do the work for which they were hired, as long as they provided these sexual services. It's hard to understand now, from this distance, why these women endured this treatment. But they needed the work, and they felt that it was the only way they could keep their jobs. Often they were supporting families, either as single parents or as partners with husbands who were in low-paying jobs. It was kind of high-class collusion—but it's hard to blame them. What finally broke this particular scheme open was that one of the black women became so incensed at her supervisor—not about the sexual favors, but about having discovered that he was stealing postage, of all things—that she reported him. And in the course of looking for the missing postage the inspectors discovered the other shenanigans as well.

These were not only incidents of racism and sexism and sexual harassment, they were safety issues as well. It was not "diversity" at that time. It was people's lives and health at stake. And the companies began to see they had a real—not a public relations—problem. When an investment had been made in hiring a well-paid woman scientist, it became overly expensive to be forced to replace her simply because the men had made her life miserable.

And there were direct costs as well. Early on, the parent company of the laboratory that had to cut holes in its doors was hit with a $50 million consent decree because of its discrimination against women, especially African-American women. This was the biggest consent decree ever awarded to that date, and it signaled to all of corporate America that the Equal Employment Opportunity Commission (EEOC) was going to be serious about this stuff.

So this was the climate that existed in the United States in the 1960s and early 1970s. By the time I completed my European assignment, some U.S. companies had admitted they had to do something, and had turned to people like the founders of NTL and other organizational development (O.D.) consultants and trainers for assistance.

## HOW I GOT INTO THIS BUSINESS

My first assignment in corporate America was in the research laboratory mentioned earlier. Along with other consultants, I worked there for eight or ten years in a program we called "Men and Women in the Work Environment," an effort focused on the white-male senior leaders. We also did team-building and development programs for women and people of color, and a program on power issues for the senior-level women.

Most of the people in these early sessions were white, but since we also required that there be a racial mix, the company would "import" people of color from lower levels of the organization. We were dealing primarily with issues of power and leadership, but there was no way we could avoid addressing the issues of sexual harassment, sexism and racism that were so obvious and so raw. We did an early version of the work that was later incorporated in our managing diversity culture-change efforts. We did standard team-building sessions, but added race and gender as components. We used our laboratory education processes in the training—a dramatic contrast to the standard stand-up lecture format that still dominated the training field. We began to experiment with processes that addressed change at the systems level and to incorporate strategic planning around these issues. We also began to understand more about the necessity of data collection and the ways that the general principles we used could be tailored to meet the specific needs of various organizations.

These years were very busy and very rich for me. In addition to corporations, I had a number of public-school districts, universities and federal agencies as clients. I was a consultant in a program in Jamaica for NTL that trained Caribbean men and women to be trainers and consultants. I did a couple of programs in conjunction with Harvard University—one on human sexuality, in Cleveland, Ohio; and another as part of an international development effort on women in development. We also did some training with the Teacher Corps.

All of this experience reinforced my belief that the ideals of our democracy had not been achieved but were achievable, and I began to be clearer about what practices and strategies were most successful in making progress toward the ideal.

In the following chapter I look at some of the theoretical bases upon which we were drawing in these years, as well as the larger historical setting within which the work was taking place.

## NOTES

1. Darlene Clark Hine and Kathleen Thompson, *A Shining Thread of Hope: The History of Black Women in America* (New York: Broadway Books, 1998), 198.

2. See Kenneth O'Reilly, *Nixon's Piano: Presidents and Racial Politics from Washington to Clinton* (New York: The Free Press, 1995), for a chillingly thorough, step-by-step account of this process.

3. It's ironic that when quotas were openly used to limit the numbers of blacks—and Jews—in educational institutions and employment there was no outcry. Now, when organizations attempt to target recruiting so that their workforce numbers reflect the numbers of workers of all groups available in the population, there is a vociferous outcry of "unfair quotas."

4. For a fascinating account of how black women have met the challenges of racism and sexism over time, see Hine and Thompson, *A Shining Thread of Hope.*

# 3

## Managing Diversity: The Beginning of a Theory

During the 1960s and early 1970s, the United States went through a period of major social change. African Americans organized more effectively than ever before to claim their civil rights. Women began to work together to push for equal opportunity. And the debacle of the Vietnam War called Americans of both genders and many races—especially young Americans—into the streets to protest what was widely regarded as a brutal and racist enterprise.

It is not possible to understand the movement that came to be known as Managing Diversity in the late 1980s and 1990s without recognizing the impact of this earlier era. In this chapter, I review four streams of thought and action that gradually came together to create the body of practice that has informed my work and the work of many other professionals: the civil-rights movements; the feminist movement; the evolution of organizational development as a theoretical and practical field; and the rise of personal growth and group process as legitimate areas for study and practice.

### THE CIVIL-RIGHTS MOVEMENT

On May 17, 1954, the Supreme Court of the United States ruled, in *Brown v. Board of Education of Topeka*, that segregated public schools were inherently unequal and in violation of the Fourteenth Amendment—thus overturning the 1896 ruling, in *Plessy v. Ferguson*, that schools should be "separate but equal."

On December 5, 1955, Rosa Parks refused to give up her seat on a Montgomery, Alabama, city bus to a white man.

And on September 9, 1957, President Dwight Eisenhower signed the first civil-rights legislation since Reconstruction.

These and many, many more actions and events changed the course of history. It is not possible to convey in a brief overview their significance to the nation, nor the enormously complicated, laborious, frightening and dangerous processes that produced them and gradually began to lighten the load of oppression.[1] What I want to consider here is the impact these and subsequent events had on the many people, both black and white, who were encouraged by the tenor of the times to feel that progress toward the fulfillment of the democratic dream was a real possibility.

The struggles of the 1950s and 1960s not only had an immediate impact on my life and the lives of my friends and family, they became the bedrock on which the theory we later called Managing Diversity was created. These struggles and the continuing patterns of discrimination and oppression in our society are indelibly etched in my consciousness. It is these memories and constant reminders that make me cringe when I come across strategies that are proposed as addressing "diversity issues" in organizations, but frame them in vague cross-cultural terms. The idea, popular in many so-called diversity initiatives, that if we just "celebrate our diversity" we will accomplish our goals, sets my teeth on edge. The notion that confronting oppression in organizations "creates division" and "stirs up dissension" demonstrates to me that the organization has not even begun to acknowledge that the divisions are there, have always been there, and have always operated to the detriment of people of color, white women and others who are not members of the dominant group. The initiative does not engender the dissension—it simply allows those who bear the brunt of discrimination to tell about their experiences and point out to the organization what changes it would need to make to enable them to overcome the barriers that prevent them from doing the jobs for which they have been hired.

Managing diversity, as we envision it, helps tensions surface so that a less tension-filled culture can be created. If we could arrive at a time and situation in which all employees are integrated in the organization, everybody has equal access to all facets of the life of the company, and no one group has the right or the ability to create policies and practices that enable members of that group to get ahead at the expense of everyone else—*then* we would have a reason to celebrate. But not before—and not soon.

Apparently, white America at the end of the twentieth century has largely forgotten those struggles that people of color and white women carried out so valiantly at mid-century. The small gains made then are magnified in the mind of the majority into a belief that the battle has been won. So it is important to review the historical record once again—and once again I must draw on my personal experience.

In my own development, I was not only following the civil-rights movements closely in the news, I was deeply involved in actions closer to home. I bought a house in the West Mount Airy section of Philadelphia, a community that was working hard to become and remain integrated.[2] I was intensely engaged in my work with the school system and the teachers' union, and with the student protest movements. And like so many others, I was reading avidly, trying to clarify for myself how we had come to the position we found ourselves in, what political processes could be used to turn things around, and how our situation fit into worldwide systems of oppression, especially of blacks. I read works such as Frantz Fanon's *The Wretched of the Earth* and *Studies in a Dying Colonialism*, which helped me understand how the colonial expansion of the past centuries had enabled the white race to empower itself and keep the masses of people of color around the globe in subservient roles.[3] Brazilian educator Paolo Freire's *Pedagogy of the Oppressed* helped me understand how education could be used for liberation, rather than for the continuing transmission of the message of domination.[4]

An especially important resource for me in my work with the school system and the teachers' union was the thought of Saul Alinsky. Alinsky's ideas on using the power of organized groups of ordinary people to counter the moneyed influence of the powerful few, although based primarily on his work with white ethnic minorities, resonated closely with our attempts to create a forum where the voices of black students, parents and teachers could be heard.[5]

And of course we were reading the African-American writers and scholars such as James Baldwin and W.E.B. Du Bois who were helping blacks recognize that we came from a noble and proud heritage, and that we deserved and could gain a noble and proud future. John Hope Franklin (who was much later, in 1996, to be appointed chair of President Bill Clinton's commission on racial dialogue) was an important contributor, as was psychologist Kenneth Clark, whose studies of the devastating effects of prejudice on children of color were powerful arguments for overturning the old "separate but equal" ideologies.[6] We read the existentialists—Jean-Paul Sartre, Albert Camus and the others—who helped make the case for the worth and dignity of each human being, even while underscoring the ways in which society as it was currently structured systematically destroyed possibilities for happiness for so many.

Much of the theory we read we were also attempting to immediately translate into practice. Mark Chesler, who has continued to do research, provide training, and publish in these fields, was an early ally when he was working under grants from the U.S. Office of Education to develop manuals on school desegregation and many other areas.[7] Chesler and other colleagues held retrieval conferences at the University of Michigan that enabled us to pool our experience as we struggled to find solutions to the new challenges posed by the desegregation movement. The issues we were dealing with in these years were the same ones we continue to confront as the century draws to a close: How can the white majority be convinced to change its attitudes and practices? Another theorist and practitioner who has been steadily working away at these concerns is Clayton Alderfer, whose works began to create a bridge from an understanding of how racism and other forms of oppression function in society to how they function in organizations—and to develop systematic strategies for changing these patterns.[8]

So there was a great deal of intellectual effort and practical activity going on, all over the country, which was taking the energies of the more visible aspects of the civil-rights movement and applying them in a quieter way to many, many aspects of life.

We cannot fail to take note of how dangerous many of these efforts were. Racism in this era was anything but subtle. Even presidents such as Dwight Eisenhower and John F. Kennedy, who were far from committed to the rightness of the cause, were forced to call out federal troops to enforce the new laws and keep the peace. A fourteen-year-old boy from Chicago, Emmett Till—who had nothing at all to do with the movement—was lynched in Mississippi for allegedly whistling at a white woman, and his murderers were acquitted by a jury in a state courtroom. In 1963, NAACP leader Medgar Evers was assassinated in the driveway of his Jackson, Mississippi, home. In 1964, three young civil-rights workers—Michael Schwerner, Andrew Goodman and James Chaney—were murdered in the same state. Freedom marchers and demonstrators were not only not defended by elected officials in Mississippi, Alabama, Georgia and elsewhere—they were violently attacked by people such as Birmingham Police Commissioner Bull Connor, who used nightsticks, police dogs and high-pressure fire hoses on peaceful protesters including groups of children.

Remember that all of this vicious violence was taking place not under some repressive dictatorship, but in the country that has always held itself up as the beacon of democracy—the "sweet land of liberty." These brutalized children and adults, blacks and whites, were *citizens* of this nation. Our society, sanctioned by our elected leaders, was allowing our brother and sister citizens not only to be denied their basic, constitutionally guaranteed rights, but to be harmed and even murdered with impunity.

Painfully, slowly, bit by bit, the federal government was forced by the blatantly brutal repression in the South to pass some legislation. In 1961, the Interstate Commerce Commission created regulations prohibiting discrimination in interstate travel—no longer would blacks have to change cars in Washington, D.C., when traveling to the South. In 1963, President Kennedy established the Committee on Equal Employment Opportunity. In 1964, President Lyndon Johnson declared a war on poverty and created a whole slew of social programs—the Job Corps, Neighborhood Youth Corps, VISTA, Head Start, Upward Bound, the Community Action Program and more. He also pushed through a reluctant Congress the Civil Rights Act of 1964, which prohibited discrimination based on race, gender, national origin and religion in many sectors: public accommodations, employment, education, and federally assisted programs. The Voting Rights Act of 1965 eliminated the poll tax. In 1968, the Fair Housing Act prohibited race discrimination in housing and real estate.

While progress was being made on the legislative front, two other forces were working to keep the nation's emotions stirred up and prevent change. Even while the Executive Office was creating progressive legislation, its own FBI was carrying out massive surveillance and harassment of civil-rights leaders; and conservative politicians, elected officials and law-enforcement agencies all across the country continued or stepped up their brutal and racist practices. In March 1965, a peaceful civil-rights demonstration in Selma, Alabama, was repressed with such violence that the day became known as Bloody Sunday. At the same time, blacks were erupting into the streets in city after city across the United States—New York, Rochester, Newark and other cities in New Jersey, Philadelphia, Chicago, Detroit. Embittered black leaders began issuing calls for revenge or for separatism, and the movement that became known as Black Power was born.

In the space of just a few years, violence took its toll of leaders, black and white alike: John Kennedy, Martin Luther King Jr., Malcolm X and Bobby Kennedy were all assassinated. In 1968, President Johnson established the national Commission on the Causes and Prevention of Violence, headed by Governor Otto Kerner of Illinois. The Kerner report concluded that the nation was "moving toward two societies, one black, one white—separate and unequal," and called for sweeping reforms in the areas of employment, education, welfare, housing, news reporting and law enforcement. The president ignored the report.

Why rehash this history now? I contend that it is impossible for anyone to deal with diversity in our organizations and our society without being in possession of the hard facts about how our country has dealt with diversity in the past—and continues to address it today. In a study published in 1997, Kinder and Sanders analyze some thirty years of survey data on racial attitudes and policies in the United States, and conclude that although the old bad days of legal discrimination and overt, violent brutality have receded, the negative attitudes that inspired these policies and behaviors have changed very little.[9]

For anyone to attempt to lead diversity training or develop a strategic initiative around diversity issues without having these facts on the table is foolish. Our history is not only real, it is alive today—in the memories of some, in the attitudes and behaviors of many, and in the policies and practices that affect us all.[10]

The Civil Rights Act of 1964 represented a leap forward in the always ambivalent record of legal redresses for the legacy of slavery. That ambivalence is evident at every stage. For example, the Emancipation Proclamation, which freed African Americans from legal slavery, was signed by President Abraham Lincoln, who could say both "If slavery is not wrong, nothing is wrong" and "I am not, nor have ever been, in favor of bringing about in any way the social and political equality of the white and black race—I am not, nor ever have been, in favor of making voters or jurors of negroes, nor of qualifying them to hold office, nor to intermarry with white people."[11] Legislation after the Civil War was excruciatingly slow in promoting either social or political equality—only political expedience or, in some cases, the sheer undeniable weight of morality, forced white politicians to move. And the gains made by African Americans after the Civil War were inexorably eliminated by the powerful regressive forces of Reconstruction—to the point that, as the twentieth century closes very few whites and many blacks do not even know about the many blacks who were elected to office, who became successful businesspeople and professionals, who bought and lived in good houses in good communities, and so forth.

So the legislation of the 1960s was not another step in a slow but inevitable march toward democracy; it was yet another effort to push back the forces of oppression. The 1964 legislation contained a very important provision, Title VII, which prohibited discrimination on the basis of race, sex, and other criteria—and provided modest remedies for those who continued to be shut out. Almost immediately the Equal Employment Opportunity Commission was flooded with complaints. The goals of the commission and its enforcement division were primarily focused on numerical targets, particularly on hiring. Gertrude Ezorsky, in her excellent study *Racism and Justice*, lays out the significant differences between individual, or overt, racism, and institutional racism: "Institutional racism occurs when a firm uses a practice that is race-neutral (intrinsically free of racial bias) but that nevertheless has an adverse impact on blacks as a group."[12] As Ezorsky shows, the legislation related to overt racism provided remedies in the form of complaints—by individual victims—about specific incidents of exclusion based on race. Such complaints are important, but have very limited value. Complainants are often labeled troublemakers, and even if the complaint is sustained their careers are ruined. Further, the complaint must prove that the employer acted specifically out of racial bias—a charge that may be self-evident to all involved but nonetheless impossible to prove. The same kinds of problems exist when the complaint relates to discrimination in housing or in education.

Recognizing that individual complaint-based remedies were very limited in their ability to reduce discrimination, the legislation also provides an active measure to reduce discrimination—affirmative action. Laws regarding affirmative action aim to significantly increase the recruitment and promotion of minorities by various means. The legislation recognizes that racist practices in segregated education; housing discrimination; last-hired, first-fired policies of employers; exclusion of blacks from white society where personal connections to jobs are made; and the refusal of unions and firms to train black youths, create the realities of a work environment where blacks remain clustered at the bottom of the occupational ladder and among the unemployed.[13] The laws aimed to diminish these effects by moving the black work force toward approximate statistical parity.

In my practice I have seen both the impressive advances that the equal-employment opportunity/affirmative action (EEO/AA) legislation has enabled, and the multitudinous ways in which employers, co-workers and society have conspired to slow or stop such progress. The enduring existence and power of racist attitudes and institutional racism are much in evidence in the attacks on and reversals of affirmative action in the late 1990s—a topic to which I return in a later chapter.

## EQUAL RIGHTS FOR WOMEN

Even while deeply immersed in the civil-rights movement, I, along with many other women, became increasingly uncomfortable with another arena of discrimination. Although women played important roles in the movement, the leaders were almost exclusively men. Black men were not particularly sensitive to the irony that while they were working for equal rights for all races, equal status was also being denied to women. This situation was not new. The Fourteenth and Fifteenth Amendments, which gave the vote to men of color, were ratified (though not widely enforced) in the nineteenth century. It was not until 1919 that a reluctant Congress, forced to recognize the contribution of women in the war effort, proposed the Nineteenth Amendment. With its ratification in 1920, it removed the injustice of limiting suffrage on the basis of sex.

As I began to consult to organizations, I became increasingly aware of the discrimination and outright abuse that women—of all races—suffered. So the work of contemporary feminists became extremely important to me and to our efforts. Simone de Beauvoir's early work, *The Second Sex*, and Betty Friedan's *The Feminine Mystique* were helpful in analyzing the history and psychology of the roles of women, as well as the ways that second-class status had been built into the structures of society.[14]

These and other feminist writers were enormously important, both to those of us working in the fields of social justice and equal opportunity, and to the lives of a whole generation of women. Although the feminist imagination was primarily focused on the situation of white women, it was also important—up to a point—for women of color. One vital and practical result of the feminist movement of the 1960s was that women were included in the equal employment opportunity legislation. In fact, as Clare Swanger points out, of the flood of complaints that were filed in the first two years of the EEOC's operation, roughly 25 percent were filed by women.[15] The National Organization for Women (NOW) was organized in 1966 and has provided leadership and direction for the movement since that time.

Of more immediate importance to my own work, however, was the research and writing of my friend, Alice Sargent. Although her contributions were cut off by her early death from cancer, Sargent's ideas about androgyny confirmed my own experience and gave me a foundation for developing educational strategies to help organizations confront endemic sexism. These concepts were spelled out first in *Beyond Sex Roles* and later in *The Androgynous Manager: Blending Male and Female Management Styles for Today's Organization*.[16] Androgyny—which basically means that we all have both male and female traits and characteristics—is a simple, almost self-evident concept, but it had a powerful impact. Today we tend to use other language—to talk, for example, of "socially constructed" gender roles. But Sargent's ideas and the work of other feminists along the same line were both revolutionary and provocative. If it were understood, for example, that men and women are more alike than different, it would be much more difficult to maintain or justify systemic discrimination.

Her work was extraordinarily significant to me personally. One of the things I've always known about myself was that I could compete with men on almost any level, athletically and mechanically, and certainly intellectually. From that early incident where my prize—the prize I had earned and the teacher knew I had earned—was given to a boy, because he was a boy, I had never been able to come to terms with what I knew about myself and what society said about me. Sargent's work was very integrative for me. It gave me a language for acknowledging characteristics that society defined as masculine, as well as those that were thought to be typically feminine. I didn't have to be ashamed of, or deny, either part of me.[17]

I have since come to realize and to use in my practice the reality that men have been taught to value only that part of themselves that is seen as masculine. This belief has forced them to deny their so-called feminine parts—their softer, feeling, emotional side. This denial, I believe, has made them focus more on power and violence and brutality, in general, and on a power-oriented rather than people-oriented style of management. This denial is also the basis of both misogyny—hatred of women—and homophobia—hatred of gays. We see these patterns being played out daily, even today. As race and gender become more available for open discussion, homosexuality and homophobia have become a new frontier on which the battle for human rights is being waged.

I don't think the split between the masculine and the feminine is there for women, especially for black women. For myself, there was a part of being a tomboy, a strong, smart girl and woman, that was OK. It was never shameful, though it was sometimes confusing. I grew up in a family in which strength was, in fact, the hallmark of womanhood—psychological and emotional strength as well as physical power. To be, to persevere, to be all-suffering, to be able to do all things, was feminine. I think that ability to embrace one's "masculine" side as well as one's feminine traits is what causes women to be less prone to homophobia than men are. It's more acceptable for women to be close friends, and it is easier to accept the idea of the closeness of two women even if it involves a sexual relationship.

While the women's movement was and continues to be important to me, as time went on it became increasingly reflective of the ideas and issues of white women. Just as the EEO/AA legislation ultimately benefited more white women than it did people of color, the feminist efforts benefited women who are white more than it did women of color. Black feminist writers such as bell hooks and Angela Davis began to express this concern.[18] As hooks more recently recalled, after the mutual advances of women's liberation and civil rights in the 1960s and 1970s, feminism gradually turned its back on women who are not white and privileged, leaving women of color marginalized and isolated.[19]

Some white feminists, however, especially those whose work also involved race and racism, began to recognize that there is a vital link between racism and sexism. My colleague, Delyte Frost, for example, in a paper conceptualized in 1973, said, "By working to combat sexism—to stop the oppression of women in our society—and not working at the same time to combat racism—to stop the oppression of people of color—white women will create a new place in our society for white women only." She continued, "This white women's place will continue to be more valued by the majority white system than is the place of women of color, who will retain a place below men of color." And she concluded, "This ultimate racist outcome will also sustain sexism, because by working for that new place for white women and not actively combatting white racism, we as white women are saying that we value whiteness above our womanness."[20] These insights have had a major impact on our work in diversity culture-change, and I will return to them frequently in the following chapters.

Another writer whose work is not specifically feminist but who had an important influence at that time is Alice Miller. Miller's studies of the profound impact of childhood abuse, the ways families and societies conspire to deny and hide it, and how violence in adults so often stems from those patterns gave us a language and a methodology for self-examination and self-acceptance that prepares us to do the work of racism and sexism, both intra- and inter-personally.[21]

Jean Baker Miller, in *Toward a New Psychology of Women*, carried some of the feminist insights further by indicating how they applied in organizational settings.[22] For example, she showed how societally produced patterns of inequality create groups that are dominant (whites, men) as well as groups that are assigned subordinated roles (women, people of color). She also indicated how these built-in inequalities result in the creation of a permanent state of conflict between dominants and subordinates. These ideas, too, have become central to our work.

A woman whose influence was felt through action rather than writing was Maggie Kuhn, the founder of the Gray Panthers. Rejecting the stereotypical view of older women as helpless and insignificant, Kuhn and her colleagues created an organization that took strong and courageous stands on issues affecting older women, and also formed important alliances with other groups in the struggle for civil rights and human dignity.[23] Her work fit closely into the other movements—civil rights, feminist, anti-war—that were insisting that all of us, as citizens, have the right to influence our government and make our views known.

## ORGANIZATION DEVELOPMENT

As the creative energies of the 1960s and 1970s began to wane (or be defeated and diffused), some of us started to look for other avenues for change. In our struggles—as people of color and as women—to assert ourselves as citizens, we were determined that the progress that the civil-rights movements and the feminist movements had made in moving us all toward more equity, freedom, liberty and justice would not be lost. As citizens, some of us believed that we had gained enough understanding of the political process, and had a keen enough sense of the workings of power, to continue to make a difference.

We discovered in the emerging field of organization development another strategy. A key thinker in this arena was Kurt Lewin. Lewin had experienced the horrors of the Nazi regime in Germany, and he brought with him to this country an intense and personal quest for justice, as well as a new concept of planned change. His work became known as systems theory or force-field analysis, and provided a very systematic—almost mathematical—way of thinking about how to move toward an ideal. He showed that a person and that person's environment interact in a learning situation, and that influencing behavior requires understanding both the individual's needs and abilities and the environment in which she or he functions. Before Lewin and other organizational theorists, we had largely thought of social change in the "Alinsky model"—that is, that the only way to move a resistant society toward greater inclusiveness and democracy was to organize large numbers of ordinary people and help them use the raw force of sheer numbers to compel the elites to share power.[24] Lewin showed us that it is possible to engage people in a thoughtful, rational way that would help move an organization toward an ideal—though it was always clear to me that it was an ideal never to be achieved.[25]

Lewin's work was complemented by the work of other theorists and practitioners in the fields of communications theory, conflict resolution, and decision-making processes—writers such as Zander and Cartwright, Blake and Mouton, Rodney Napier and many more.[26] In the field of management, these writers brought a new, more humanistic perspective, which countered the mechanistic time-and-motion studies that had been dominant in the past. They were showing that organizations could be improved by paying attention to the psychological processes of individuals and groups, and by engaging workers and group members themselves in the effort—an approach that came to be known as participatory democracy.

Another important theorist whose concepts have been and continue to be influential in our work is Edgar Schein.[27] Schein and others theorized that organizations have identifiable "cultures" that develop over time and reflect the values and norms of the founders and the controlling members. These values and norms become deeply embedded in the policies and practices of the organization and are exceedingly resistant to change. They theorized that change could, however, be effected by paying careful, methical attention and by applying the principles and techniques that came to be known as organization development, organization behavior and—much later—change management.

These techniques, which were originally developed to study and guide organizations in general—not specifically to address issues of discrimination or oppression—gave us tools that have proved to be effective in that arena as well. The field—which has come to be known as process consultation—begins with having a clear contract with the client, and then moves on to gathering data in a variety of ways. In our work we use both written surveys and face-to-face conversations in focus groups, as well as observation of people at work and review of demographic and other company data. All of this documentation is gathered to give the company an assessment of whether the situation about which the leadership is concerned really constitutes a problem; and, if so, what its dimensions—the scope, the depth, the breadth—seem to be. This assessment is then followed by recommendations for change.

In the early phases of organization development as a field, the process tended to stop at that point, with perhaps some follow-up from time to time to see how the recommendations were working out in practice. As the field matured, we began to understand that more was needed to bring about lasting change, so training strategies such as team building and conflict resolution processes were added into the mix. Over time, we began to realize that the process that we later called culture change was a much bigger effort involving strategic planning, measurement, benchmarking and much more—a process that began to be seen as an "intervention" into the daily life and culture of the organization.

## GROUP PROCESS AND THE PERSONAL GROWTH MOVEMENT

Concurrent and intertwined with the evolution of the field of organization development was the emergence of group dynamics and group process theory, and the movement that was sometimes known as "personal growth." Humanistic psychologists such as Abraham Maslow, Carl Rogers and Frederick Perls emphasized the worth of the individual and the value in looking inward for meaning.[28] Therapists, teachers, consultants, clergy and many others began to look at the interaction of the individual and society in a different way, placing more emphasis on the importance of the growth and development and creative potential of the individual, and less on the authority of tradition or societally imposed restrictions. Emerging from this sea of change was a whole new set of concepts and practice, the training group (or T-group), the laboratory method and human-relations training.

Closely associated with the National Training Laboratories (now known as the NTL Institute for Applied Behavioral Sciences), these concepts were developed by Lewin and other founders of NTL: Kenn Benne, Lee Bradford, Bob Chin, Ron Lippett and others. The basic premise was—and remains—that participation in a facilitated group not only results in new and powerful learning at the individual level, but that the process changes the group as well.[29] The movement's academic arm became known as action research, which dominated studies of management for decades.

I became personally involved with NTL and this movement in the late 1960s. I still have a vivid memory of my first experience in an advanced human-relations laboratory. This two-week session was led by Oron South (who was much later to become the first editor of our firm's publication, *The Diversity Factor*), Lindy Sata and Hal Kellner. Kellner, who was Jewish, had experienced many of the same kinds of discrimination that I, as an African American, had encountered. I had been from the beginning resisting the group, staying self-righteously distant and being miserable. At some point Hal addressed me directly, challenging me with the notion that my resistance had to do with my fear of acknowledging and risking my sense of control and power. He suggested that we explore this issue by using a technique that was frequently employed in Gestalt work. He put me in the middle of the group and invited the other members to turn me around—not hurting me in any way, but making it impossible for me to be in control of the situation or even of myself. I became indignant and very angry, both with Kellner and with the group. But as he asked me to share the experience with the group, I realized for the first time in my life how angry I was, how angry I had always been; how much racism had hurt me. It was an incredibly powerful and emotional experience. I understood, for the very first time, that I was not responsible for the feelings of inferiority I had held. I suddenly saw that I wasn't inferior, that I had been treated in a way that made me feel small and demeaned. And that it wasn't that I hadn't done enough or been good enough—but that society had created a whole system that gave me these messages.

It was a life-changing experience, which gave me an understanding of my own worth and potential—and also, over time, helped me see how this kind of process could help people come to terms with the impact of bigotry, prejudice, racism and sexism.

The group-dynamics field was complemented on one side by the theory and practice of adult education, following John Dewey; and on the other by the personal-growth movement, with its center in California-based institutions such as Esalen, the Western Behavioral Sciences Institute, and the Center for Studies of the Person. Gradually the branches of the movement diverged. Human-relations training maintained a strong connection with the social-justice initiatives of the civil-rights and feminist eras, whereas the personal-growth emphasis became increasingly centered on the individual—leading to charges that it spawned the "me" generation. In its more absurd manifestations the personal-growth movement became deflected into drug abuse and New Age irrelevancy.

Another unexpected consequence of the popularity of these trends was the explosion of a population of people with little training and few skills who saw in the "do your own thing" approach the opportunity to make a quick buck. Although the movements in their purer form stressed the importance of the individual, the need for critical thinking, and the responsibility of each person for her or his own education, the atmosphere of freedom and "anything goes" also allowed for the rise of gurus—some of them absolutely nutty—and a training technology that was riddled with gimmicks, content-deficient audiovisuals, and poorly designed and tested group exercises. Some of this technology is still evident in today's diversity movements. Another consequence, which also has its echoes in the present time, was the decline in the importance of degree requirements and professional certification as criteria for performing work. Fields such as counseling, education, social work, human-relations training, the various psychotherapies and "creative arts" therapies were particularly vulnerable. However, then as now, much of the force of the resistance to this new cadre resulted more from the desire of the credentialed establishment to protect its turf than from a genuine desire to protect the unwary public. In any case, the positive aspects of these movements generated an approach to human learning and organization change that has proved to be extremely powerful in our work in helping organizations ameliorate systemic oppression and discrimination.

## CLOSING THE CIRCLE

As we moved into the 1970s and began our work with large organizations, the four themes outlined above—civil rights; feminism; organization development, action research and participatory decision making; and human-relations training and personal growth—began to provide a basis for understanding how racism and sexism functioned in the organizations, and for devising strategies aimed at reducing their impact. Although it would be another decade or more before this understanding resulted in a fully articulated and tested theory, we knew we were onto a new, exciting and challenging enterprise.

## NOTES

1. See Kenneth O'Reilly, *Nixon's Piano: Presidents and Racial Politics from Washington to Clinton* (New York: The Free Press, 1995), for an account of the involvement of the presidents in the struggle for racial justice.

2. For an account of the Mount Airy community efforts, see Lois Mark Stalvey, *The Education of a WASP* (New York: William Morrow, 1970).

3. Frantz Fanon, *The Wretched of the Earth*, preface by Jean-Paul Sartre, translated by Constance Farrington (New York: Grove Press, 1963). *Studies in a Dying Colonialism*, translated by Haakon Chevalier (New York: Monthly Review Press, 1965).

4. Paolo Freire, *Pedagogy of the Oppressed*, translated by Myra Bergman Ramos (New York: Continuum, 1970).

5. Alinsky's book, *Reveille for Radicals* (New York: Vintage Books, 1969), was especially helpful.

6. Among the numerous works of John Hope Franklin, see *Color and Race*

(Boston: Houghton Mifflin, 1968) and *From Slavery to Freedom: A History of African Americans*, with Alfred A. Moss, Jr. (New York: Alfred A. Knopf, 1994). See also Kenneth Clark, "Desegregation: An Appraisal of the Evidence," *The Journal of Social Issues* 9, no. 4 (1953); *Prejudice and Your Child* (Boston: Beacon Press, 1963); and *Dark Ghetto* (New York: Harper and Row, 1965).

7. Among his more than 175 publications, see in particular Chesler's *Vital Problems for American Society*, co-authored by J. Winter and J. Rabow (New York: Random House, 1968), and a series of articles on planning educational change and school desegregation in the late 1960s and early 1970s.

8. See, for example, Alderfer's *Existence, Relatedness, and Growth: Human Needs in Organizational Settings* (New York: The Free Press, 1972) and *Learning from Changing: Organizational Diagnosis and Development* (Beverly Hills, CA: Sage Publications, 1975), with L. Dave Brown.

9. Donald R. Kinder and Lynn M. Sanders, *Divided by Color: Racial Politics and Democratic Ideals* (Chicago: University of Chicago Press, 1997).

10. There is, of course, an enormous body of literature that reviews these times and these issues. For a brief but more comprehensive review than the one provided here, see Clare C. Swanger, "Perspectives on the History of Ameliorating Oppression and Supporting Diversity in United States Organizations," in *The Promise of Diversity*, edited by Elsie Y. Cross, Judith H. Katz, Frederick A. Miller and Edith W. Seashore (Burr Ridge, IL: Irwin Professional Publishing and NTL Institute, 1994).

11. O'Reilly, *Nixon's Piano*, 43.

12. Gertrude Ezorsky, *Racism and Justice: The Case for Affirmative Action* (Ithaca, NY: Cornell University Press, 1991), 9.

13. Ibid., 32.

14. Simone de Beauvoir, *The Second Sex*, translated and edited by H. M. Parshley (New York: Alfred A. Knopf, 1953); Betty Friedan, *The Feminine Mystique* (New York: Norton, 1963).

15. Swanger, in Cross et al., *Promise of Diversity*, 8.

16. Alice Sargent, ed., *Beyond Sex Roles* (St. Paul: West Publishing, 1977), and Sargent, *The Androgynous Manager* (New York: AMACOM, 1981).

17. Another writer whose work complements Alice Sargent's is Rosabeth Moss Kanter. Her books, including *Men and Women of the Corporation* (New York: Basic Books, 1977), began to help identify the patterns of sexism that are endemic in our organizations. Her film, *The Tale of O*, which describes graphically the functions of "ingroups" and "outgroups," has been very influential in the field.

18. See, for example, bell hooks, *Ain't I a Woman? Black Women and Feminism* (Boston: South End Press, 1981); *Feminist Theory: From Margin to Center* (Boston: South End Press, 1984); *Talking Back: Thinking Feminist, Thinking Black* (Boston: South End Press, 1989); and Angela Davis, *Women, Race and Class* (New York: Random House, 1981).

19. bell hooks, *Outlaw Culture: Resisting Representations* (New York: Routledge, 1994).

20. Delyte D. Frost, "A Special Place for White Women Only," unpublished paper prepared for Elsie Y. Cross Associates, Inc., Philadelphia, PA, 1973; revised 1976, 1987.

21. See, for example, Alice Miller, *Prisoners of Childhood*, translated from the

German by Ruth Ward (New York: Basic Books, 1981); *For Your Own Good: Hidden Cruelty in Child-Rearing and the Roots of Violence*, translated by Hildegarde Hannum and Hunter Hannum (New York: Farrar, Straus and Giroux, 1983); and *Thou Shalt Not Be Aware: Society's Betrayal of the Child*, translated by Hildegarde Hannum and Hunter Hannum (New York: Farrar, Straus and Giroux, 1984).

22. Jean Baker Miller, *Toward a New Psychology of Women* (Boston: Beacon Press, 1976).

23. See a biographical account in Maggie Kuhn, *No Stone Unturned: The Life and Times of Maggie Kuhn*, with Christina Long and Laura Quinn (New York: Ballantine, 1991).

24. See Alinsky, *Reveille for Radicals*.

25. See Kurt Lewin, *Field Theory as Human Science: Contributions of Lewin's Berlin Group*, compiled by Joseph de Rivera (New York: Gardner Press, 1976); *The Conceptual Representation and the Measurement of Psychological Forces* (Durham, NC: Duke University Press, 1938); *Resolving Social Conflicts: Selected Papers on Group Dynamics*, edited by Gertrud Weiss Lewin (New York: Harper, 1948).

26. See, for example, the work of Alvin Frederick Zander, including *Motives and Goals in Groups* (New York: Academic Press, 1971); *Groups at Work* (San Francisco: Jossey-Bass, 1977); *Making Groups Effective* (San Francisco: Jossey-Bass, 1982); and, with Dorwin Cartwright, *Group Dynamics: Research and Theory* (New York: Harper and Row, 1968). Also see Rodney Napier and Matti K. Gershenfeld, *Groups, Theory and Experience* (Boston: Houghton Mifflin, 1973).

27. See, for example, Schein's early work, *Organizational Psychology* (Englewood Cliffs, NJ: Prentice-Hall, 1965); *Personal and Organizational Change Through Group Methods: The Laboratory Approach*, with Warren Bennis (New York: Wiley, 1965), and his later books, *Organizational Culture and Leadership* (San Francisco: Jossey-Bass, 1985) and *The Art of Managing Human Resources* (New York: Oxford University Press, 1987).

28. See, for example, Maslow's seminal work, *Toward a Psychology of Being* (Princeton, NJ: Van Nostrand, 1962); Rogers' *On Becoming a Person* (Boston: Houghton Mifflin, 1961); and Perls' *Gestalt Therapy: Excitement and Growth in the Human Personality*, with Ralph E. Hefferline and Paul Goodman (New York: Dell, 1951).

29. For a summary of the history of NTL and a brief overview of this process, see Edith Whitfield Seashore and Judith H. Katz, "NTL's Road to Multiculturalism: A Diverse History," in *The Promise of Diversity*, edited by Elsie Y. Cross et al. (New York: Irwin, 1994). Some important texts from this period are Kenn Benne, *Group Dynamics and Social Action*, with Leland P. Bradford and Ronald Lippett (New York: Anti-Defamation League of B'nai B'rith, 1960); *The Planning of Change: Readings in the Applied Behavioral Sciences*, edited by Warren G. Bennis, Kenneth D. Benne and Robert Chin (New York: Holt, Rinehart and Winston, 1976); *The Laboratory Method of Changing and Learning: Theory and Application* (Palo Alto, CA: Science and Behavior Books, 1975); *T-Group Theory and Laboratory Method: Innovation in Re-education*, with Leland P. Bradford and Jack R. Gibb (New York: Wiley, 1964). Also see Jack R. Gibb, *Trust: A New View of Personal and Organizational Development* (Los Angeles: Guild of Tutors Press, 1978).

# 4

## From Theory to Practice

Some years ago, on a long airline journey across the United States, I fell into conversation with the man seated next to me. After the usual exchange of pleasantries, he began to tell me about his life and his problems. I participated in the conversation by listening and being very attentive to his every gesture and providing the kind of unobtrusive responses that helped him tell his story. After we had been engaged in this interaction for some time, it suddenly occurred to me that he was not paying any attention to me at all. This was not a conversation we were having; it was a facilitated monologue. So I interrupted. "Look here," I said to my very startled seatmate, "I'm finished with this. I don't want to do this any more."

"What have I done?" he said, in great bewilderment. "Have I said something to offend you?"

He was completely unaware of the roles we had been playing. It was obvious to me, however, that we were reproducing in this simple interaction gender patterns that are invisible to almost all of us, almost all the time. The incident also emphasized for me how these patterns undermine all our efforts to create more equitable workplaces and a fairer society. It was a small but dramatic illustration of what happens in organizations when men and women are working together.

In a work team, if men are not listening to women, or women are facilitating men in their conversations rather than making their own contributions, the team is not functioning as well as it might if all individuals were being heard. The impact this situation has on women is to make it clear to them that their ideas don't count: "You're not important here. Don't talk. Don't share what you know—just help the men convey their ideas." This happens even when a woman or several women in a group have more information or ideas than the men, and even when the women are further up in the hierarchy.

Another example of this is an experience I had in a train station not long ago. I was sitting on a bench near a group of people—one woman and three men—whose conversation I could not help hearing. It was evident that they had not known one another previous to this encounter, but it was obvious from the introductions that the woman was the expert. She was introduced to the others in terms of her degrees and publications and her expertise in the subject under discussion.

It was fascinating to watch what happened. As the conversation evolved, the three men began to talk to each other. Little by little their expert—the woman—was left out of the discussion. The men—quite unconsciously—moved closer to one another, forming a tight circle from which she was excluded. I could no longer hear their words, but it was easy to imagine that they were making decisions on the basis of their own information—without regard to the fact that they were ignoring the very person they had gone there to meet, the person whose knowledge they needed to help them make the right decisions. It was impossible for her to insist on being heard. What could she say? "Hey, guys, I'm over here!" It would have been rude and awkward in the extreme.

In situations like this there is almost never any intention on the part of the men to exclude the women; they aren't thinking to themselves, "This woman is stupid. Why should we listen to her?" It is just the habitual pattern of communication between men, one that gets played out over and over in formal and informal settings. Similar habits and patterns recur in conversational groups and work teams that are multi-racial.

As my colleagues and I began to work on these issues in corporations in the 1970s and early 1980s, we became increasingly aware of how the power dynamics of traditional patterns of interactions had created systems of privilege for some—especially for white men—and had barred others—white women and men and women of color—from equal access to opportunity and power. We worked with many different organizations during these years, with a variety of populations. In this chapter I review the strategies we developed in relation to, and in partnership with, three of these groups: college students; people of different races in the corporate setting; and women and men in various companies. Many of these strategies have become key components of our ongoing work aimed at ameliorating racism, sexism and other forms of discrimination and oppression in organizations.

## STUDENT DIALOGUES

One of the immediate results of affirmative-action legislation was the gradual increase of people of color on college campuses. As in all affirmative-action efforts, the focus was on giving more students of color opportunities to have a college education. Very little attention was paid to what their experience would be once they got in the door. Naturally, there were problems.

We were asked by several of the colleges in the Pennsylvania state system to come in and help them resolve conflicts. One instance is typical. One of the larger state institutions, a school with some 3,000 white students, had admitted a rather small cadre of blacks—around fifty or so. As the college defined the problem, the blacks had created a situation in which there were racial incidents, fighting and so forth, between the whites and blacks. We were asked to investigate and cool things off. My colleagues and I designed a simple program in which we brought small groups of white and black students together for three-day weekends, in a modified T-group format. The focus of the sessions was racism. We made sure the work was serious but not threatening, helping the students get to know each other and understand the issues of racism by providing simulations and activities, and then helping them discuss and understand what they had learned. The spirit of the sessions was wonderful. The students were eager and enthusiastic learners, and not so steeped in the culture of racist attitudes and behaviors that they were too defensive to learn.

We ran these workshops for more than a year. Early on, it became evident to the students and to us as well that it wasn't the new African-American students who were causing the problems—it was the hostile white students. The colleges had no more prepared the white students for learning with and living with the black students than they had prepared the African-American students for succeeding in this new environment. So my colleagues and I—Delyte Frost, John Leeke and others—realized that we could not help the institutions resolve the problem they had identified if we were not able to help them understand what the problem really was. We began to strategize with a staff member at one of the colleges, a black woman with some background in organization development, about how we could get the president and the administration, and some of the faculty members as well, involved in the process.

We developed small efforts, and just kept working away at it bit by bit. There was some federal money in those days that the schools could use to support the process. The president of this college finally agreed to pull together a group of administrators, and we developed a team-building process with a special focus on race. We met with this group

several times, maybe every other month for a year or so, and they gradually began to understand how the college's policies and practices were
creating the problems, and that they needed to review them carefully to
see where they could be changed. One of the things they learned was
that the root causes did not rest with the students at all. They had to
look at the lack of diversity among the faculty members and in the administrative personnel and curriculum, as well as at the problems that
resulted because the group of students of color was so small that they
were not able to support and protect one another well.

Looking back, over a distance of almost two decades, I am struck with
two things. First, some of the strategies and actions that came out of this
initiative have become standard practice in many diversity efforts, especially in corporations. But second, I am dismayed to realize that there
has been little progress in these areas in the university and college setting.

Institutions of higher learning, in the last half of the last decade of the
twentieth century, have launched dialogue programs, student workshops
and gender- and race-focused initiatives that have the same concerns and
use the same techniques we were using in these early times.[1]

Similarly, there is as much resistance now as then to recognizing that
we cannot expect students to solve the problems for the rest of us. It is
counterproductive, if not hypocritical, to wring our hands over hostility
and violence between groups of students when we have not resolved
issues of imbalance of power and authority among our faculty and administrative groups.

Another factor has held true over time: Money talks, in diversity work
as everywhere else. Even though various colleges in the state system
looked at the results in that first institution with interest and attempted
to emulate them in their own organizations, once the federal money
dried up, the efforts faded away.

If our institutions of public education and of higher learning had recognized, in those early days of affirmative action, that it was important
to invest in educating, supporting and challenging faculty, administrations and students around issues of race, I firmly believe we would be
in an entirely different place in this society today. If the process that
began to open doors to people of color had been supported by processes
that enabled them to succeed, that helped white students and white faculty recognize their own bigotry, and assisted administrations in removing policies and practices that were based on a white-male norm, we
would not be revisiting the affirmative-action debate at this point.

This pattern of paying attention and then turning away is a constant
and dramatic component of intergroup relations in the United States. It
is the reason I contend that it is not possible to address "diversity concerns" in organizations without paying attention to the historical context

within which the current reincarnation of the pattern is occurring. Unless we understand that advances made during periods of high activity, such as Reconstruction, the 1940s and the 1960s, were always followed by periods of reaction and reversal, we are doomed to repeat the cycle. It is this historical reality that leads us to call for "amelioration" of racism, sexism and other forms of oppression—rather than a more hopeful call for overcoming them.[2]

## MANAGING AND WORKING IN A DIVERSE WORK FORCE ENVIRONMENT

At the same time that affirmative action was prizing open a few more doors in higher education for students of color, people of color were also beginning to gain access to better-paying jobs with more potential. Corporations were finding that they needed help "managing" the new workers—nearly always the problem was defined as residing in the people of color themselves, not in the discriminatory systems into which they were hired.

While we had many contracts during this time, in this section I describe one contract that extended over a period of several years, beginning in the early 1970s, and illustrates the concepts we were exploring and the processes we used to help participants in workshops come to terms with the realities of racism as well as sexism. The work was focused primarily at the individual level, although there were several aspects that represented group-level involvement and some initial steps toward systemic remedies as well.

The contract I am describing was with a major oil company. The company had hired a number of white women engineers and a few African Americans; but the new hires were having extreme difficulty in being seen as professionals, and several had left. When management calculated the expense of replacing them, and recognized that they had both a moral and legal obligation to continue bringing in minorities and women, they realized that they would have to put some time and energy and thought into figuring out how to make sure these professionals were integrated into the organization. At the time, I'm sure, their idea was that the new hires would simply be "assimilated." That is, with some assistance from management and maybe from outside consultants, they would learn to dress, behave, act and think as much like white men as possible so that, leaving aside the inevitable physical differences of race and gender, the workplace would look and feel pretty much like it always had.

One example that sums up their expectations was an anecdote that was repeated with pride frequently in our early days there, about a black man who was so smart that he learned to speak Polish (Poles being the dominant group of white men in the company). It was a long time before people realized that the black man should be able to just be himself— not a black man pretending to be Polish. The company learned pretty quickly that assimilation wasn't the way to go. At the prodding of an internal organization development consultant who was aware of the issues and knew about things that were going on in other companies, they invited us to come and give them some help.

One of our initial clients there was a specific refinery in that system. The manager of the refinery, a white man, was a very quiet, unassuming person; but from the beginning he understood the issues and he understood our point that the problems would not be resolved at the individual level alone. He knew something about individual psychology, and intuitively, I think, he believed in justice. He was very smart and also very brave. We wrote a number of proposals, similar to the following abstract:

> This presentation introduces a program for managing diversity within work groups in the Technical Division at XXX Refinery. It proposes that the ability to work with and effectively manage people who are different in terms of race, gender, experience, age, religious background and job roles results in a more constructive work force, develops managerial skills, provides managers with an increased capacity to manage conflict, and ultimately increases productivity.

This proposal, submitted in the early 1980s, went on to point out that the work force was becoming increasingly diverse in terms of race, gender and other factors.

> It is critical that supervisory personnel and others develop new skills to manage and work effectively in diverse work group situations, to minimize the negative impact of behavior based on assumptions and stereotypes, and to capitalize on the benefits inherent in diverse work groups. This program is designed to give supervisory personnel and other employees some of the insights and skills needed to be effective in this changing work force. The workshop [training sessions] provides a groundwork, which will be supplemented by on-the-job coaching and follow-up meetings which will provide support and feedback to participants.

The proposal outlined the various segments of the program, in addition to the educational and awareness workshops.

The refinery manager and a senior vice-president came out very strongly as advocates of the approach we proposed. The senior vice-president saw the issues as moral and ethical concerns, and drew on his own religious convictions in taking on the matter with real passion. And the refinery manager joined him. I think it was their clarity and their certainty that carried the day.

From our previous experiences we recognized that nothing solid would happen unless this top management group came to "own the work" themselves—to take it on as a management issue, not just a question of education and awareness for the lower echelons. We insisted that the entire management group participate in the workshops, and they—much to our surprise—agreed. Our concepts of the work had evolved to the point that we now realized it was important for both the participants in the workshops and the trainers who assisted them to be thoroughly mixed by race and gender. At the refinery, as in every organization in the United States then (and in most today), it was impossible to put together a mixed group of top managers because they were all white men. So we insisted then—and continue to insist—that they reach out to other segments of the organization to find white women and men and women of color to join them. This was very difficult, and as time went on became increasingly burdensome for those invited, since they often were asked to participate in one workshop after another. Sometimes they got battle fatigue, with all this educating of their white male bosses. But mostly they hung in and made major contributions.

We began the process by conducting individual interviews with the white-male top managers, and with the invited white women and men and women of color. And then we started the work by bringing in the data from the interviews and helping the group understand how the company and its management practices were viewed by the different constituencies. As the work progressed we designed and implemented another very useful strategy. Every vice-president who participated in a workshop was asked to nominate another white man, someone who reported directly to him, to go to a subsequent session. Prior to the workshop, we created trios consisting of the top manager, his direct report and a consultant. In a one-hour interview the top manager discussed the workshop with his employee, sharing with him what his own experiences had been and what his expectations were of those who reported to him. After each workshop, the trios met again and reviewed the experience and discussed the implications of what the men had learned for the running of their particular business units.

These were very powerful experiences—but also, of course, very cumbersome, logistically; and expensive. Eventually the trios were replaced by group interviews; and the trained external facilitators were replaced by internal human-resources people, who often did not have the same skills or experience. But we were able to test the model as a strategy, and we saw that it was very effective in getting top managers and their direct reports intimately involved in the work, and that it enhanced their understanding of the issues, both cognitively and affectively.

It is important to note here that we had designed and were implementing this work, "Managing and Working in a Diverse Work Force Environment," almost a decade before the publication of the Hudson Institute's "landmark" study that predicted the rapid change in the demographics of the U.S. work force.[3] It was becoming clear to us, from our experience in corporations and from following the national trends, that the workplace was already diverse by race and gender and would become more so as time went by.

We also recognized that U.S. companies, created by and in the image of white men, were completely unprepared to welcome or even tolerate the new workers who would be needed. We understood that we would have to find ways to engage the white men in a process that would seem to many to be not only counterintuitive but also threatening. They would have to be able to understand racism and sexism as objective facts that operate outside of individuals as well as within them. And they would need to learn that they could choose whether to become champions in the cause of eliminating discrimination and oppression, or retreat into denial, anger and destructiveness.

It was not just the white men who were unprepared. Members of subordinated groups often develop patterns of collusion that may become habits that persist to the detriment not only of the individual but of the individual's identity group as well. For example, a pattern of overly aggressive or inappropriately timed outspokenness on the part of a woman—whether black or white—feeds into a stereotyped view of nondeferent women as "pushy" or "bitchy," and is used to negate the valid and appropriate claims of women in general.

There were many other concepts that we recognized as relevant and built into the workshops and the diversity program, in general. One important aspect was the function of power and authority within the workshop group, which reflected and commented on the way lines of power and authority operated in the real-life workplace. In the following section I explore this topic in more detail.

## MEN AND WOMEN IN THE WORK ENVIRONMENT

One of the least recognized but most important impacts of the affirmative-action and equal-employment-opportunity legislation was the increase in access for women—especially white women—to colleges and graduate schools, and to jobs in the corporate world. Much of the attention of organization-development consultants during the late 1970s and the 1980s was directed to the concerns raised by women who were hired into corporations—and then harassed, ignored, overlooked and demeaned.

My colleagues and I developed and implemented a training initiative that we called "Men and Women in the Work Environment," which we facilitated in some half-dozen or more corporations over a period of more than a decade. While the initiative was tailored to the particular needs of each corporation, there were many common elements. In this discussion, I draw particularly on our experiences in one specific company; but a similar account could be written for many others.

This company, a highly specialized research and development facility, had conducted a very aggressive recruiting campaign and had hired a qualified group of women engineers. As in the case of the universities and the black students, corporations at this time had little awareness that recruitment was just the beginning, not the end, of the process. After a frustrating period during which the women attempted to do the jobs for which they were hired and were very qualified to perform, but were prevented at every turn by abuse, harassment and neglect, they initiated a class-action suit which resulted in the company's being hit with an expensive consent decree. Soon after, we were hired by senior management to consult to the company to try to resolve some of the communication issues and head off any possibility of further legal and financial damages.

My colleague Eileen Lang and I, with help and support from the internal human-resources staff, designed a three-day awareness workshop focused on gender discrimination and sexual harassment. We drew heavily on Alice Sargent's concepts of androgyny, and emphasized the ways men and women are socialized in this culture—and every other culture—so that men's views, concerns, needs and experiences are valued more highly than women's.[4] Women in those days—the late 1970s and the 1980s—were imbued with feminism. Especially those who had fought their way into college and graduate school, and then into professional positions in the corporate world, were very clear about their goals. They wanted equal rights, they were demanding respect and dignity, they wanted the same pay, the same access to promotions, the same ability to succeed that their male colleagues had.

It is important to emphasize here that these workshops, like almost all the work that was going on at the time, were focused on the individual. Although we were already aware that there would be no permanent change unless the norms, practices and procedures of the organization were corrected, the companies had not yet begun to think in those terms. Later we were able to build our work around the concept that change must happen at three levels—certainly at the individual-awareness level, where prejudice resides, but also at the group level, where prejudice results in discrimination, and at the system level, where discrimination is embedded in every aspect of the organization's norms and practices.[5]

## Communication Patterns

These "Men and Women in the Workplace" workshops were very exciting. They were primarily focused on helping the participants learn to see the patterns of communication that men and women unconsciously adopt as they relate to each other. I often referred to my experience in the "facilitated monologue" with my airline seatmate as an example of how we fall into these ways of relating in our everyday life.

These intensive three-day sessions included many of the components that became standard practice in our work: stand-up lectures; facilitated exercises; simulations; small-group and large-group work; lots of processing of the learning as we went along; careful attention to the dynamics of the group and the experience of each individual in it; and a scrupulous commitment to our pledge that no one would be harmed, either psychologically or professionally, by their participation.

Of the many components that were incorporated, one stands out as both particularly effective and demonstrative of the goals of the work. In an exercise that had been designed by a colleague early on, we asked the members of the group to divide into pairs, each pair including a man and a woman, and for forty-five minutes to interact with each other *in reversed roles*, following the typical behavior patterns I described above in the train-station incident.

Usually the participants started out with a certain degree of skepticism: "Oh, this is simple-minded stuff. We're just playing games." But as the minutes went by, the task became more and more difficult. The women found it very hard to maintain dominance in the conversation, to keep the focus on themselves. The men found it equally difficult to play the "facilitative" role and "help" the women keep the conversation going. We had already pointed out to the group the characteristic dynamics between men and women—how a woman often signals an intense interest by a certain tilt of the head, or by encouraging vocalizations, or by a slight inclination of the body toward the male speaker. So the pairs tried to include these in their exercise as well. When the time was up, we helped the members of group understand what they had learned. They all always agreed that they were shocked at how difficult the task had turned out to be, at how uncomfortable they were in the other role—and how it helped them realize what their customary communication styles actually were.

This exercise, and the entire workshop session, had profound effects on the men as well as the women. Men often reported later that it was the first time they understood what their wives had been telling them for years—that they really didn't listen to them. Some men reported that they went home and asked their wives to practice the "reverse role" exercise with them, and that this new insight had a major and positive impact on their marriages.

The impact was even more powerful for the women. They could see their own patterns of behavior in the exercises, and often were very angry when they realized how readily they had fallen into this facilitative, subordinated role. We began to talk with them about how, by employing these kinds of behaviors, they colluded in their own degradation.

This concept of collusion became a central tenet of all our work—not just on gender but on race and other kinds of discrimination and oppression as well. It became obvious to all of us that patterns of abuse could not continue if people who are abused could stand firmly against them—and join with other subordinated people to refuse to accept them. But there are many reasons, some conscious but many unconscious, why people collude in their own oppression. The first and most obvious is self-protection. Nearly all of us want most of all to live our lives with as little aggravation and pain as possible. We "go along to get along." When we must live in an atmosphere of hostility, disdain, degradation and discrimination, it is a natural human instinct to hunker down and minimize the enemy's opportunity to attack us. In many situations, this instinct for self-protection is based on actual life and death situations. Many women are battered by the men with whom they share their lives. Many African Americans have been set upon, tortured, lynched, shot by police and brutalized in countless small and major ways throughout our history—for several centuries with the explicit permission of the law. Jews throughout history have been brutalized, the Holocaust being just one of the genocides they have suffered. And there are countless other examples. In such cases, collusion may be seen as a mark of sanity.

In other situations, however, the motives for collusion and the ways it manifests itself are more subtle. In the corporate setting, for example, it is easy to see a woman or a person of color putting up with abusive language, customs and practices in the interest of appearing to be a "real team player." Here collusion may take the form of internalizing the stream of abuse, swallowing the rage in the interest of saving the job or hoping for advancement. Or it may be done simply in the very human hope of being liked, being accepted, being seen as a person who wants to cooperate rather than as a "troublemaker" or a "pushy broad."

There are other forms of collusion as well, some less justifiable. Some people—perhaps those who are clearest about the evil intents of the abusers—simply figure out how to use the situation to their own advantage. It's the "Step'n Fetchit" mentality—saying "Yessir" to the oppressor's face, and reserving the negative thoughts and actions for private times and places. I believe for many people this becomes a way of life of which they are not aware. "Getting over" becomes such a habit that they may be driven to this kind of behavior even when it works against their own self-interest.

In my view, collusion is a concept that applies only to people who are assigned subordinated roles in society. It is a dynamic of the oppressed. In the dominant group, these dynamics *are* oppression—sexism, racism, heterosexism and so on. The influence of collusion is an important factor in all our work, and I return to it often throughout this text.

The workshops just discussed were focused on gender issues, and that remained the central theme. Nonetheless, it became apparent, when there were both white women and women of color in the sessions, that there are differences in how we are socialized. It became strikingly evident that white women are socialized, by and large, to be accommodating and deferent to white men, whereas black women—at least in my generation and the generation preceding me—had been socialized to be strong, powerful, independent and forbearing.

It is easy to see that there are sociological and economic bases for the differences. It is much easier for white men than for black men to establish themselves in well-paying jobs and thus to claim the role of head of household. White women have much less to lose, from an economic standpoint, by being deferent than they have from demanding equal treatment in the home and in the workplace. Black women have been in the work force by sheer necessity for generations. They have had to learn to rely on themselves to a much greater degree than have white women. These facts are not, perhaps, as true today as they were two decades ago, but I believe they are still significant.

Much of the motivation of the companies for "doing something" to improve relations between men and women derived from the new legislation prohibiting sexual harassment in the workplace. Whereas abuse of women may always have been regarded by some as morally and ethically reprehensible, now a company that allowed it to continue without challenge could face stiff fines. Nonetheless, it persisted then, and it continues today.

When we began the "Men and Women in the Workplace" workshops, we drew on feminist literature and concepts to help our participants understand that sexual harassment is not a sexual dynamic as much as it is a power dynamic. Every man is not a harasser or a potential harasser, but because the environment allows men to assert their power over women, an environment is created in which sexual harassment is the order of the day.

We worked on this concept in many ways in every workshop, and both men and women were able to see how the dynamics operated in their specific situations. Here is one of thousands of examples that could be given. In those days, a hospitality suite was always provided by the company at the end of the workshop each day. Liquor and wine flowed freely, and the participants and consultants relaxed together after hours of intense interpersonal interaction and cognitive learning. In this particular workshop we had been having a powerful discussion of sexual harassment, so the topic was very much on people's minds. As the evening went on, a man began to harass one of the women in a very aggressive and offensive way, perhaps partly due to the influence of alcohol.

The next day, a man who observed all this asked me privately whether he should bring it up in the session. I encouraged him to do so, and he did. It created a very powerful, real-in-the-moment illustration both of the actuality of how sexual harassment operates and of how it can be challenged and reduced, if not eliminated.

This example illustrates several things. First, no matter how clearly the case is made on a cognitive or intellectual level, actual behavior is not apt to change unless there is a direct, personal and emotional connection with an individual. Second, it should not be the task only of the person who is harassed to take responsibility for challenging the harasser when there are others who witness the action. The fact that the witness was another man, not the woman who was targeted or even another woman who had observed the situation, created a dynamic that was very powerful. It takes extraordinary courage for a man to "step out of the box" in situations like these; often, it is very difficult for such a man to see how it is in any way in his own self-interest to break ranks and call attention to himself in defense of someone who is not a "member of the club."

A third point that the incident illustrates is the importance of careful, experienced facilitation of such emotionally powerful situations. In a later chapter I review what we believe are the educational and experiential criteria necessary for training and consulting in diversity initiatives. At this point I will only observe that in our experience, the person responsible for guiding the discussion around an explosive issue such as sexual harassment must have a broad theoretical understanding of the topic—including the power and authority dimensions—as well as a deep experiential recognition of her or his own attitudes around gender and sexuality.

The trainers or facilitators who guide such work must have had experiential training that enables them to operate on many levels at once. They must be able to watch the dynamics of the group for their gender (and race) outcomes. They must be alert to the emotional status of all the individuals in the group and be able to take quick action if they spot someone who is in distress or who has psychologically left the scene. And they must be closely attuned to the dynamics operating among the members of the training team as well, sensing when their colleagues may have been drawn into the issues under discussion and making sure that *all* participants—whether facilitators or workshop members—are comfortable or protected.

The "Men and Women in the Workplace" initiative, like the work in colleges and the "Managing and Working in a Diverse Work Force Environment" strategy, remained focused primarily at the individual level. However, when these issues are addressed effectively, it becomes evident to participants as well as to facilitators and administrators that they spring from a much deeper base than the interaction between individuals alone. From time to time, women would express their anger over disparate rates of pay, or about not getting promotions due them. But there was no mechanism in place to address the problems—so the same issues came up in workshop after workshop, with no way to begin to resolve them. These experiences confirmed our recognition that no real change would occur if organizations continued to commit resources solely to individual education and awareness. Yet even today, many companies have begun or are beginning such work, failing to take account of what is by now a solid body of evidence that education and awareness—what is usually called "diversity training"—does not, by itself, pay off in the long run. To achieve lasting change, the company must be willing to address systemic issues of how power is held and used in the organization.

## POWER AND AUTHORITY

Issues related to the distribution of power came up over and over again, in quite predictable ways. When I was leading the workshop myself, I could predict that at some point, early on, a senior white-male leader in the group would challenge my authority by confronting me on some point. A kind of fight would ensue, which proceeded on two levels—the ostensible point raised by the white man, and the invisible but powerful question of my authority versus his. Usually the discussion would come to a point at which I was "winning"—naturally, since the topic inevitably related to my area of expertise—and I would make sure that it resulted in a draw, so that both of us retired from the field as victors.

What was important in these interchanges was not the matter at issue, or whether he won or I won. What we were dealing with were authority questions: Who is in charge here? Who is in charge in this company? Who is in charge in this society? I also knew that it had to do with the phases of group development.

One theory of group development observes that in every group there are people who are independent—who make up their own minds and can challenge or support the authority figure; dependents—people who always support the authority figure and want to be told what to do; and counter-dependents—people who challenge the authority figure consistently. The theory proposes, and we knew it to be true from our own experience, that if you can capture and facilitate the independents to take up positions of visibility and authority in a group, the dependents will give up their dependency on the leader (or at least go along with the independents), and the counter-dependents will stop railing against the authority figure—in this case, the workshop staff and its leader.

In nearly all of these early workshops, these issues of challenging and reestablishing lines of power and authority almost always emerged toward the end of the first day. At this point, we asked the participants how they felt the workshop was going; how they were feeling individually; and how they felt the group as a whole was doing. These seemingly casual check-ins elicited the power and authority issues. Often the groups would use this time to criticize the staff because the workshop, in their view, wasn't going well. They could always cite specific reasons, but whatever the reasons, the process served the purpose of challenging our authority and allowing the group to begin the process of reconstituting the power dynamics and assuming responsibility for its own welfare.

It was obvious to us, and became obvious to most members of workshops, that this realignment was a metaphoric example of the kind of readjustment of responsibilities and power structures that would have to be undertaken in the organizations of the future. Whereas in the past white men could take it for granted that they would be, or report to, the "men in charge," now they would have to consider the possibility that the "men in charge" might be women; or they might be men of color. Similarly, white women and women of color could no longer assume they would report to a white man—so the strategies of collusion, deference or helpfulness they had adopted, consciously or unconsciously, in the past might in the future be increasingly counterproductive. They might be reporting to a white woman or a black man or a black woman. They might end up being the boss themselves, and have to learn strategies of leadership that would require quite different approaches. All of these challenges, in addition to the more obvious issues of the "isms," had to be addressed as we assisted the corporations.

We continued to run education and awareness workshops, focused primarily on individuals, in numerous organizations. At the same time, however, we were consulting to leadership teams and helping them review their policies and examine how those policies were implemented. They often formed themselves into what has since come to be called a diversity council, and took the task very seriously. The diversity council would examine, among other things, a company's recruitment strategies and conclude that it was not appropriate to go out and hire white women and people of color without a systematic plan. They then developed strategies that helped them expand their recruiting networks and begin to identify a diverse pool of well-qualified candidates. This allowed them to begin to overcome the serious deficits of tokenism or quota hiring, and to bring in diverse candidates who had a good chance of succeeding in the company.

Companies were also, of course, very concerned about retention and the revolving-door syndrome. In those days, jobs were plentiful and people could move around fairly easily. So there was a constant stream of people who were recruited, hired, oriented and trained, but, facing ongoing harassment or lack of progressive development opportunities, were soon seen departing. We recognized that this pattern would not be broken unless the company was able to change its practices around performance appraisal and promotions. We also knew that the stated policies and practices were only half the problem. Even more critical, and much more difficult to affect, were the unspoken norms, expectations and attitudes that really drove the process and determined who would advance in the company and who would be left behind. To meet this challenge, our consulting team developed a strategy that we called the "Managing Diversity and Performance Appraisal Process." The strategy was conceptualized and defined by our colleague, Kate Kirkham, and the following description is based on her paper.[6]

### Revising the Performance Appraisal Process: An Example of Policy Shift

As Kirkham says, it is crucial that the performance appraisal process be closely integrated with the overall objectives of the Managing Diversity initiative. Without a unified approach, paying close attention to diversity alone in the performance appraisal process might seem to indicate preferential treatment of men and women of color and white women.

As she points out, the roles of the manager, the employees and the top-management committee or board overlap in the appraisal process. It is this interlocking at different levels with the various steps of the appraisal process that constitutes the appraisal system. However, the focus of this particular strategy was on the individual manager.

There are three stages in the process: appraisal preparation, conducting the appraisal, and appraisal outcomes. A manager's behavior in conducting the performance process is influenced by how she or he thinks about the job, the expected products of the position, and the employee's relationship to the tasks and the organization. Kirkham notes that all three stages must be reviewed in order to modify outcomes. Addressing each of the stages, she says, "clearly conveys that increasing effectiveness in managing diversity and appraising 'different others' involves more than watching the different other more closely."

In each of the three stages, the strategy proposes specific steps the manager should take; the issues of diversity that relate to each stage; and the specific actions required by the manager.

As we identified the steps necessary for an appropriate performance-appraisal process, it usually became obvious to us and to the management of the company that the standard appraisal process did not, in fact, work in an objective and professional way for *anyone* in the company. Few managers were able to describe the job content of the employees in their charge or list the specific "norms" or standards the employee was expected to meet. Little attention had been paid to a systematic data-gathering process, or to the company's guidelines for ranking, rating and completing the forms provided for management development and recommendations for promotion. Most managers failed to engage their employees in serious discussions about their performance on the job, either for the purpose of correcting deficiencies or planning for the future.

Most decisions on who was to be advanced in the company were based on familiarity, comfort level and general expectations rather than on actual performance. When the new process was implemented, the "myth of merit" was readily seen to be just that—a myth. White men who were much less competent and motivated than others in the work group—white women and men and women of color, but also white men who did not "match the image" of the executive—were routinely promoted while more ambitious and productive "others" were passed over. So the second aspect of the strategy we developed turned out to be useful not just to those who were different by race or gender, but also to those who were just different from the cookie-cutter image of the successful manager.

Kirkham helped us move the initiative forward by describing a series of concepts that clarify how diversity issues play out in organizations. These include the following:

*Like me.* Managers are likely to value the performance of those like them more than they value the performance of those who are different. Since most top managers are white men, this leads to a replication of one style of management and to the continuation of preference for one group. If careful attention is paid to describing the job content related to *results* rather than appearance, it is easier to see the contributions of all employees, rather than just those of the employees who are most like the manager. It is important to recognize that the tendency to favor those who are "like me" is as apt to result from lack of awareness as it is to derive from intentional bias.

*Informal Network.* Expectations about job tasks and priorities are often communicated informally through conversations with managers or peers. Employees who are "like" the manager are more apt to be included in informal networks, often centered around participation in sports, social clubs, or simply casual conversation "normed" on common experience. White women and people of color are often blocked from having access to these informal interactions, and thus lose out both in terms of specific information related to the job and in having the opportunity to form comfortable personal relationships.

*Past experience.* When a manager compares the contributions of individual employees, he or she bases the evaluation on past experience of good or poor performance. When the manager's experience has been with homogeneous groups, the perception of adequacy of performance may be based on style as much as substance. Stereotypic expectations— what one *expects* of a person of a particular race or gender—may have more impact on perception than actual observation of what that person is accomplishing.

*Superstructure.* This is the vicious circle phenomenon. There are so few men and women of color and white women in top management that no one is accustomed to thinking of them in these roles, so no one perceives that they are qualified for or aspire to these roles. As a result, managers do not have that possibility in mind when carrying out performance evaluations or career development planning.

An example of this was a myth that was widely believed regarding Asians and Asian Americans. The stereotype was that they might be excellent scientists or mathematicians, but they weren't good managers. This myth was sometimes supported by consultants who promoted a cross-cultural approach to diversity—they held that the deference that was expected in Asian culture was what prevented people from that group from being effective managers. Somehow the fact that Pacific Rim countries were experiencing an enormous economic boom as a result of the successes of companies led by these "ineffective managers" didn't do much to correct the view from this side of the ocean.

*Perceptions and feelings about differences.* Managers who have been responsible for leading a homogeneous work group usually have little perception of how they perceive minorities and women, or of how those perceptions affect their evaluations of their job performance. The manager must take responsibility for ensuring that the evaluation is not determined by his or her own biases or prejudices.

*Beware of others' biases.* How and when a manager obtains information from others who have knowledge of the employee's performance can also be influenced by race and gender. Data may not be accurate because of bias, lack of experience, or the fear that information will be seen as being racist or sexist. Thus the reports by others may be either unwarrantedly negative or unwarrantedly favorable—based solely on the respondent's attitudes toward different others.

*Fear of expressing.* Discomfort in appraising people of color or white women can lead to the respondent's being either too general or too specific in recorded comments. The fear that any notation of difference will be seen as racist or sexist can prevent accurate and appropriate documentation of behavior and weighting of factors. A white-male manager will customarily draw on more informal information in evaluating other white men; yet in describing women and minorities, this information may not be available, or the manager may feel uneasy in using it.

*Hiding issues of diversity.* A common defense mechanism used by managers who are uncomfortable working with people who are different is, "I don't see you as black" or "I don't think of you as a woman." Since this is obviously untrue, this denial affects the final outcome. An employee's race and gender must be a comfortable part of the evaluation process and the general discussion. Unless it can be included naturally in the process, the information will either be overused (for example, the pretense that all female employees are "superwomen") or underused (the typical stereotypes related to racial and gender bias).

*Failing to provide honest feedback, both positive and negative.* A manager who is uncomfortable in leading a diverse work group may find it very difficult to have to discuss employee performance with the "different others" in her or his charge. This discomfort will color the interaction—sending unintended messages about how the individual was treated or how fair the system really is.

In the process we designed, as described by Kirkham, each of the steps and the relevant issues of diversity were matched with specific actions that the manager should take to improve the overall effectiveness of the performance evaluation process. For example, we pointed out that each manager needed to review the key tasks and the weighting of the factors listed for the job involved in the review—rather than just going through a pro-forma checkoff of generic listings and evaluating by comfort level. We also suggested that the managers review the assignments of personnel in the work group, and note the frequency of interaction with employees, in order to determine if *informal access* to information and opportunity had been made available to women and people of color, as well as to white men.

Managers were also expected to consider the opportunity for advancement to higher-level positions for *all* employees, and to articulate standards for competing for those positions in a way that made clear that race or gender characteristics were not valued differently—that is, that all individuals would be competing based on actual job performance and potential.

This approach to rethinking the performance appraisal process was one component of a very effective strategy that we continued to refine and tailor to the specific needs of the organizations to which we consulted, and that became a vital component of the diversity culture-change process itself.

The process was, however, sometimes derailed by events in the company that had nothing to do with diversity. For example, at the refinery discussed earlier, we continued to do education and awareness workshops, and to consult to and work closely with the management board, for several years; and both they and we could see that progress was being made on the issues they had identified. But then there was a series of personnel changes. The manager who had championed the initiative was promoted. The CEO was transferred. And the internal consultant—a white man—with whom we had worked most closely was fired for reasons that had nothing to do with this effort.

What happened next was very typical of that time, and often happens today as well. The internal consultant was replaced first by a black woman from the EEO and affirmative-action function, who was smart and committed but had no background in systems theory and—even more important—no access to the board. She was soon replaced by a black man, with the same limitations on access to power, and no vision. So the whole effort just fell apart—time, money and energy invested with far less results than could have been realized had the leadership looked at the effort as "a business issue" rather than an incidental concern.

Of course, not all was wasted. There was demonstrable progress in terms of an increase in the awareness of a large number of managers; better results in terms of retention and promotion; and the development of more effective policies and practices. Also, the improvement in this one refinery was observed by other organizations in the system, and we were invited to consult to a number of these as well.

Much of the work in other organizations was similar to that just described. There were, however, some additional developments that were important. For example, we were invited to consult to a plant within the chemical division of a large company, in the deep South. This was one of our first experiences of working directly with southern "good old boys." We learned then, and have had it confirmed over and over, that contrary to the stereotype, many of these southern white men have a particular insight into issues of race.

I'll never forget one person from this plant, a huge, six-foot, six-inch white man with a deep southern drawl—a blue-collar worker, not a college-educated manager—who immediately saw the issues, saw his own complicity in racism, and was not afraid of confronting both his own history and the culture of the plant and the area.

One of the new elements we designed with our partners in that plant was a peer-counseling system. The managers told us that there were a lot of complaints from employees. Some seemed to be about discrimination, but others were just general complaints. The managers were having trouble telling which was which. There was no union at that plant, so there was no effective avenue by which complaints could surface, be investigated and be resolved.

Together we developed a fairly simple but powerful process in which we trained a group of line employees to listen to complaints of their peers and work with them and their managers to resolve them. The counselors were not given extra pay for this effort, but the company provided released time for both the training and the counseling. The process was very, very effective and much appreciated. With our help, the counselors were able to begin to identify which complaints were really about discriminatory practices, and which were more general. The number of complaints was reduced, and those that continued to surface were more readily and appropriately resolved. The managers were grateful because the workplace was more comfortable and productive. And the counselors received new skills which stood many of them in good stead in gaining promotions or in other jobs.

Nonetheless, our work at that plant and most other companies at the time was heavily devoted to ongoing education and awareness. There was little recognition in most companies then—and in most companies today—of the complexity of the issues of discrimination in the organization, or of the determination, courage and commitment of time and money that would be required to ameliorate racism, sexism and other forms of oppression.

Nevertheless, there were other bits and pieces of work that we were able to do in those early days that were more systemic. In several organizations we assisted in the development of what are now known as employee networks—groups of African Americans, senior women, technical employees and so forth—which were very helpful both to the members and to the organizations, and many of which continue to exist today. In one company, I recall, we were asked by a group of black women who had formed an employee association—recognized and supported with some money by the company—to help them strategize on their career paths and develop themselves into more confident and competent professionals. This was very important and useful work, and helped many of these women overcome barriers and make their way slowly up the corporate ladder. Again, if more companies had recognized the importance of such efforts early on, we would not now be scrambling to find white women and people of color to fill top management positions, nor would there be such competition between companies for the best and brightest minorities and white women.

Neither should we minimize the importance or the impact of the training workshops. Even in settings where the work was not particularly intense, where we were working with a few trainers and large groups—forty, fifty, sixty people diverse by race and gender—and the focus was more discussion than experiential interaction or action planning, people would emerge from the experience saying it had changed their lives. We cannot forget how rare—then as well as now—are opportunities for diverse groups to explore differences of race and gender in a setting that is comfortable, nonthreatening and supportive of genuine learning. These workshops also helped us, as consultants and trainers, deepen our theoretical understanding of the issues and hone our practical skills. As time went on, we became more and more aware of how difficult the issues are, how powerful the emotions surrounding them, and how much personal and professional competence is demanded of trainers and facilitators who choose to help people explore them.

## ABUSIVE PRACTICES

I cannot close this review of the 1970s and early 1980s without a look at some of the uglier aspects of what was happening. My recollections fall into two categories: (1) the eruption of various forms of abusive "training" and, (2) the destructive impact of the common practice of appointing someone—usually a white woman or a person of color—to take major responsibility for a diversity initiative on the basis of "identity group" alone, without regard for that person's experience or competence in the field.

Organization development, experiential education and group process as fields of study and practice were, as I have pointed out, products of the 1960s and the 1970s. They were not widely understood, and were often abused by individuals and groups. While many of these charlatans are now gone and forgotten, a few are still around. And organizations that have no experience in working to resolve issues of discrimination are still sometimes taken in by grandiose claims or flashy packages.

Of many examples that could be cited, here are some samples. In one corporation where we were asked to work on gender issues, another consultant had been brought in to assist the company with its problems around racism. This particular man's mode of operation was to assume the power position in the group, standing in the front of the room, and starting a rant about racism. He would identify a scapegoat—always a white man—and accuse him of everything: of being a racist, being evil, shameful, whatever. He would actually yell at him, curse him and keep him in the spotlight for what must have seemed like hours. The other participants were naturally terrified, fearful that if they protested they would be the recipients of the same abuse. After several hours or even a day or two of this kind of abuse, this "trainer" would gradually shift his strategy and become the loving, forgiving father who would absolve the scapegoat of his sins and offer redemption. To my knowledge, this was the sole intent and outcome of the training. To be sure, it created a powerful emotional effect. But at what great cost, both to the identified target and to the group at large! And it added fuel to the fire for those who were suspicious of any experientially based training and hostile to efforts—no matter how valid—to attempt to eradicate discrimination and oppression in organizations.

Another common practice was the use of highly manipulative and cruel group processes. This was the heyday of the EST movement, devised by Werner Erhard, which persists to this day and is probably the best-known example of such work. I had direct personal experience of a movement of this type when I was consulting to a manufacturing plant in the Northeast. We were doing pretty good work on racism and sexism, beginning to see that the senior management was open to working on a wider initiative, and we had the opportunity to help them make real progress on resolving the issues they had asked us to help them with.

However, the human-resources manager who had responsibility for working most closely with us had become a devotee of one of these abusive systems, which I will call "Concepts." She kept urging me to sit in on one of the Concepts workshops, because she was determined to incorporate their work in the diversity effort in the company and she wanted my support. Finally I agreed—with considerable trepidation.

It was a very, very frightening experience. There was a large group of people, 250 or more, in one room, with a leader standing in the front and someone in the back of the room at a huge console. This device manipulated the entire environment—it raised or lowered the temperature, created sounds that were coordinated with the presentation, and was aimed at creating an effect that I can only describe as brainwashing. The entire goal of the event was to seduce participants into giving up their common sense, their ability to make individual decisions and to tell right from wrong, and to enter into an authoritarian ethos where the will of the leader could dominate and overwhelm the desire and ability of individual participants to make their own judgments. It felt to me just like the images of fascist leaders commanding total obedience from robotlike followers. I was terrified.

The whole thing was a kind of pyramid scheme. Participants were seduced into selling products and workshops devised by the founders, and the proceeds from these sales flowed back into the founders' pockets. Innocent people—people who had been sent by corporations or who came on their own, seeking some kind of external meaning or validation to their lives—would give up any pretense of rationality and fall in with this scheme.

I couldn't stand it. Even though the pressure for conformity was very powerful, several of the participants seemed to be able to see through the trickery, and we managed to find and support one another. As the session concluded, we just refused to give in and walked out the door.

In spite of my vigorous protests, however, the company bought into the Concepts ideology and began to send a few people, and then for a time even made attendance mandatory. The whole thing collapsed over two incidents. One participant was so distraught that he committed suicide, and his wife sued the company. And a vice-president of the company attended, was horrified by the experience, and stopped the whole thing—and fired the woman who had promoted it.

There are two things that this horrifying episode illustrates. One is that it is relatively easy for people with no experience in intergroup relations, group process and organization development to get caught up in techniques that may seem similar to the positive things professional consultants and trainers do—but are actually the reverse images. They take the power of group dynamics and use it in the service of what can only be seen as evil. Where our work requires and helps participants to explore their own attitudes, biases and behaviors and make their own determinations about whether to change and how to change, work like that promoted by Concepts aims to prevent critical thinking and subvert common sense and individual responsibility.

The second thing is that the deliberate or inadvertent use of destructive techniques can distract an organization from the necessary work of diversity. When there are no experienced and competent managers and consultants to guide the effort, it can become an "anything goes" situation. And the end is far, far worse than the beginning.

Another kind of abuse has been, and continues to be, the damage that results from targeting someone—a member of a subordinated group—to head up an initiative simply because of their membership in that group, regardless of whether the person has the background or skills required. In one company to which we were consulting in the very early days of our diversity work, there was a black man from a line position who participated in some of the workshops and became very excited about what he saw. Because there were so few people of color in the corporation, and it was important to have their leadership in diversity initiatives, the company asked him to get some training and take on responsibilities in these areas. The demands of the position quickly exceeded his training and competence, and he began to feel increasingly insecure and inadequate. He was positioned by the company as someone with expertise and knowledge, and he felt under increasing pressure to demonstrate that he did indeed have them—all the while recognizing more and more that this was not true. Eventually he left the company and became an independent consultant.

We worked together a great deal over the next few years, even partnering with other consultants in an effort in which a number of leading corporations got together to sponsor workshops in which promising candidates of color were provided with special developmental opportunities to help advance their careers and succeed in the face of the ongoing and powerful barriers that they faced. His competence increased, but he became more and more disaffected with the idea that the United States would live up to its democratic ideals. He began to believe that it was not only not possible for him to make a difference, personally—but also that change itself was not possible. He began to believe that the evils of racism and other forms of oppression were so inherent in the capitalist system that there was, literally, no hope here. He decided that he could be of more use, and have more personal satisfaction, if he went to a developing country to work. And so he did—and continues to make his contributions there.

In his case, I think we can honestly say that racism—not blatant, in-your-face "I hate you" racism, but patronizing, heedless, unthinking, unaware racism, which surrounds and affects us all—broke his heart.

## NOTES

1. For an overview of some academic programs, see the special issue of *The Diversity Factor* 5, no. 1 (Fall 1996).

2. For a helpful review of the patterns of forward movement followed by resistance and retreat, see James W. Loewen, *Lies My Teacher Told Me: Everything Your American History Textbook Got Wrong* (New York: The New Press, 1995). Loewen reviews twelve textbooks in current use in high-school history classes and compares their contents with primary documents in American history. He demonstrates that the standard practice of textbook writers is to present U.S. history as a steady progression toward greater equality, led by a stream of heroic politicians and statesmen. Loewen's point is that not only is such a misrepresentation of our history dishonest, it fails to provide our students with sufficient understanding of the reality of the struggles that have been required—and are still required—to maintain this fragile democracy. Loewen also compares our historical records with those of other countries to debunk a favorite American myth, "We are certainly flawed, but we're better than everybody else."

3. William B. Johnston et al., *Workforce 2000* (Indianapolis: Hudson Institute–U.S. Department of Labor, 1987).

4. See Alice Sargent, *The Androgynous Manager* (New York: AMACOM, 1981).

5. See Kate Kirkham, "Dimensions of Diversity: A Basic Framework," unpublished paper prepared for Elsie Y. Cross Associates, Inc., Philadelphia, PA, for a full description of these concepts (1986).

6. See Kate Kirkham, "Managing Diversity and the Performance Appraisal Process," unpublished paper prepared for Elsie Y. Cross Associates, Inc., Philadelphia, PA, 1983.

# 5

## The Theory Evolves

As the previous chapters demonstrate, by the late 1980s we had helped many companies and other organizations begin to look at their issues of discrimination and oppression. Our experience in working with hundreds of people in workshops also helped us test our theories and come to understand them more fully as they evolved in practice.

It was becoming increasingly clear to me that this work is ultimately about helping leaders have the skills and the courage to manage effectively in a new, much more diverse environment. It is about helping them understand the true meaning of citizenship, in our organizations and in our society. To me, citizenship means equality. Citizenship means being a full member of this family called the United States. The denial of citizenship is most blatant in the ongoing fact that white immigrants are assimilated within one or two or three generations, whereas citizens of color whose families have been part of this nation for almost three hundred years are still excluded from many aspects of our society— aspects that others take for granted.

My whole life work, as I reflect on it, has been to help people and organizations overcome the denial of citizenship and fulfill the real promise of the democratic ideals on which this country was founded. I believe that, at some level, every American wants the giant wound of oppression healed. Even though we will never be able to remove the scars, we can work to try to prevent them from being reopened.

But the prospects for success do not seem bright. There is currently strong pressure for the revocation of rights that were gained during the civil-rights period. Hard-won voting rights are being narrowed. Housing is becoming more, not less, segregated. Public education is inexorably moving toward resegregation. Affirmative action is under constant attack, and is losing the battle in many spheres. There is a disproportionate rate of incarceration of young African-American men and Latinos. Income inequality has increased exponentially—and class divisions are wider than at virtually any other time in our history.

These concerns have led us to define our work in different terms from those prevalent in the common parlance of diversity. We have chosen the language of our definition very carefully. We propose that "Managing Diversity aims at the amelioration of oppression based on differences of race, gender, age, ethnicity, various physical disabilities and sexual orientation." Racism and sexism are the most evident forms of difference and are visible. Managing Diversity means acknowledging and valuing the differences of race and gender in particular and moving toward integration. Difficult as the other issues are, in our society racism and sexism are the most pervasive forms of oppression, the most difficult to talk about and to change. Therefore, in our view, working against racism and sexism gives managers skills for acknowledging the merit of and developing the uniqueness of all people.

One of my frustrations with some of the work that is done in the name of managing diversity is that it focuses on much more trivial matters. In many organizations diversity efforts are little more than activities—ethnic dinners, celebrations of all kinds of holidays, or other kinds of "cultural issues." Such efforts are often mounted in an attempt to appear "inclusive" and—mistakenly, in my view—to deflect what is perceived as the resistance that results when the real issues are approached directly.

How can such initiatives get to the heart of the matter? What is wrong in this country is that people are denied access to organizational power and political power on the basis of skin color and gender. People who are, under the Constitution and under the law of the land, full citizens are excluded from equal employment opportunities, promotion based on merit, equal access to good housing and education, and on and on—not on the basis of lack of intrinsic intelligence, or lack of ambition or pride or ability, but simply on the basis that we are perceived by the white majority as being inferior because we have dark skin tones—or because we are women. This denial of equality is supported by government policy and action, by the courts, by business organizations, by educational, religious and social organizations—in short, by every institution of our common life.

There are many connections between efforts aimed at achieving broader social justice in society and our efforts at organizational change and managing diversity. But the two are not identical. At one level, democracy and capitalism are separate and competing ideologies, and global capitalism departs even further from the ideals of democracy. The current retreat from market regulation strikes at the very heart of the idea that one function of a democratic government should be to promote social and economic justice. However, even within the free-market rampage are found the seeds of its own correction—markets, whether free or regulated, need consumers and employees, and they require a society not distracted by riot and rebellion in order to continue on a steady course of increasing profitability.

Since I have opted to consult to corporations, I am constrained by the realities of corporate culture. Our contract with our business partners is to help them achieve their own goals regarding equity in the workplace. Aiming to achieve social justice is, in my view, a political stance. Corporate management, however, views its primary responsibility as enhancing the return on investment to its stakeholders.

Sometimes people who are drawn to this work become confused about these matters. Even people who are employed by organizations, particularly people of color, forget that our client is the corporation itself—not the identity group or particular individual who has been aggrieved. We enter into contracts with companies, and those companies are specifically dedicated to the goals of capitalism—to maximizing profits, to enhancing return on investment to shareholders, and to winning out over the competition.

It may well be that if more and more people in a corporation begin paying attention to issues of equity, the company will become more humane. But that does not mean that it will become a democratic or socialized system. We are not working to dismantle hierarchy or, within the corporate structure, to redistribute income or even reallocate power.

We are working to provide more equal access to power and its privileges. We believe that no one group—in our society, white men—has any innate claim to these privileges. There is no rational justification for the fact that all the top positions in the hierarchy are held by members of that one group. Such limitation is not only unfair, it is short-sighted and ultimately "anti-capitalistic": that is, it robs the company of resources that would help to maximize profits, enhance return on investment, and win out over the competition. Since our work aims to help white women and people of color gain access to more power and more opportunities *within* organizations, it inevitably follows that there is some fallout toward helping these subordinated groups gain access to more power and more opportunities in society at large. This is a consequence that I enthusiastically applaud, and which, in other aspects of my life, I enthusiastically work to achieve. But it is not the goal of corporate-based diversity initiatives.

## RACE AS ALLEGORY

Even within the limited goal of "shattering the glass ceiling" or "cracking the cement floor" of U.S. organizations, we are confronted with an extraordinarily difficult challenge. Relations between people of different races—particularly between white people and African Americans—are so intensely charged emotionally and so tangled up with our shameful history of slavery and subsequent abuses that it is very difficult to come to terms with the present realities.

As we work with ordinary people at all levels in organizations we become aware that the numbers of those who are truly in the dominant group are very small. Most people, of whatever race or gender, but especially the working classes or lower classes, have been treated very badly. The amazing thing is how successfully the concept of divide and conquer has functioned to keep the oppressed groups apart and at odds. In our education and awareness workshops—the basic building block of the Managing Diversity intervention—we see that race provides a symbolic way of representing how patterns of dominance and subordination, power and authority, and resistance work throughout organizations and society.

In every workshop we use a staff group that is mixed by race and gender. There are many reasons for this choice, but one of the most important is that it provides a mechanism for illustrating the power dynamics of race and gender. As I pointed out in the previous chapter, in the small-group setting of the workshop (usually about twenty-four participants and four staff members), the whole concept of authority and power plays itself out visibly and immediately. The majority of the staff—usually one white woman, one woman of color and one man of color—represent subordinated groups. The one white man on the team represents the dominant group. The group of participants comes together as a collective of people who don't know each other.

As the work begins, the conversation and interactions function on two different levels simultaneously. On the first level, participants share their daily experiences in the company. They are always different—but also always the same. That is, the experiences that the individual participants have had fit into patterns of discrimination and oppression that recur repeatedly in organizations and in society.

For example, a black man may recall that a watermelon was left in his locker. Another person tells of a time when "nigger" was scrawled on his car. Many women speak of finding sexist notes posted on their computers. A white man may report that his tires were slashed when he intervened on behalf of a woman who had protested harassment. Many people describe company conventions as orgies of lewd behavior, complete with company-financed strip shows.

Even while the recitation is going on, interactions are taking place among the participants, among the members of the staff, and between participants and staff. These interactions are posing another level of questions—raising issues that the participants are not yet aware of, but that are usually quite obvious to the members of the staff, who have seen them surface in hundreds of such sessions. The issues begin to form patterns and lead to highly predictable outcomes.

Some of the issues that arise relate to authority. "Where is the power in this group?" "How do I respond to power?" "How do I bring my typical way of responding to power and authority into this setting?" "How do I behave in *this* group?" The way we structure the dynamics of the group means that participants will find their usual expectations of authority upset. Instead of finding the white man in charge, they may discover that it is a woman of color, or a white woman or a man of color. Since all of us have grown up expecting that if there is a white man in a given situation, he will be in charge, this shift creates a kind of cognitive dissonance. People lose their bearings. They don't know exactly how to act, where to look, what to do. This discomfort is not generated by the staff. We don't harass people, or accuse people of being racist or sexist or anything else. We simply shift the ground of assumptions slightly, so that people have to find new ways of relating and understanding power.

Since every group includes some people who are independent, some who are dependent, and some who are counter-dependent, these roles get further complicated by the dynamics raised by dissonant race and gender power relationships. It often works out that there are a number of white men in the group who are counter-dependent. They resist everything that is going on. No matter what the staff does, it isn't right, or it isn't fast enough, or it's too disorganized, or they've had a better experience in some other diversity workshop. The independent members, at the same time, are saying, "Well, I'm learning something and I'm beginning to think differently." And the dependents are saying, "Would you please shut up and let the staff go on with their work?"

It gets more and more complicated. A counter-dependent white man, watching an independent white man, may become very confused. He will wonder why the independent man is in alignment with the woman staff leader. If the independent white man is someone who has authority in the organization, the counter-dependent man really begins to sweat. Quite often, he will transfer his resistance to the white-male staff member. He can't resist the white man who is in an authority position in the organization—that's much too dangerous. But he can—and this happens over and over—begin to challenge the white man who is a member of the consulting team.

The role of a white man as a member of a mixed staff in this work is very tricky. By yielding the dominant role to someone else—a black woman, an Asian-American man, a white woman—he deliberately steps outside the parameters of the old boys' club and confounds the expectations of the group, especially of the white men in the group. There is no ready-made role for this staff person. If he has not come to terms with his own identity and his own feelings about race and gender, he may well come across to the white women and people of color as whiny, self-serving and unattractive—at the same time that he is dismissed by the other white men as a traitor.

It takes a great deal of work to develop a mixed staff of people who are clear about their own identities and their own issues; who have learned to work together effectively in the tinderbox of emotions, feelings and concepts that the workshop represents; and who understand at the cognitive level the important psychological, historical and sociological issues that the workshop addresses. These are skills and competencies that are not readily apparent to someone who has never experienced them. Therefore, it is understandable that newly appointed diversity managers have difficulty in knowing how to identify consultants who have the expertise they need. I return to the topic of criteria for the development of diversity trainers and consultants in a later chapter.

## LEARNING ABOUT RACE

We all take in messages—stereotypes—about race before the age of judgment. These messages come from all of the institutions in our society, from our family members, our peers, our colleagues, from school, church, governmental bodies—and mostly from the media. Since we are little children when we begin to receive them, we are completely unaware of their meaning or impact; we just absorb them. We have no way of saying to our mothers, when we are three or four or five, "It's wrong for you to think that black people are violent."

These stereotypes—of other races and our own race as well—get submerged in us and become unconscious. I often ask people to interview their children to find out what their attitudes and beliefs are, and they are absolutely shocked at what they hear. This has not changed over the twenty or more years we have been investigating it.

We have found that helping participants understand the stereotypes that they have always had requires other than rational approaches. Because the messages are taken in so early, they are not readily available to the conscious mind. We use a variety of what are often called projective devices—techniques that function like Rorschach tests and elicit powerful, deeply buried memories and feelings.

The same patterns appear over and over. White people can seldom talk about what they learned about being white, because white is "normal." It's like fish in the water—they aren't aware of the water at all. The exercises also show, dramatically and tragically, that we all learn the *same* things about race, whether we are white or of color. For the most part, the early messages teach people of color that they are inferior—they also teach white people that people of color are inferior—and they teach both groups that whites are superior.

But people who are white and people who are black (or other people of color or Hispanic) do something very different with the messages. Being taught that one is inferior has very negative consequences for a subordinated-group person. We either learn to overcome those messages, or we succumb to them, or we find a variety of responses somewhere in between. White people, however, tend to obtain a very unrealistic view of themselves and of their abilities and their worth in comparison with people of color, unless they work very hard to drown out these early messages.

In the workshop, as the members of a small, five-to-seven person group begin to share with one another and with a facilitator what they've done and what they've learned, an amazing thing begins to happen. They have shared a human experience that is almost always emotional, that is deeply metaphorical, and that is genuine. The experience and the sharing of the feelings around that experience reduce the tension and the fear people have of being able to talk about race. They form a strong interpersonal connection around a topic—race—that is usually so terrifying that we are afraid to discuss it. White people often feel that they have, for the first time in their lives, faced up to the shame and guilt they have inside themselves around racial issues. The process is very restorative—they relieve themselves of the need to hide their attitudes and their feelings.

African Americans and members of other subordinated groups may feel that they have, again often for the first time, faced up to the pain and anger inside them—and they are stunned to realize that facing it, and sharing it with the "enemy," didn't destroy them.

When the groups are joined together in a plenary session, we always find that the messages that have been shared in the small groups are very similar from group to group. The messages about dominant groups—about whites—are that they are superior, better, more educated, more powerful, than subordinated groups. But that's not all; the messages also indicate that whites are viewed as undemocratic, mean, thoughtless and rude when it comes to their treatment of subordinated groups.

Messages about subordinated groups—not just blacks but other people of color, Latinos and Latinas, Asian Americans, Native Americans and others—are ubiquitous and easily captured: messages that characterize the other as inferior, dirty, lazy, always late, and so forth. As more peo-

ple of color who are not African-American come into this society, we
begin to see that there is a slight differentiation between the stereotypes
between groups, but there is also a great deal of overlap.

In the workshops, people who come from other countries, who were
not socialized in the United States, are asked to talk about what they
learned about race in their own countries, and what they learned when
they came to the United States. If they came to this country as adults,
they may be shocked to discover that they have learned the same racist
stereotypes as U.S. citizens, and that they have brought them with them
to their new home. They also begin to realize that these stereotypes have
been reinforced when they take up residence here. In fact, some people
say that they didn't have much information about racial stereotypes until
they arrived—but once here, they were thoroughly indoctrinated in
American attitudes.

In addition to experiential exercises, we also use videos and other techniques to give workshop participants more information about the topic.
When we present the facts about what every African-American person
and many other people of color experience in this society daily—no matter how they look, how they behave, how educated they are, how they
speak—white people are *always* amazed, surprised and confounded. This
news comes as such a shock to them—you can hear the emotion in their
voices when they talk about it.

The culmination of this process of exploration asks the participants to
talk about how these same messages about race play out in their own
company. It is quite amazing how the group members, who may have
come into the session defensive, closed, bored or fearful, now are able
to speak quite freely. Any number of people, whites as well as blacks,
will talk about what they know goes on that is racist in the company.
They can give example after example, and there is no doubt in anyone's
mind that the situations are based on racial and racist stereotypes, or
that they exist in every corner of the company.

I should say that the process isn't always as perfect as I am suggesting
here. There are still some people who deny what is being demonstrated,
or people who insist that these things are all in the past—and these are
both white people and people of color. Some people find it too frightening or too threatening, and shut down or become angry. But in the
vast majority of situations, the process works as I have described.

Going back to the roles that people take on within any group setting,
the experiential exercises and simulations we use help to move all the
members toward assuming a relationship of interdependence. They have
moved from being individuals who are relating primarily to a person
who is in a position of power and leadership, to being individuals who
are relating to one another—who can have conversations, who can share
feelings, who can work together to solve problems. In the business set-

ting, they can begin to see that these issues, unresolved, have a negative impact on the company's ability to do business. They begin to see that in spite of the messages the groups have received, as individuals they are much more alike than different—and that they each have important contributions to make to the common enterprise.

One final point, somewhat more speculative. I feel that the work we have done over the years has shown us that this question of inclusion and exclusion is very basic. As we talk with the participants, and watch them learning to talk openly with one another, we are struck over and over with the longing we all have, as people, to be intimate and to be loved. Much of the fear we have, I believe, of talking about difficult topics like race and gender and sexual orientation and physical ability comes from our belief that talking about them will separate us from one another and make affection and intimacy impossible. My experience, though, is just the opposite. I have found that nothing—except sex— promotes intimacy more quickly than does talking about race.

## DEEPER MEANINGS

After years of seeing these patterns appear over and over again in workshops and seminars, I have begun to realize that attitudes about race play an important role in the psyche of our society. These attitudes seem to arise from what the psychologist Carl Jung called archetypes— innate ideas or patterns in the psyche, which are expressed in dreams or art as certain basic symbols or images.[1]

Many archetypes deal with our most primal needs and relationships— dependence on the mother, the need for safety and security, the urge for sex, the fascination with and fear of death, and many more. If you trace the relationships between whites and blacks in this society back to the days of slavery, we are, in many, many cases, the children of the same father. As we all know, many of the slave masters had sexual relationships, either forced or consensual, with slave women. The white slave master also allowed or forced his male slaves to have sex with the slave women, because he wanted to increase his human property by having more children, whom he could then sell for profit.[2] The white slave master was, then, selling his own children. Or he allowed the female children to grow up on the plantation, and then raped them, too. Thus not only were slavery, adultery and rape institutionalized—but also incest.

At some macro-level such institutionalized abuses *must* have an impact on the body politic. In our work, we have found that people have some dim awareness of this, of these atrocities and how they have impacted our public policies and our laws and the norms of our societies. But who among us is willing to look at such things? Yet they creep up, in our workshops, and people begin to acknowledge them.

These facts and their implications are completely antithetical to every-thing that our society is supposed to stand for—to our belief in life, liberty and the pursuit of happiness. Imagine what facing up to them would require of us—we would have to admit to what degree we are and have been living a vast lie. Following out the lines of these impli-cations leads to strange and often quite frightening places. It explains the whole sexual aura that has surrounded black women and continues to surround us. It has something to do with the displacement of sexuality from white women to black women; it has something to do with the notion of the southern belle who was pure and on a pedestal. It has a lot to do with the competition of white men with black, the envy of white men for African-American men, the sense of sexual inferiority that led white men for so long to bar black men from competition in professional sports.

It also—horribly and tragically—underlies the lynching of black men for supposed insults to white women. Think of the terrible irony of this, when we have at every hand—in the mixed race of so many black people in this country—the evidence of the result of white men "insulting" black women in the most dastardly ways possible.

I think it's all based in fear and in religious and political control. This may seem far-fetched and speculative, but one can see how it plays out in actuality. In the early days of our country, poor white indentured servants and black slaves and some Native Americans cooperated to resist the abuses of the white landowners. But by clever, devious and cruel means the power elite contrived to separate and thereby disem-power the working-class groups, creating the whole concept of a "white race" to use the working-class whites as a buffer to keep the working-class blacks and Chinese and Hispanics—and even the Irish—from having access to power and goods and services.

And the same patterns are operating now as our politicians battle over our census. By controlling how we count, the power elite can control who gets counted. By assuring that people of color, the poor, the im-migrants and others who are disenfranchised are undercounted, those who are in power can avoid sharing power with them—thus maintaining the status quo, as far as possible. At this moment in our history, it is a losing strategy. The sheer growth of numbers of people of color will bring about a change in the power structure. The question in the last hours of the twentieth century is, Will we who have been subordinated learn how to work *together* for the common good? Or will we simply replicate the patterns and systems that have been used by the dominant whites, to try to raise our own group (or ourselves, as individuals) and keep the others still at the margins?

## EXPERIENTIAL EDUCATION

I have given this long discussion of race as an allegory for the American condition because understanding race, racism and the dynamics of subordination and dominance is crucial if the reader is to grasp the intent and methodology of our work. The basic education and awareness workshops, and other workshops we have designed as part of the Managing Diversity and diversity culture-change process, have one overarching goal: to explore issues of bias and prejudice, discrimination, and racism, sexism, heterosexism and other forms of oppression.

The workshops employ the basic methodology of T-groups, or laboratory-education groups, but are differentiated from these by the focus on a specific topic. The traditional T-group is a self-contained experience; the point of the process is that the individual comes to understand how group dynamics work, in practice, and how he or she functions within that setting. The Managing Diversity education and awareness workshop, in contrast, aims to provide participants with a direct experience of how a group that is mixed by race, gender and other identifiable characteristics functions; how the individual functions in that setting; and how those dynamics replicate patterns that exist within our organizations.

Thus the workshops provide learning at three levels: the individual, the group, and the organizational or societal. Over the years we developed a framework for exploring these issues, which has been most succinctly defined by our colleague Kate Kirkham in the paper referred to in the previous chapter.[3] Kirkham suggests that in order to help participants talk about issues of race and gender and the workplace we need to help them achieve a *breadth of awareness* of the complexity of the issues, and a *depth of understanding or insight* into their significance.

In the workshop, we help individuals recognize that the issues are not just interpersonal. Through the various simulations and exercises, as well as lectures, we enable participants to broaden their awareness to a recognition that different *groups* have different experiences in life, and thus different responses to members of other groups and to situations. The policies and practices of *organizations* reflect and replicate the biases, prejudices and discrimination that evolve from differential group experience and the different degrees of power held by the various groups. Further, the organizations themselves reflect and replicate the norms and expectations of *society*, which also embodies long-held attitudes, policies, preferences and barriers based on race, gender and other differences. Each aspect of this dimension—breadth of awareness—can be identified with basic problems in managing diversity: *prejudice* in interpersonal interaction; *discrimination* in intergroup behavior; and *racism, sexism, heterosexism and other isms* in organizational dynamics and in society.

Comprehending the breadth of issues is a part of the competency required as a colleague in a diverse work force. The relationship between co-workers who are different (the interpersonal aspect) is embedded in how groups are valued, how interaction is structured in critical internal systems such as performance, promotion and so forth, and conditions in the larger society. When an individual is "stuck" in any one place—is unaware of the nature and extent of the other issues—her or his effectiveness in working with others is reduced.

The second dimension the workshop illustrates is the need for a *depth of understanding*. As Kirkham points out, individuals respond to these issues in various ways. First, we react *cognitively*; that is, we respond in an intellectual or "thinking" way. As we gain more insight into the issues, we are able to respond *behaviorally*—that is, not only to change our thinking but to change our actions as well. Finally, if the process is successful, we achieve change in our *attitudes, feelings and core values*. That is, we not only learn to think and behave in new ways—which could be the result not of real learning but of responding to what we think the company expects of us—we perceive issues of race, gender and other differences in a whole new way, and we begin to live on the basis of different feelings and values.

Using both dimensions helps the group and the facilitators identify what is going on as the workshops proceed. For example, we check to see if some individuals are stuck at the interpersonal level—are they defining everything in terms of one-to-one experiences? Do some participants seem to recognize that racism and sexism exist in the organization at levels beyond the individual? Are all or most of the members able to recognize their attitudes, feelings and core values? Are there differences in this regard between the various groups—is the work more difficult, for example, for white men than for black men, for men in general than for women in general, and so forth? Using both dimensions also helps to identify what strategies may be needed to create change in this particular organization.

Kirkham also points out that the simple framework, which can be diagrammed and kept in view throughout the workshop, has three specific uses: as a personal checklist, as a diagnostic and intervention guide, and as a map of the territory. Understanding the "map"—or the overall view of the Managing Diversity intervention—is especially helpful for majority-group members. Since few whites, and especially few white men, have had the opportunity to hear at first hand the experiences people of color, or women, have in organizations, they are most apt to get "stuck" at the individual level—becoming defensive, guilty, hostile or confused. When they are able to see that this is a stage in a well-defined journey, they are less apt to stay bogged down in these reactions and more able to move on to form partnerships and receive new learning.

The education and awareness and other diversity workshops are entities in themselves and can be viewed separately from the individuals who participate in them. Each group has a character, a style, a personality and a set of dynamics similar to those of other groups but distinctive for *this* group. The dynamics that exist in such groups mirror, in a highly concentrated and intense way, dynamics that exist in every organization. As suggested above, issues of dependence and counterdependence are always evident, as are needs for inclusion, intimacy and affection.

Conflict is inevitable, in the group as in the organization. In each group, too, as in every organization, certain roles are always assumed by one or more individuals: leader, follower, gatekeeper, clarifier, supporter and so forth. There are also specific and predictable psychological processes in evidence in the group, such as transference and displacement, integration and differentiation, and others, that also occur (but less observably) in daily interactions in organizations.

The role of the trainer in this kind of experiential education is a kind of paradox. She is there to facilitate group interaction and to offer expert information on the topic of managing diversity. But she is also there as a participant in the group, acknowledging and sharing feelings, attitudes and ideas about the topic.

The classical experiential education trainer has the same dilemma— being a member of the group while serving as group facilitator. The Managing Diversity group trainer, however, has intensified both roles in a domain in U.S. society which is fraught with feeling, ethical and legal issues, personal prerogative, ignorance, taboo, fear, pain, competition for the spotlight, symbolic representation of deep psychological issues (archetypes, redemption, collaboration, betrayal, shame, guilt and so forth), religious conflicts (over issues such as homophobia and misogyny, for example)—not to mention "the bottom line." It is obvious that learning to be a competent trainer in a Managing Diversity setting requires intense effort including cognitive understanding of history, economics, sociology and psychology, skill in leading groups, and thorough awareness of one's own attitudes, prejudices, behaviors and beliefs around the issues addressed. It is not a role that can be adequately filled by someone who is simply chosen for it from a line position, or from human resources, because he or she is a person of color, or because she is a woman. Anyone, regardless of race or gender or sexual orientation, *can* learn to do it. No one—again regardless of race, gender or sexual orientation—can do it without adequate preparation.

As I pointed out earlier, one of the most important functions of the

Managing Diversity education and awareness group is to replicate the ways in which power and authority exist and operate in organizations. We use various exercises and simulations that allow people to "try out" what it feels like to occupy different positions of power.[4]

These simulations provide a very powerful demonstration of the principles of organizational dynamics. Participants are able to see that it is not necessarily individual prerogative or merit that dictates what happens in an organization. What happens is predetermined by the way the organization is structured and by the luck of the draw. In the simulations, how each person behaves, the goals and strategies of each group, and the overall outcome are determined not by the competence or personality of individual participants, but by where they are placed in the organization by the random assignment of the exercise. The simulations have very dramatic implications for how race and gender and other differences play out in organizations. The process works just the same no matter who participates in it. We've done it with groups who are all African Americans, all women, all whites. It becomes crystal clear that it is not education, not merit, not competence, not niceness, not attractiveness that matters—it's a question of where you are assigned in the game (and thus in the organization and society) at the outset.

Participants get the point immediately. They can see that in society and in the organizations, people of color, women, people with disabilities, and people who are "out" as gays and lesbians automatically "draw" the chips that assign them to one of the lower groups. In a simulation, when a CEO's luck of the draw places him in the lowest group, and he experiences the dynamics of being an outsider—a subordinated-group member—he is almost always shocked and astounded. He recognizes that his achievement is not based on his individual merit alone, but on whether he drew the chips to send him to Harvard, to grow up in a middle-class or upper-class neighborhood, to have the opportunity to attend quality schools, to have access to various kinds of cultural enrichment and opportunities for experiences that led to being very competitive for entry-level positions—and on and on.

When we ask participants to give examples of how the principles play out in the company, they never hesitate. They will say that the senior executives never try to find out what's going on at the bottom of the organization. They acknowledge that middle managers typically block information (especially bad news) from going up the chain to the top, and also block information in general from going down to the lower groups. They note that their middle managers feel so threatened that they contrive to prevent others—white women, or people of color or lower-class white men—from succeeding.

Another striking learning is that one carries the self-identity based on one's original assignment (in life, in the organization, in the simulation) throughout one's life or career. A lower-level person who is able to reach the top of the organization still is apt to behave like a lower-level person. A black man, for example, who reaches the top has already made some deals and trades with people down at the bottom, so he must be accountable to that group. But he must also behave in such a way at the top as to engender trust and maintain his position—because the men in charge can eject him easily. So he is pulled in both directions all the time—a very stressful life.

Most white women and most people of color in our society are in the lower groups. Even within the financial industry, for example, where about 72 percent of the people are women, they are concentrated at the bottom of the organization. The top groups are made up of white men who want to hold on to power. The middle ranks are also mostly white men who don't want to give away any of their power by opening up their ranks to women.

I should stress here that I am describing the way the dynamics of oppression play out in *this* society. In another society—say an all-black country like Nigeria—the same dynamics obtain, but have to do with class or religion or gender. I contend that the same dynamics of oppression exist in all societies. In our society it is particularly and peculiarly focused around race. But gender cuts across every society.

The exercises and simulations we employ are not ends in themselves—not games we offer for the amusement or amazement of the participants. At the end of every simulation, we ask the workshop participants to gather again in small groups to talk about how they can apply what they have learned in their own organizations. They come up with incredible recommendations based on their understanding of the need for structural change—not just individual shifts in "hearts and minds." They often say that they now see that it is the communication patterns within their organizations that block the ability of senior managers, for instance, to get information from below; or they understand that middle managers, because of their precarious position in the organization, tend to keep the flow of information stuck at their level. These insights and recommendations often become the building blocks of a strategic plan around diversity—the basis for a culture-change initiative.

It is important to bear in mind that the education and awareness workshop and the other workshops we facilitate (performance appraisal, leadership development, champions, training of trainers and many more) are *components* of an overall organizational change intervention. In the following chapters I present two case studies of such interventions, which illustrate the function of the workshops in the effort. To conclude this chapter, however, I highlight how some of the roles managers and consultants play, in relation to diversity initiatives, replicate in real time the dynamics we illustrate in the simulations.

## ROLES OF MANAGERS AND CONSULTANTS

As our work progressed in the last half of the 1980s and the early 1990s, our client base expanded to include many separate companies within large multinational corporations. Having by this time facilitated hundreds of workshops with thousands of participants, in dozens of companies, we had acquired a lot of experience in the strategies that would lead to success and those that blocked progress.

One factor that always had great impact was the role played by the internal consultant or manager who was charged with responsibility for the effort. We found that these roles fell into clearly distinguishable categories and were fairly predictable.

First, in every organization, there is a person or group of people who function as *gatekeepers*. The gatekeeper often has direct access to the CEO, and appoints himself or herself to keep the CEO from hearing bad news or receiving too much disconcerting information. Often the gatekeeper takes up a position of competition with us, the outside consultants— even while the company is negotiating with us to help them address very serious problems.

In many cases, unfortunately, these gatekeepers are people of color or white women who have worked themselves into key positions by ingratiating themselves with the people in power. They are people who were assigned to the "lower groups" in society and still carry that self-image with them into their new positions. They are easily threatened and regard any strategy that is apt to create disequilibrium in the organization with suspicion and fear. Since our work deals so directly and so persistently with race, gender and other difficult identity issues, it is also very often personally threatening, since it may require that the manager confront his or her own pain around these issues and acknowledge that she or he, too, has been wounded by the sexist and racist systems of the organization.

There are a variety of reasons why people of color and white women are chosen by corporations for these positions. They may be chosen because the white men who are the leaders in the organization genuinely believe that no white man could be asked to take responsibility for a diversity effort because no white man really understands the issues. These white men may have just begun to see that people of color and white women have had different experiences in life and in the corporate world than themselves, so they make a logical leap to assume that white men can't really "get it."

A second reason is that few senior executives are willing to concede the importance of power dynamics in bringing about organizational change around issues of race, gender, sexual orientation or other forms of oppression. They certainly understand these dynamics in other aspects of the organization—for example, when they are trying to develop leaders or launch a reengineering effort. But they don't make the connection around diversity. So they select people who lack power and access to power—very often someone at a fairly low level in the human-resources function.

I have had a good deal of success in arguing with corporate leaders that the people most able to head up diversity initiatives are powerful, senior-level white men who are "fast trackers." These people are recognized by the work force as being of consequence in the organization, and their appointment says to the employees that this is a significant intervention and that management expects the same kind of compliance with it as it does with all other initiatives.

A third reason is much less positive. Often, unfortunately, a low-level white woman or person of color is assigned responsibility for the initiative because the white leaders have no real commitment to it and expect it to fail. I once worked with a company where the person responsible for the diversity effort was a mid-level African-American man. He was genuinely interested in the work, and he wanted us to succeed. But he was terrifically insecure in his own position, he did not have access to the top of the organization, and he constantly misread all the signals— signals that were perfectly obvious to us from our years of experience with other such organizations. So he spent his time coaching us endlessly on how to behave, how to dress, how to position ourselves. We had no choice but to work in such a way that we moved him aside—to go around him, or rely on our own experience to get to the top of the organization. We had no ill will toward him, nor he toward us. But his lack of experience, skill and power actually led to a prolongation of the start-up of the intervention—and to increased costs to the company. In other cases, such an appointment has derailed the entire effort and left behind a residue of anger or disappointment that may take many years to overcome.

Another phenomenon is the presence of internal consultants and managers who lack the skills necessary to manage the initiative. Since the function of "diversity manager" or some such title is a relatively new position, there are few if any criteria for who should be selected or what they should do once they get there. Many people who hold these positions are white women, or men or women of color who have been chosen *because* of their race or gender, not because of their competence in the field. In the majority of cases they are individuals who have been in the human-resources function, have little or no power in the organization, and are thrown into this responsibility with no staff, few resources, and no experience or training in dealing with race and gender issues.

In a number of cases, too, we found that the internal person, even while discussing possible collaboration with us, is actually promoting another consultant who would do work that is more multicultural (and less threatening) or would keep the initiative at the "ethnic dinners and activities" level—work that does not really raise the issues or attempt to change the power dynamics in the organization.

Fortunately, however, there are many other people in organizations who do see the issues, have the courage to take a stance, are willing to take the risks necessary to let the problems come to the attention of the CEO and other top managers, and have enough self-confidence to work with the external consultants—either our firm or another—as partners. If the culture-change initiative is to succeed, that partnership must be strong. We bring to the interaction years of experience and information about the issues of race and gender, about how groups and systems function, and about how they can be changed. The internal consultant or manager brings her or his knowledge of the organization, including both the factual information of the parameters of the problems and a more informal awareness of the norms, expectations and political realities of how things get done.

Both are crucial to success. Where we have found such partnerships, and top management has made and held on to a commitment to the change they say they desire, we have been able to help the organization go a long way toward creating a new, more inclusive culture.

In the following chapters I review two of these. In closing, however, I want to point out that even where initiatives have been aborted at the education and awareness level, value has been added to the organization. When we think back over these more than two decades and recall the thousands of people who have worked with us—and cried, laughed, struggled and learned with us—we realize that they have returned to their duties with a different perception and more awareness of how racism and sexism and heterosexism and other forms of oppression play out in daily life and in the life of organizations. I often meet people, as I travel around the country, who tell me that they were in such-and-such workshop, and that it changed their lives. Even without the kind of support from top management that we seek, without the continuity and consistency that we know is important, they have been able to translate their learning into new ways of working and living. In spite of all evidence to the contrary, as the forces of regression try to pull us back to a world of white-male domination and narrow-minded bigotry, there is hope.

## NOTES

1. See, for example, Carl Jung, *The Archetypes and the Collective Unconscious*, translated by R.F.C. Hull (Princeton, NJ: Princeton University Press, 1968).

2. Many texts document this history. One excellent recent source is Darlene

Clark Hine and Kathleen Thompson, *A Shining Thread of Hope: The History of Black Women in America* (New York: Broadway Books, 1998). Another reliable text is *Slaves in the Family* (New York: Farrar, Straus and Giroux, 1998), in which author Edward Ball, a white man, traces the historical record of his own slave-holding ancestors in South Carolina, and seeks out his relatives who are "black" descendants of the same people.

3. See Kate Kirkham, "Dimensions of Diversity: A Basic Framework," unpublished paper prepared for Elsie Y. Cross Associates, Inc., Philadelphia, PA, (1986).

4. For another version of these concepts, see Barry Oshry, *Seeing Systems: Unlocking the Mysteries of Organizational Life* (San Francisco: Berrett-Koehler, 1996).

# 6

## "Jaraco Corporation": A Case Study in Culture Change

In the previous chapter, I reviewed a few of the concepts that inform our work at the individual and group level. In the education and awareness workshops, we aim to help individuals come to terms with their own attitudes toward people of the other gender and people of other races, sexual orientation, ability levels and so forth. We also provide structured events that enable workshop participants to experience in simulations the ways power dynamics based on group membership operate in organizations and society. As the descriptions suggest, facilitating these processes requires both an in-depth knowledge of the historical and sociological facts of oppression and extensive training in the processes of adult and experiential education.

In this chapter I turn to an even more difficult challenge—how to analyze and change the culture of an organization so that long-standing practices, policies and norms that favor one group over another are removed, and new ones put in their place. I use one organization, to which we consulted for a period of eight years in the late 1980s and early 1990s, as the focus of this discussion. Many of the concepts, however, are those we use regularly in many companies, and some of the examples could be drawn from virtually any organization.

### "JARACO CORPORATION"

In the mid-to-late 1980s more and more U.S. companies were beginning to recognize that doing business as usual was becoming less productive. Our firm received many invitations to submit proposals for providing assistance to companies in addressing their "race relations" issues, or their "status of women" concerns. Few of these translated into actual contracts, since most companies were still looking for quick fixes or public-relations ploys. A number did, however, engage us, and we were increasingly busy.

One day I received a call from the vice-president for human resources for "Jaraco Corporation," a mid-sized firm that was one of many companies in a major multinational corporation. He briefly described the company, and told me that the president had heard about my work and wanted to talk to me about their problems in retaining blacks. Would I come up and talk with them about the issues and how we might help them? In those days it was still possible for me to respond to such a request personally, so in a few weeks I made a quick trip to Jaraco, which was headquartered not too far from our offices. The president and the vice-president of human resources and some other top executives received me cordially and laid out their dilemma succinctly.

"We've hired lots of blacks here," the president said. (In those days the business world was only concerned about African Americans and still called us blacks.) "And we've done our best to keep them. But our efforts have not paid off. Either they can't seem to do the work, or if they are more competent, they just leave. This is not acceptable to me. We know that the market for our products includes many blacks, and that market is growing. If we don't understand what our own employees want and need, how can we be sure we understand what our potential black customers will buy?"

He told me that his goal was to have a black man on his board as soon as possible. He had been able to develop white people, including white women, and see them advance to board level. But so far he had not had the same success in enabling a black man to succeed.

Well, of course I first had to have a conversation with him about his assumption that the only blacks he needed to be concerned about were men! Once we got that resolved, he went on to confide that his motivation was not simply altruism or increasing his company's profits. As it happened, the parent corporation had a goal statement in place that indicated that diversity was important in the system. This president was both ambitious and smart. He felt that Jaraco was the best company in the system, and that if the parent company wanted its executives to demonstrate that they were addressing diversity, he was going to be the best in meeting that expectation, along with all the others.

I assured him that his needs and concerns were very familiar to me, that we were having some success in addressing them in other companies, and that I would be glad to work with him to find a match between our competencies and his goals. We discussed the work we were doing in other companies, and I told him that at the outset I would want to have him and his direct reports participate in one of our three-day education and awareness workshops. I was pretty blunt—I said that unless he was firmly committed to the work, unless he and his staff felt that what we were doing was *their* intervention, he would be wasting the company's money and all of our time. I shared some of my experiences in other settings where the lack of buy-in at the top undermined the entire initiative, and the effort degenerated. The focus had to be on change at the "system level"—not on changing individual hearts and minds. The expectation of an initial three-day commitment was just the beginning.

Right away he balked. "Three days?" He was incredulous. "Why the hell do you need three days? I can't ask these executives to spend that much time in some touchy-feely seminar." I'd heard that before—many times. I began to collect my things.

"Wait," he said, "let's talk about it. Maybe I just don't understand."

So I explained to him the purpose of the workshops: to develop a sense of community, some trust, the ability to talk about uncomfortable issues like race. The vice-president, another white man, joined in to confirm what I was saying and encourage him to at least consider it. The president began to waver—it was clear he could be convinced. But I had to hit him with another tough reality. "We can't do this work unless there are some people of color and some white women in the workshop," I said, fully aware of what this would mean for him.

"Well, that's impossible," he protested. "We're all white guys on the board—well, there's one white woman, from public relations. This just can't happen."

So we talked about how to create the necessary situation—again, an easy conversation for me since we have to make these adjustments in every company.

"Well, George," I said (by this time we were on a first-name basis— he called me "Else"—which nobody but my brother has ever called me). "Here's how we'll do it. You identify some black people, men and women, in your organization, and you offer the invitation to them, directly, yourself. You assure them that you really want them there, that you want to hear from them, and that there will be absolutely no negative consequences for them if they participate."

"Oh," he said, quite relieved. "Sure. I can do that."

So he was pretty much on board. But some of the other executives in the room were not at all happy about the idea of having to go off for three days and put themselves in the hands of this uppity black woman and go through who-knows-what kind of mickey-mouse experiences. The tension in the room was palpable. But Jack, the VP, and President George kept talking, and it became clear to everybody that George was going to go ahead whether they liked it or not. So they gave in. But George wasn't going to make it too easy for me, or let his staff think he was a soft touch.

"OK, Else," he said. "Here's the deal. If you can hold our attention for three days, you've got the contract. And the way you'll know you've succeeded is if you can keep us in the room, not running off to the phones or back to our offices at every break."

"Done," I said. "But with one stipulation—you've got to schedule this workshop off-site, somewhere far enough away that you *can't* slip back to your offices."

"Fine," he said. Then he turned to his VP. "Jack," he said, "this is your project. You make it work."

After that session Jack and I knew we were under the gun. We put our heads together and got things rolling. First I said, "Jack, you have to select these black people and white women very, very carefully. We want people who are not intimidated by these executives, we want people who know the issues already. And they have to be willing to speak up—we can't have a bunch of shrinking violets in there." He agreed, and pulled together a top-notch group of participants for this crucial workshop.

But we also knew that we had to do some other crucial preparation. We had to give these executives information about their organization that would demonstrate how the issues existed there. We had to collect solid data and organize them in a way that they could relate to—and would not be able to discount. So we proceeded with our customary data-collection process. We also met with all the board members beforehand, interviewing them about their views, attitudes and expectations. So we knew when we went into the workshop what to expect—where the strongest resistance would lie, who we could count on to get the ideas quickly and be supportive, and who would be in the wait-and-see group.

In addition, we interviewed all the people of color and the white women, in small groups. We helped them understand what their role would be, the kinds of support we would give them, and the range of dynamics they could anticipate during the sessions. We reassured them as well as we could that there would be no retribution—although we also had to be up-front that all we had was the president's word. You can never make an absolute guarantee to people that there is no risk whatsoever in their participation.

## LEARNING FROM EXPERIENCE

We went into this top-level workshop with a team of our most experienced consultants—a black man, a white woman, a white man and myself. We used our standard design, as described in Chapter 4.

Education and training workshops, like everything else in this work, can be either incredibly effective or incredibly difficult. This one was exceptional. The hand-picked white women and the African Americans used the preparation we had given them perfectly. They really told it like it was. They used specific examples from their own experiences in the company—though the same kinds of examples could be given for every company in the United States.

Some pointed out the pay inequities between whites and equally qualified blacks. They talked about living daily with demeaning and degrading language, of not being included in social activities, of being talked over or ignored in meetings. They discussed specific and frequent instances where they were overlooked for promotions or special assignments. They patiently pointed out how the white men in the company played golf together and—just incidentally, of course—talked about business and made informal deals during the round. Since men of color were generally excluded from the country clubs where their white co-workers played, this seemingly apolitical pastime effectively removed them from the arena where the informal power arrangements were carried out. And since women were never invited to play, both black women and white women were also excluded.

This exclusion from informal social activities such as golf also carried over into a lack of mentoring in more structured settings. White men with similar backgrounds, experience and competence found it much easier to get the attention of a powerful mentor, who passed along to them the same kinds of assistance, encouragement, tips and contacts they had received from their own mentors. Without such assistance, people of color and women got stuck in lower levels and often experienced burn-out or lost interest in the work.

Another factor that worked against the success of members of subordinated groups was the simple matter of how people were expected to look. The assumption, especially by white men, was that the more a person looked like a white man, the more successful he or she would be. In Jaraco, sales and marketing was the most important department, and there was a consistent (although unspoken) expectation of how an effective salesperson looked—handsome, tall, clean-cut and, most of all, white and male. No black person could meet these expectations—he might be handsome, tall and clean-cut, but he couldn't be white. And of course black women were off the radar screen altogether. White women were at least visible, but were frequently chosen for their attractiveness rather than their competence.

Like most companies, Jaraco thought it was doing the best it could under the circumstances. They would try to find men of color who looked like dark-skinned white people; or they would seek out blacks with very light skin. The problem with this (in addition to the absurdity of it) was that every other company was using the same tactics, so these pseudo-whites would get gobbled up very quickly by competitors. The result at Jaraco was that there were no African-American men in the sales and marketing division—therefore they couldn't get to the board, since that was the traditional route to advancement. There were several blacks in finance, more in research, and one in human resources; but none in either marketing or sales. Examples such as these, and many more, flew thick and fast as the workshop progressed. We, the consultants, captured all of them and put them up on newsprint all around the room.

George provided excellent leadership throughout the sessions. He did not sneak away to take phone calls or to respond to urgent matters back at the office. He stayed for the full three days—so of course his direct reports had to be there, too. And it wasn't just for show. The president really heard what the participants were saying, and quickly put two and two together: If people were having such unpleasant experiences, it was no wonder they wanted to get out. So he could see how the way the company did business had to change—and why it was going to take a lot of time and effort to make that happen.

## SYSTEM-WIDE CHANGE

We signed a contract and got started. Over the course of the eight years that we worked with Jaraco, many initiatives were carried out simultaneously. In this discussion, I highlight specifically the company's attempts to address its race and gender concerns, and show how these efforts led to a recognition that addressing these issues required much more than education at the individual and group level. The leaders came to see that discrimination and oppression, around race, gender and other forms of difference, are woven into the fabric of the corporate culture— and that no lasting improvement could be achieved unless the culture itself could be altered.

Once we got off the ground, the president wanted to fix things fast. Having had his own eyes opened in the initial workshop, he was determined that everyone in the company should have the workshop experience, and we were soon frantically trying to deliver services fast enough to be sure that happened. We quickly scheduled all the senior-level people and moved on down through the ranks. By the time the intervention was over we had facilitated workshops with all the top management, nearly all the middle-level managers, and a respectable number of the operations-level people.

In addition to the standard introductory awareness workshop we also offered sessions specifically devoted to race. George had been right in sensing that there was something very wrong in the way they were hiring and developing their employees of color. It soon became apparent to us that there were many managers in the company who were deliberately or inadvertently sabotaging his efforts at bringing more African Americans into the organization. There were several aspects of this.

First, the company was both a research and development organization and a sales company. It is very difficult even today to find African Americans in biomedical research, anywhere; at that time there were probably only three or four black Ph.D.s coming out of the graduate schools each year (and in 1999, with affirmative action under attack, there are even fewer). It was true that the pool of potential recruits was very small. So it was inevitable that, with a specific goal of hiring as many African-American scientists as possible, some were hired who were not very competent—just as there were white scientists hired who were not very competent. In this situation, as throughout corporate America, mediocre white men were able to survive; mediocre women or people of color could not.

But as the examples given above demonstrate, there were also problems in the sales and marketing divisions, with far less justification. Even though there was an adequate pool of qualified candidates of color (and white women) for these positions, people were hired who were not much more competent than the black researchers. It was obvious that there was some deliberate undermining of the effort.

It was another example of the typical vicious circle. A white manager, feeling pressured to do something he didn't believe in or want to do, would say to his staff, "OK, I've got to have some black people here, go get me some." And they would get his unspoken message clearly: "Get me the least qualified candidates you run into, and we'll prove that they can't be developed. They'll fail, the company will have wasted a lot of money—and management will get off my back." So we designed workshops to address race, racial attitudes, expectations, bias and prejudice, first for the president and his direct reports, and later for the work force in general.

Following four additional introductory workshops with vice-presidents, directors, and white women and men and women of color, Jack, at my suggestion, organized a Managing Diversity Steering Committee and charged it with hearing recommendations, planning activities, recommending actions to the board, and general oversight of the initiative. A women's forum was organized, which met three times with the president and the steering committee.

In the forum women shared their experiences, and it became clear that the patterns of discrimination around gender were just as serious as those around race. The women's forum asked that we develop some special workshops on gender issues. A pilot gender workshop was held for the Managing Diversity Steering Committee and was repeated for the board shortly thereafter.

The situation for women at Jaraco was probably no worse than in most U.S. organizations at the time—but it was bad enough. The women reported that they were not seen as credible employees, especially in the R&D area. They were not receiving promotions to positions of power and influence—there was a very rigid glass ceiling at Jaraco—and women universally received lower pay than men holding the same positions. Married women with children were almost entirely discounted; there was a strong cultural norm that the company came first, and an assumption that mothers would not or could not make that commitment.

And there was an ongoing, almost invisible stream of sexual harassment that flowed throughout the entire culture. As the women in the workshops began to talk more openly, they recounted incident after incident. Women in the field sales force told of constant harassment by doctors, in hospitals or private offices. They were reluctant to report these incidents to their managers, fearing that the situations would be seen as their own problems. And their fears were well grounded. The managers were generally reluctant to confront the doctors for fear of losing business, and often the women were coached to either put up with the harassment or to try to devise strategies to get around it, such as making appointments with the nurse rather than the doctor, or trying to be sure a nurse was present during the meeting. At the same time, women were being counseled to dress in ways that made them look more attractive. And there was a lot of collusion going on. Women naturally wanted to get ahead, to be successful—so they would adopt the looks and manners that seemed to be expected.

I remember going to one of the national sales meetings—one of those big events with several hundred people, including advertisers and other vendors. The women were dressed to the nines, and the level of sexual tension was high. It was just like a bazaar, a sexual bazaar. And it wasn't subtle. For example, when people were being recognized for top performance, the vice-president who was handing out the awards would pat the men on the back, shake hands, and say great things about them and their work. If the award was being presented to a woman he would give her a kiss and a vigorous hug, and make comments on how beautiful she looked.

But we had been having meetings with the women for some months by this time, and many of them were beginning to see the issues in a different light. During the convention, a group of them pulled away from the large session and had a little caucus meeting on their own, which they invited me to join. If you ever want to see a group of nervous men, imagine that setting. The men didn't know what was going on, but they knew there was plenty the women could be saying—and none of it would make them look good. And they were right. The women had achieved that state of awareness, and a sufficiently critical mass, where

they were able to be candid about what was happening both at the meeting and in the company in general, and begin to develop a strategy for
bringing the problems to the attention of management. Just the fact that
they caucused had an immediate effect. As I recall, one of the vice-
presidents was alerted, right there in the general sales meeting, and
elected to make a general statement of support of the women and go on
record saying that they were within their rights.

Later on in the intervention, after the culture-change process had begun
to take hold, I went to another national sales meeting, and the atmosphere
was quite different. I remember one incident in particular. A consultant—
not from our firm!—was at the microphone and began to make lewd jokes
and comments about women. One of the managers got up, right in the
middle of this meeting of hundreds of people, and said, "We will not tolerate this kind of behavior here. If you want to continue to work with us,
you'll have to change your style right now." The man was absolutely
shaken. If I remember correctly, he just stopped his presentation and sat
down. Later he came back and apologized to the group.

This is a very important illustration of how difficult it is to change the
culture of an organization, because the abuses of the old culture extend
into every facet of the way people interact. That the abusive individual
was challenged by a high-level executive—and a white man—demonstrated to the group that such sexist and harassing behavior was no
longer a "women's problem" but a company-wide problem. Only when
leadership sends such signals can change really happen.

In those days, many of the issues around gender resulted from the fact
that the men still hadn't learned to see women as equals. Many—probably most—of these executives had wives who didn't work. The men
were the breadwinners, the heads of household, and they just assumed
that women were not interested in the business world—or if they were,
they were not as competent as men. So a fair amount of the conversation
at this point was around gender roles. There was discussion of men
needing to take more responsibility for child care and home mainte-
nance—but it was still at the level of "men helping women" rather than
taking on equal responsibilities at home and at work. It is important to
remember that women are no more equipped to deal effectively with
abusive situations than are the men; we all grow up and live in the same
culture. In general, at Jaraco, the women had put up with the sexual
harassment, as women do everywhere—until it accumulates beyond the
point of endurance. The women at Jaraco colluded in their own degradation, as women do in any situation where they feel powerless. They
colluded because they wanted to succeed, they wanted to be part of the
team—and in many cases they were actually afraid of speaking out.

Sometimes they were unable to change. I remember one young woman
in the operations department, on the fast track—a person who was seen

as the woman most likely to make it to the executive suite in the company. She was being coached by men to behave like a man, and she took the advice literally. She wore very severe, tailored suits, she presented herself in a very masculine manner, and she had little patience for the complaints of other women. When the culture began to change, she was left with a major dilemma. Her behavior patterns had become so much a part of her demeanor that she literally did not know any other way to act. She did not know how to respond to the new norms that encouraged women to be themselves rather than trying to be proto-men. She never made the shift, and she did not succeed in the new culture. She was one of the casualties of change, and we were very sad that we had not been able to help her find her way.

## TAKING STOCK

At one point, even while the various workshops and other efforts were humming along, it became clear both to Jack and to me that although most of the initiative was going wonderfully well and people were responding positively, there was something missing. I didn't sense that much was happening in the organization itself. People were becoming more aware of their own attitudes and behaviors, and white men were learning about the real experiences and perceptions that people of color and white women had of the company and their place in it. But it was still pretty much "business as usual" outside of the workshops.

"Jack," I said, "I think the problem here is much deeper than we thought. I think it's in the culture itself. We're probably wasting time and money unless we can figure out how the culture keeps reproducing these patterns of discrimination."

He agreed, and also confided that there was some discontent on the management board with the effort—a general sense of not having accomplished all that they had hoped, and a lack of direction in how to proceed. We decided to bring the board together again to explore these feelings. I suspected that they had not been sharing with one another what they were doing—that there was no interaction around the entire initiative. So we asked them just to talk about what their successes had been up to that point. I thought this would be a simple exercise that would take about fifteen minutes; once the ball got rolling, however, it turned into a session that went on for a couple of hours.

We captured their reports on newsprint and put them up on the walls for review and comparison. Both we and the executives were surprised, not only with how many individual items—seventy-eight!—were listed, but with how much overlap there was from department to department. It became obvious that much had been happening—we just hadn't been hearing about it. The most significant of the seventy-eight items can be summed up in a few categories: improvements in recruitment, promotion and retention; participation in diversity programs and workshops; development of specific diversity skills and changes in policies and practices; and improvement in the company's reputation as a diversity-friendly organization. Each of these deserves some comment.

One of the strong motivating factors that had led the president to engage in this effort had been his concern over the high rates of turnover of people of color and white women in the organization, and his inability to move white women and people of color into the executive suite. Now the president was able to report that there had been four promotions to board level since the beginning of the Managing Diversity initiative— three white women and one person of color. Other executives also reported progress. One said that five people of color were promoted in his division when they were ready, with no fanfare or demands for unusual proofs of competence. Another pointed out that the recruiting effort had improved remarkably. Recruiters were not only bringing in more *numbers* of minorities; the individuals hired were more competent—indicating that resistance was softening and more people were trying to do the right thing for the right reason. A third board member provided statistics on improvements in retention rates in his area—and other members documented similar improvements in their own arenas. Several managers said that their divisions were committed to going over "head-count" to attract high-quality minority candidates.

Further, all the executives reported that their employees who were people of color seemed more energized. Where they had previously felt stuck at a lower level, they now seemed to anticipate the possibility of advancement—and thus were more strongly motivated to make their full contribution.

A major challenge in any organizational development effort is getting employees and managers to attend workshops or other educational opportunities. At the beginning of this initiative, we worked with the company to design strategies that would make participation attractive to all groups. During the board session, we were glad to hear that special efforts were no longer necessary; the executives reported that people were looking for opportunities to attend workshops, and that in some cases there were waiting lists for upcoming sessions. They felt that most of their employees were convinced that the company was sincere in its effort to reduce racism and sexism in the organization, and that the workshops were important components of the overall effort. Some groups that were created in the workshops continued to meet on their own once the sessions were completed, enhancing their understanding of the issues and exploring more effective ways of working together across differences.

One report that surprised us, because we had not been involved, was that *all* the divisions had held follow-up meetings, building on the heightened awareness of the initial workshops. These sessions were focused on the development of diversity skills and action planning.

Other accounts were of less measurable improvements. Some executives reported that managers in their divisions were now openly discussing issues related to race and gender, while others gave examples of how incidents of racism and sexism were being challenged when they happened—in the moment, rather than being allowed to fester and cause resentment. They reported that the recognition in the organization of strong commitment at the top meant that it was no longer legitimate to say, of a diversity-related proposal, "It can't be done" or "That's not how we do things here." Some said that communications between people of color and whites—particularly in the field-based sales organization—had improved dramatically.

One of the most important changes in policies and practices was reported as having diversity-related concerns built into the performance-appraisal process. As a result, the company now had specific measures to reward good performance in this arena, as well as ways to penalize those who refused to take it seriously. One division—operations—had established a formal mentoring system, signaling a recognition that the traditional "golf-based" culture operated to exclude people of color and white women from progressing in the company. Development and succession plans were now reviewed to identify possibilities of exclusionary or discriminatory patterns. Advisory groups were reported as having been formed in several divisions, and charged with responsibility for carrying the initiative forward. Further, several executives reported that community outreach efforts had been strengthened. Managers had also begun to take responsibility for identifying contractors and vendors who shared Jaraco's commitment to equity.

All members of the board agreed that Jaraco now was seen as an organization that was "diversity friendly"—that it was "doing the right thing about diversity." This was not an opinion based on rumor or wishful thinking. An EEOC investigation of a class-action suit, which had been initiated prior to the diversity intervention, had been called off, with the agency citing "progress made" as the basis for its decision. All agreed that there had been a reduction in lawsuits—a clear indication that the initial investment in the Managing Diversity initiative had already begun to pay off. In fact, the company had recently won an award in recognition of its track record as an equal opportunity employer—an instance of "toast, not roast" in this area.

This session had a dramatic effect. With the evidence of progress laid out before us, we had a strong platform from which to launch our next steps. Building on these successes, we asked the executives to strategize on what needed to be done. First we suggested that they consider what they wanted to gain, and what they needed to improve, at the personal or individual level. The responses were varied, but all indicated that they were ready to "move from intellect to action" and needed to be able to communicate to their employees that they were genuinely committed to the effort. In addition to acknowledging that they still had a ways to go in being aware of their own biases and the impact of subtle behaviors, they emphasized that they needed to know more about how to intervene or challenge others when they made racist or sexist remarks in a social setting. They indicated that they were ready to learn new skills for being competent in diversity-related arenas. These top-level, predominantly white-male managers recognized that they still needed help in getting other men to stop their "locker-room" behavior—telling off-color, sexist or racist jokes, leering at women, and exhibiting other demeaning or harassing behavior.

At the organizational level, the group acknowledged that they needed to find more structured ways to measure progress, including monitoring changes in the perceptions of white women and people of color about the progress of the company in becoming more inclusive. They indicated that it was important to them to get managers to take ownership of the effort, as well as to be accountable for change in their immediate areas or work groups. They also were able to begin to see what systems, patterns of behavior and practices were still in the organization that created subtle barriers for people of color and white women, and recognized that they needed more information about this.

## TOWARD CULTURE CHANGE

So we began to strategize about how to give them the data they needed, and how to use that information to move the work forward. Our colleague, Delyte Frost, was using a design in another company based on Edgar Schein's definition of culture. Schein says that culture is made up of beliefs, basic concepts, heroes, or role models, and so on, all of which give meaning and purpose to our lives. Schein proposes that culture is both formal and informal.[1] Delyte's design used Schein's concept of culture to help the organization identify those beliefs, basic concepts and so on, all of which we began to think of in terms of the organization's norms—its panoply of "shoulds" and "oughts" that governed expectations and behavior.

We felt that if we could assist the organization in identifying the norms that actually guided the day-to-day operation of the company, we could then also help the leaders determine which of these norms were positive and should be preserved, and which created barriers for white women and people of color, and advantages to white men—and should be changed.

They agreed, and we got right to it. We assembled the leaders of the organization and asked them to identify the norms in the culture—just to list off the top of their heads what were the accepted practices, attitudes, behaviors and expectations in the company.

We were all surprised at the results. As the group generated more and more examples, the consultants were kept busy trying to keep up with the flow and getting it up on the wall. We later divided into smaller groups and continued the process. By the time we finished, we had more than one thousand norms!

Some of these norms exist in any U.S. organization, and some were specific to Jaraco. Here are just a few selected examples:

- Work gets done better in groups that are alike.
- Winners don't make mistakes.
- "Excellent" performers develop selves.
- People in power make decisions.
- Jaraco is the best in the industry.
- Short-term profit is the primary motivator.
- The company comes first, over family, leisure time, etc.
- White men set the standards.
- People of color are not competent.
- Women should be in supportive roles.
- The right appearance = credibility.

The most powerful thing about these lists of norms is that there was a consensus that these were, indeed, the patterns that made up the culture. That is, white men as well as white women, women of color and men of color all agreed that the lists of norms accurately described the company.

Having all these data, of course, presented us with another challenge— what to do with them. We could see that the repeated elements looked like the beginnings of patterns, and it seemed likely they could be analyzed to create a picture of the company's culture that might serve as a kind of mirror.

A Jaraco statistician took a look at the material and saw that it could be broken down into categories or dimensions and analyzed by computer. When she gave us the feedback, the patterns were obvious to everyone. We now had a clear definition of the company's culture, created by its own management board and diversity council, that could be used as a diagnostic tool in the attempt to change those aspects of the culture that were not healthy. The challenge of controlling the data was further complicated because the company had simultaneously contracted with another consulting organization for a large-scale employee survey; some of those data paralleled or expanded our own.

But how to use this powerful tool? We wondered how different groups in the company would compare in terms of their perception of how the identified norms advantaged or enabled some groups and disadvantaged, or created barriers, for others. So we created another session, this one specifically designed to collect such perceptions. We created five groups—senior white men, other white men, white women, African-American men, and African-American women—put them in separate rooms, and for a full day asked them to work with the norms. Which of these, we asked, create enablers for one group and barriers for another? We didn't load the questions by indicating our own expectations. We asked each group to start from ground zero.

If the first session, which created the lists of norms themselves, had been eye-opening, this one was earth-shaking. There was almost absolute unanimity among the groups. Of the sixty-nine or so categories that we were working with, there was dissension on only two. On the rest, all five groups agreed. For example, in regard to some of the examples given above, the analysis demonstrated the following:

- "Winners don't make mistakes." Participants agreed that this norm created a barrier for *everyone* in the organization.

- "'Excellent' performers develop selves" and "People in power make decisions." These norms were perceived as being "enablers" for white men and barriers for everyone else.

- "Jaraco is the best in the industry." Yes, participants agreed, this is the perception—and it is a positive aspect of the culture for all of us.

- "Short-term profit is the primary motivator." This norm was seen by everyone as beneficial only to one group—senior white men. For everyone else, all agreed that the emphasis on short-term profit formed a barrier to success.

- "The company comes first, over family, leisure time, etc." All agreed that senior white men, and those few black men who were at the senior level, benefited from this norm. But for everyone else—including white men and black men who were not at senior levels, and who were less apt to have "stay-at-home" wives, this norm was recognized as creating significant blocks to progress.

- "People of color are not competent." No one denied that this perception was, in fact, generally held in the company and formed an important and negative norm. All further agreed that this view helped white men and white women, and was seriously detrimental to men and women of color.

Collecting and analyzing the data was almost like following the clues of a treasure hunt or solving a mystery. Now we had, spread out before

us, a definitive portrait of the culture of the company—and it was obvious to everyone that most of the spoken and unspoken norms of the
culture advantaged white men and created barriers for people of color
and white women. And everyone agreed that this was a real picture of
the true culture. When we fed this information back to the management
board they were stunned. Of course Jack—who had known more or less
instinctively all along—was very excited because the data confirmed
what he had been trying to say. But George was equally charged up. He
could now say to his white-male colleagues, "See, here's the evidence.
What are we going to do about it?"

Before we had this documentation, in spite of all our efforts, the general assumption was that it was the individual behavior of white men
that created the problem, or the lack of competence of white women or
people of color, or that it was the policies and practices and systems that
had to be changed. Now we could see why the very real efforts the
company had made in recruiting people of color and white women, and
in developing and promoting them, were not working as well as they
had hoped. They were being defeated by an invisible, all-pervasive network of norms and expectations that very effectively screened out the
very people they were trying to bring in and keep.

## USING DATA TO CREATE CHANGE

Once again we were faced with the necessity of helping the company
understand how to use this very powerful information. Jack and I envisioned a series of intensive culture-change workshops, involving top
managers of the company, in which we helped them not only understand
the norms and how they functioned in the culture, but also how their
own attitudes and behaviors helped to perpetuate the discriminatory
patterns that the norms reflected. To provide further assistance to the
managers, we used a 360-degree feedback instrument we had developed
that gave the executives personal feedback on their performance. On the
basis of evaluation from supervisors, peers and subordinates, the managers were able to pinpoint specifically how they benefited from the
norms and how they participated in the ways the norms functioned to
limit the success of their colleagues and employees who were not white
men. The combination of the two sets of data—the general data about
the company, and the specific information about each participant—created very powerful workshop sessions, perhaps the most intense we
have ever facilitated.

I must emphasize once again that in attempting to provide a linear
account of the development of this process, I cannot fully convey the
complexity of the enterprise or the degree to which the entire company
was involved. In addition to the components mentioned here, many

other groups had formed and were meeting: groups of men; women in management; people of color in management; dialogue groups; leadership team-building sessions; inclusion of diversity in sales-training sessions; integration of diversity and quality initiatives; and much more. Nonetheless, as we track the culture-change process per se, the next milestone was the development, with the culture-change committee and the management board, of a definition of what the new culture should look like once we got there.

After many hours of collaborative work, the group identified eight aspects of the culture that needed to be improved: power relationships; leadership models; informal relationships; valuing of employees who are different by race and gender; work and family expectations; decision-making processes; the general work climate; and performance standards, rewards and recognition.

A few details give an idea of the whole:

- *Power*: The vision of the new culture perceived a "power spiral" rather than a hierarchy. Power would be shared throughout the organization, and all members of the community would have equal access to it.

- *Leadership*: Recognizing that the old culture's norms provided systems that enabled white men to move more easily than others into leadership roles, the new vision proposed that there would be mentors and role models for everyone. It was also recognized that there should be champions and supporters throughout the organization, and that management must be the primary champion. Further, in the new culture all managers would be evaluated and held accountable for modeling the new way of doing business.

- *Informal relationships*: In the new culture, there would be no more "golf-club" power plays. Informal interactions and relationships would be encouraged and fostered across diverse groups, and exclusionary banter would disappear. Further, informal coaching and counseling would be available for all.

- *Valuing of all employees*: After all the listing of norms, and reflection on who most benefited from the norms of the old culture, it was only a small step to recognize that in the new culture the white male model would no longer be the only image of success. Not only would all individuals be judged, respected, valued and accepted on their own merits—not on the basis of gender or skin color—but the ability to so value others would be incorporated into formal processes, such as promotions, appraisals, audits and so forth.

- *Work and family*: In the new culture, greater support would be given to "the 'family' side of work and family, and to personal life for men and women."

- *Decision making*: Since the new culture was envisioned as less hierarchical than the old one, teamwork and shared responsibility for decision making were seen as increasingly important. Initiative and creativity—rather than the ability to simply follow the rules—would be encouraged and valued. Since initiative and creativity are risky, there would need to be an increased tolerance of mistakes, and the ability to give timely, appropriate and constructive feedback—across all differences.

- *Work climate*: Trust, openness, cooperation, thoughtfulness—these were seen as the hallmarks of the climate in the new organization.

- *Performance standards, rewards and recognition*: This important area received the most attention, with fifteen different components being cited. Again, the emphasis was on setting and following objective standards—standards based on merit and competence, not on cronyism or personal favoritism. It was also made clear that the standards to be set would be high, and that excellence would be expected of everyone.

With such a utopian vision before us, it became evident to all that we needed to have some large-scale, significant event to bring all the many facets of the initiative together and allow us, as a consulting firm, to sign off on this effort and move on. The steering committee—now renamed the culture-change committee—took responsibility for designing this symbolic event, which was to be called "Celebrating Culture Change."

"Celebrating Culture Change" was a grand celebration, and highly publicized. The entire operation of the plant was closed down. The culture-change committee took a very courageous and visible role in leading the organization in activities that focused attention on the changes that had been made and needed to be made. The central hall of the modern glass headquarters building was festooned with tastefully—and expensively—developed banners promoting the vision and goals of the new culture. The press came and the whole enterprise made a big splash. It was very exciting and important.

The efforts of Jaraco to change its culture and ameliorate the impact of racism, sexism and other forms of oppression were more thorough than those of any other company we had worked with to that date—or that we had heard of. The event brought the initiative powerfully to the attention of the entire organization in ways that the previous ongoing but piecemeal efforts the management team and the culture-change committee had made had not been able to do. And there were, I believe, major and long-lasting effects.

However, no corporate initiative operates in a vacuum. While the management board was receiving and thinking about the information we had discovered, many other things were also demanding their attention. At Jaraco, as at many other companies, a dramatic downturn in business began to erode the management team's ability to address issues—such as diversity—that were more nebulous and seemed less immediately crucial. A very promising product was found to have serious defects, the company was sued, they had to settle with a very large payment, and there was a tremendous amount of bad publicity. From being one of the stars in the corporate firmament, Jaraco was now off the screen in the parent company. George was "promoted" into a dead-end position in another sector, and there was some indication that corporate felt he had become overly involved in the diversity effort, perhaps at the expense of more bottom-line concerns. A new president was brought in from outside the company who had had no previous experience with this kind of work and little patience for it. He had a lot on his plate, too, trying to restore the company's credibility in the marketplace. He didn't actively oppose the initiative, but his tepid support allowed the resisters, who had been biding their time while George was in charge, to come forward and reassert their power.

In addition, some of our strongest supporters had moved on. Two of them, a white man and the white woman who had provided the internal O.D. support, were tapped to lead the development of a new research and development firm—an assignment into which they carried their learning about and commitment to diversity. They engaged us to work with the new company, and we assisted them there for a number of years.

After this, there was a period of confusion and adjustment. The vice-presidents who had been supportive became less clear about how to proceed without George's leadership. Other people who had resented our influence took this opportunity to attack. One person who consulted to the parent company, who had never liked our work and functioned as a gatekeeper to the presidents and some of the vice-presidents in the family of companies, undermined us at every turn. Jack, too, was under attack and eventually followed George out of the company.

During this period of dissolution the work didn't so much come to a stop as begin to go around in circles. By this time we were also feeling pressured because our work at Jaraco had led to our signing contracts with a number of other companies in the parent corporation, so we were spread fairly thin. A number of the Jaraco vice-presidents asked us for proposals for how to move the initiative forward, but then failed to respond to the suggestions. Finally I lost patience and wrote them a very critical letter—a letter I now regret. We had worked so long and so hard together that they experienced what I thought of as a diagnosis of problems as a rebuke. And they justifiably resented it and were hurt by it. From that point on the process began to peter out.

## LESSONS LEARNED

As I have emphasized in the above account, this description provides a linear narrative of the Jaraco initiative, for the sake of clarity. In real life things do not happen so neatly and with such clear cause and effect. In addition, there were many other facets of the diversity and culture-change effort, more than we are able to describe in this review. A few, however, deserve a brief mention because they serve to illustrate some of the complexity and challenge of such an effort.

One of these is the structure and roles of affinity groups. During our work at Jaraco and in subsequent initiatives at other companies in that system (some of which continue to this day), we often helped the companies respond to requests from various groups to form employee networks or affinity groups. While these are quite common in corporate America today, and some have existed for three or more decades, in these companies they were just getting started.

Networks or affinity groups are voluntary organizations of subordinated-group members who have been discriminated against. They are an important ancillary structure for a diversity effort because they help to raise the awareness of the dominant-group members and, most important, they provide a support system for the subordinated members. They enable women, people of color, people with disabilities and others to learn from one another and become more competent employees—thus helping their members become integrated into the work force.

One important aspect of such groups is that their members are often mentored by senior executives, and that increased visibility and support has helped many white women and people of color move to high-level positions. Sometimes minority-group members are afraid to speak out or take risks, because they feel they will be punished or lose stature—particularly if the risk doesn't pay off. Affinity groups provide a safe arena where very competent, very articulate, wonderful people can support each other, and together they can become more visible to members of the senior management group—who are delighted to come to know them, what their concerns are, and what they have to offer.

In many organizations the leaders of the affinity groups are invited to participate in or provide input to the diversity council or to particular task forces. Some companies have developed structures that create a direct line of communication between the CEO or president, or his top management team, and the affinity groups—so that their concerns and suggestions can be conveyed directly, without being screened or diffused by lower-level managers who may have a vested interest in this information not reaching the top of the organization.

Such groups play an extremely important role in helping to break down the barriers that prevent successful integration of people of color and white women into the multiple layers of corporate management. Their value is usually recognized by the company with both financial support and the provision of meeting spaces and, in some cases, released time from paid assignments to conduct work related to the group's mission. Such groups may go astray, however, when the group or its leadership becomes confused about either goals or strategies. The clearest differentiation, perhaps, is between the appropriate role of the affinity group and the stated—and legally recognized—role of the union. A union specifically exists to counter the power of the corporation, to distribute some of the wealth the corporation creates, and to make sure that working conditions are fair and decent. Unions are directly and intentionally concerned with power and the balance of power between workers and management.

Affinity groups are not designed to upset the balance of power, but rather to assist the company in its stated goal of broadening the base of power to include more people who are not white men. The purpose of the group is to help its members be, and be seen as, competent, loyal employees. The group is neither an advocate for the rights of its members nor an activist in the more general sense.

Occasionally a consultant may lose sight of her or his appropriate role in relation to the affinity group. Whatever we are asked to do, our contract is with the company—not with a particular group. When a consultant who is a person of color works closely with a group of people of color, problems may occur if a relationship arises in which there is too close an identification between the consultant and the group. When this happens, the group may lose sight of its appropriate role and begin to act more like a union—that is, to be advocates for a particular cause or their particular group.

The temptation to become overidentified with the people with whom one is working is very strong, not just in work with affinity groups but in consulting work in general. In my own experience, in reflecting on the Jaraco years, I can see points at which the other consultants on our team and I may have allowed ourselves to confuse the respect and professional interdependence that is appropriate in a close working relationship with personal friendship. While this may happen in any kind of ongoing consulting work, it is especially difficult to avoid in diversity work, where emotions run high and interactions of necessity go far beyond the usual limited range of the business environment.

At Jaraco, I believe that this overidentification led us to put too much emphasis on developing too small a cadre of leaders. We did not take as much care as we might have to identify other potential champions who could have carried the work forward when the key leaders moved on. We could also have avoided some of the sense of hurt and betrayal that remained when the initiative was sidetracked, and we moved on to other assignments.

One of the things that the Jaraco experience made even more clear to me, and which I have attempted to carry forward into our work with other clients, is that all of this is about partnerships. Our contract—not the legal contract, but the psychological agreement—is to help the company do its own work. If the organization wants to address the impact racism, sexism and other forms of discrimination have in its culture, we stand ready to utilize all the skills and knowledge we have to help it achieve that end. We can bring together all our tools—education, awareness, consulting, data collecting, analysis, looking at policies and practices, strategizing around culture change, assisting in performance assessment and so on—and put them at the service of the company.

But only the company and its leadership can lead the way. Our responsibility is to assist them in getting where they want to be: we can help them engage many people in the organization; we can help them look at themselves to see how their own attitudes and behaviors get in the way; we can help them see what has to be changed in order that an increasingly diverse work force can work well together and be more productive—and make more money. Once this is in place, the process that leads to significant changes in attitudes and behaviors throughout the company can take hold.

At Jaraco, if we had been more steadily conscious of this responsibility, I believe that we could have engaged the vice-presidents in a process of diagnosis, at the point at which confusion was the greatest, and they would have been able to arrive at next steps that would have been appropriate for them as we moved on to other assignments. All this learning has served us well as we have moved on to assist other companies and to continue to develop our own knowledge and skills.

The Jaraco experience also had more direct benefits for us. We received a lot of press attention for the culture-change initiative. A major West Coast newspaper published a long article in its Sunday magazine section, and various women's magazines and local newspapers also covered the events. I received innumerable invitations to speak at professional organizations, using Jaraco as a case study. And even more important, we received a flood of invitations to meet with the leadership of other companies to explore their diversity needs and concerns. What we learned at Jaraco, as well as at the many other companies to which we were consulting at the same time, has given us a solid basis for the work of the 1990s.

## NOTE

1. Edgar Schein, *Organizational Culture and Leadership* (San Francisco: Jossey-Bass, 1985).

# 7

## White Men as Champions

Think about this situation:

> John Smith, a white man, has been manager of an important technical division of a Fortune 500 company for the past five years. His division has been quite successful. He has been able to recruit and develop a highly skilled work force and has created an atmosphere of easy camaraderie. Most people seem to like working there and respect his leadership.
>
> There is just one problem. Nearly all the people he has hired are white men, very much like himself, with similar backgrounds and shared experiences. The company has recently undertaken a diversity initiative, and John has been told that he needs to put much more emphasis on finding candidates who are white women or people of color. Further, he has learned that in the future his performance appraisal will include his ability to create successful integration in his division and enable all his employees to progress at equal rates.
>
> John is baffled and angry. He feels that he has been a good manager, has been playing the game as he had learned it, and had good results. He resents being asked to change what had been very successful strategies and to try to work in a way that he doesn't understand and doesn't believe is necessary anyway. His frustration is communicated to his employees, and the performance of the division quickly deteriorates. John is called on the carpet by top management and informed that he is no longer meeting expectations and must get his act together if he is to succeed.

There are thousands of John Smiths in corporate America, and one of the major challenges of a diversity initiative is to recognize their needs and their strengths, and integrate them into the effort. In a 1992 article on our work by *Los Angeles Times Magazine* writer J. P. White, the dilemma of the white man is aptly summarized:

> I'm a WASP whose ancestors stepped off the Mayflower. My historic dispensations—including 24-hour-a-day affirmative action 365 days a year—are gifts I don't even have to open. I'm certain they are the qualifications that got me my corporate job, right out of graduate school, English degree in hand. Now, in my staid, nearly all-white Midwestern suburb, I realize I'm struggling to define a place for myself in America's diversity.[1]

Like many white men, Jay White asked, "What can managing diversity do for me?"

In our work, we begin with an understanding of how the situation of an individual John Smith or Jay White fits into the overall historical and cultural situation in which we find ourselves. First we have to recognize how patterns of dominance and subordination exist in society and in our organizations, and how they function to prescribe roles for people, depending on their "identity group"—male or female, white or of color, straight or gay, able-bodied or disabled.

In every society there is a group that is dominant and other groups that are assigned subordinated roles. In all societies, men are dominant, women subordinated—the difference from country to country is a matter of degree. In every society there is also a group of men who are assigned the dominant role in contrast to groups of men who are subordinated. The basis may be class or caste or color; but the fact of dominance and the kinds of power that dominance enables are the same from culture to culture.

In the history of the United States, white men have been and continue to be the dominant group. It is no accident, and no reflection of innate merit, that all our presidents have been white men. Nor is it coincidental that all but a small percentage of top leaders in corporate America are members of that group as well.

White men are not only the present leaders of our corporations; it was white men who largely made up the salaried work force from the beginning of the industrial era. The corporations of today reflect standards set by those white men—standards that indicate who should make decisions about who is in and who is out, who is competent and who is not, what constitutes merit, and what is the appropriate behavior (and appearance) for a manager.

The John Smiths of our corporations had no direct part in creating this structure. Like all the rest of us, they simply entered into the culture and assumed the role assigned to them. *Whether they like it or not, they are members of the dominant group*, just as white women and people of color, whether they like it or not, are assigned to groups that are subordinated to the dominant one.

Saying that the dominant group is made up of white men is just one fact. It does not mean that all white men are powerful or accepted by the elite group of white men or have equal opportunities. It does not mean that white women have no part of the dominant group attitudes and behaviors around race. Or that men of color do not share some of the dominant group's attitudes and behaviors around gender.

Saying that white men constitute the dominant group simply states the fact that the power in our society and in corporate America resides with white men. Individual white men are as powerless—and blameless—in regard to this fact as individual people of color and white women are in regard to the fact that their groups have been assigned subordinated roles.

So how is change to happen? Should we look to the members of subordinated groups—gays and lesbians, for example, or people of color, or whites from the working classes—to change the structures of society and of corporations? Or do we look to those who now hold the power, and expect them—and help them—understand why and how they need to use that power to create more open, more democratic, more equitable, and more productive organizations?

In my experience, there are countless white men in positions of power in the institutions of our society who are caring, intelligent, thoughtful, full of feelings, and who want to do the right thing. Many of them are extremely smart, insightful, literate and resourceful. Most (though of course not all) have attained their positions because they are shrewd, hard-working, competent and quick to understand the implications of situations with which they are confronted.

What these well-meaning white men often do not have is any experience of what it means to be a member of a subordinated group. They have been busy developing themselves, creating careers, working themselves into positions of power, and keeping their eyes on the bottom line. As I talk with many of them, I understand that they have thought very little about the issues. They do not see that their behavior and their actions and their leadership could bring about changes that would dramatically alter the life and work experience of people who have been excluded from access to power and success. They may, however, recognize that such change is desirable and would benefit not only those who have been excluded but the entire organization.

I do not see white men as the enemy. Over the past thirty years I have met and worked with an amazing array of white men in very senior positions who have welcomed me as a partner in this work. They have been open to learning from me and my colleagues what it means to be a member of a dominant group, and how they can use their good fortune and their skills to make better organizations and a better society.

In the early days of our work, the senior men we encountered tended to be conservative, part of a lifestyle that included a stay-at-home wife and an aggressive, the-company-is-my-life attitude toward business. In the 1990s, we are finding men coming into positions of power who have a different background. Many of the most successful executives now are white men who grew up in the 1960s and 1970s, who either participated in or were sympathetic to the powerful pro-democratic movements that forever changed the landscape of this nation. Whether or not they were activists themselves, they felt connected to the movements and shared the common hope that out of this upsurge would come a better society for all our citizens.

Many times we walk into a workshop to find, among the diverse group of participants, a bunch of white guys who fit all the stereotypes of the Organization Man. They dress alike, they wear their hair in the same clean-cut styles, they have that polite "Yes, sir" demeanor that has earned the trust of their superiors. They are, in short, the model by which all others are judged.

But when we begin to talk, when they begin to put together the things they are hearing from their colleagues who are women or people of color with the ideals and visions they had in their earlier days, the stereotypes begin to fall away. They get excited. They put their intellect to work on the task, and they find the courage to put themselves on the line for something they now see they believed in all along.

And then they are unstoppable. Over and over I see these youngish white-male managers and executives recapturing a part of themselves they thought they had had to give up. They see themselves again as part of something bigger than themselves—bigger than just making more money and buying grander houses and more cars—and now, wonder of wonders, they are in positions where they actually have the power to make change.

I think these men are actually our best hope. With their leadership and their help, the rest of us—those who have been assigned subordinated roles—can carry the ball. But without the passionate belief and help—and courage—of the people who are in positions of power and authority, nothing will really change.

Even though they are just now beginning to be seen in considerable numbers, I've worked with such men throughout my career, not just in recent times. Even in the earliest days, in the 1970s and early 1980s, I encountered top executives who clearly saw that racism and sexism undermined a lot of the business efforts they were making in the company. At the beginning they were often asking us for help that we didn't know how to give. They already understood, intuitively, that their problem was systemic; but we were only prepared, at that time, to deliver workshops that stayed at the level of individual awareness.

These white men came from various backgrounds and had very different personalities and styles. But on reflection, I can see that they all shared certain characteristics that enabled them to be effective in leading a diversity effort:

*Courage.* For any white man, taking a stand for more inclusion and equity means risking the wrath of other white men, both peers and subordinates. All the men leading the organizations that chose to work with us exhibited, in greater or lesser degree, the ability to take risks and trust that things would work out in the long run.

*Self-confidence.* One advantage of being a member of a dominant group is that you have not had the history of self-doubt that comes from a lifetime of rejection. The men we have worked with not only have made it to the top, they have generally had a sense that they deserve to be there. They understand power, because they had to understand it to get it; and they know how to use it.

*The ability to interpret.* We bring to the partnership a knowledge of the history and sociology of discrimination, an understanding of how systems work, and competence in using the principles of group dynamics and group process to help people change. The white-male leaders we work with bring their intimate knowledge of their organizations. They know the language, the white-male lingo, and they can translate our sometimes abstract concepts into the concrete expressions of daily work.

*Empathy or a sense of justice.* Some people really feel the pain of others. Others have a more abstract indignation at what they perceive as injustice. Few of the men we work with have both—but one or the other will serve to get the job done!

*Commitment.* Diversity is one area in which taking a public-relations approach becomes counterproductive in a hurry. The white men with whom we work—those who are successful—have understood that putting themselves on the line for this initiative is going to mean holding on for the duration. It is one of those clichés that happens to be true—unless the leader is committed and stays the course, no lasting change can occur.

*Willingness to hear the truth.* In many ways, life in the executive suite is lonely and isolated. Few employees are willing to take the risk of carrying bad news to the boss, with the result that the boss often is the last to know what is going on in his own company. The white men we have worked with, to one degree or another, have made sure that they hear *all* the news that's important. Many have participated in workshops in which white women and people of color have spoken candidly about their experiences and their pain and rage, and these men have also been able to speak candidly about the impact this information has had on them.

*Sufficient patience to let things happen.* Patience is not the long suit of most top executives. They are used to moving fast, giving orders and expecting them to be carried out forthwith, and seeing results. Nearly all the white men we have worked with have started down a fast track at the outset—"Let's just get this done!"—and we have to help them slow down and wait for results. Developing people is more like tending gardens than creating products; there has to be a nurturing climate, time to grow, and the patience to wait for the fruit to appear.

I don't mean to suggest that my life has been filled with interactions with white knights in shining armor. For every CEO who shares our vision and signs on to do the work with us, there are probably a dozen who don't. From time to time we have gotten caught up in what seemed to be a promising endeavor, only to see it disintegrate around us.

One example illustrates the point. We were engaged by the CEO of a large multinational financial organization, a white man with a firm moral compass, who saw that changing the culture of his company was the right thing to do and set about trying to do it. He never asked us what the business reasons were—he just knew it was the right way to go. We got started with a fair degree of optimism, and all seemed well.

Only a few months into the contract, however, this CEO left and was replaced by a man with very different values. He was personally rude and crude, very aggressive, and didn't care about anything except how much money he was making and how much market share the company could get. He hated the idea of affirmative action, and always translated whatever we said into quotas or preferences. He participated in a workshop, but was sarcastic, inattentive and disruptive throughout.

He did not challenge the contract. But it immediately became evident that he had no passion for the work. He saw that there was lots of turbulence in the system that needed to be calmed, and he also knew that many other companies were "doing diversity" and he wanted to be part of the scene. Also, I think, he really didn't know how to stop what was already in motion.

That lack of commitment allowed the naysayers and underminers to appear from every direction. The CEO brought in an O.D. consultant whose interest was strictly instrumental; he recognized "diversity work" as the thing to do, and he wanted to check it off and make himself look good. To make things worse, we had to work through a vice-president in human relations who was a competent person, but not skilled in this area. So we were stuck with a CEO who didn't give a damn about the work, an O.D. person who was duplicitous, and an HR liaison who was well meaning but inexperienced in the area.

Our contract was to train the 300 senior managers, and we fulfilled that obligation. We eventually were hired by other segments of the company, where there were senior white men—and one lone senior African-American man—who knew this was going to help the climate of their divisions. But there was never a corporate commitment, and the initiative gradually wound down.

An interesting thing about this company is that it often appears on lists of the "fifty best companies" for their diversity records, and had been on such lists even before we went there. Knowing what we do about its management and its practices (and those of many other companies that appear on these lists), we have to wonder what criteria are used to make the selections!

Another example illustrates the kind of leadership a white man who is committed, who is himself decent and honorable and caring, can provide. In a leadership training session the president of a regional bank organization—a man who had recently signed up to do the work, and brought a sixties-type passion to it—began to exhibit a great deal of intolerance for other white men who he felt were not getting on board as quickly as he expected. At one point, in a workshop with his senior direct reports, he targeted one man who was well known in the company as a racist and a blocker. Right in the middle of the session he began to berate him and even threaten him: "If you can't toe the line, you can't work here!" and so forth.

I was horrified. Here was this powerful white man, in front of a group of white men and white women and people of color, who all worked for him and worked with one another every day. I could not allow the situation to continue—even though the president was our client and I knew that confronting him risked wrecking the entire intervention.

But I felt I had no choice. I just stood up, right in the middle of his tirade, and told him he had to stop. "We have to give people a chance to change," I said. "We have to give them tools and support. This is inappropriate—you just have to stop."

To his credit, he heard me and even thanked me for standing up against him. And the other man, the one he was attacking, was a changed man from that day on.

The point is important. We cannot assume, because a person exhibits racist or sexist or other kinds of unkind or even cruel attitudes and behaviors, that he is beyond hope. Each person has his own history, and operates within the framework of his upbringing and his social situation. An intervention must be able to give the person grace—provide some space for growth and change. It must *not* allow someone to be used as a scapegoat. And our leaders must also be able to accept some grace—to recognize their own limitations and move on to more effective behavior.

One final example. Many years ago, we were running a workshop for lower-level employees—supervisors or below—and we had been warned that one of the men who was coming was very hostile and angry and inarticulate. And it turned out to be true—he was disruptive and ugly, and he wouldn't stop talking, though what he said was not very coherent.

Even through the anger and the attacks, though, we could see that this was a man in pain. We began to ask him why he felt so angry, and he gradually was able to tell bits and pieces of his own history—life with an abusive and racist father, and much more. Then he suddenly said that when he was in the service his life had been saved by a black soldier—a man who was a member of a race he had always believed was inferior and not worthy of his attention, let alone his gratitude. It became painfully obvious why this white man was angry and confused.

Little by little, as we talked, he began to see that the pain he felt was very much like the pain that women or people of color feel—his recognition of that mutual pain made a bridge that he could walk over. It was like a revelation to him; he never considered that a black person who experiences segregation or who is discriminated against could feel the same anguish that he felt. He had thought only, "Nobody wants to hear about me; they only want to hear about *them*." His anger and hostility were cries for attention, for concern, for caring. Once he experienced that, he became a dedicated ally in the work and a much less hostile person in general.

People talk a great deal about the angry white man, or the resistance of white men to diversity efforts, and so forth. But in our experience, the anger is overstated, and the resistance provides opportunities for growth and learning for the entire group. There's a theory in group dynamics that if there is a conflict—a fight—with a powerful person in a group situation, and the facilitator, who is the most powerful person in the setting, engages the person directly but doesn't—metaphorically, of course—"kill" him or her, the other people in the group will not be afraid to engage in the work. They feel reassured that nothing terrible will happen to them, and that the facilitator has the ability to assure their own safety and that of the others in the group. It's the theory of dependence, counter-dependence and independence that I discussed earlier. It is a very useful and positive strategy for helping white men understand and resolve their issues in doing this work.

Over time, we find that there are fewer instances where such interventions are necessary. In most workshops now there will be a small but critical number of white men who come into the session already clear about the issues and willing to talk about their feelings, and who are very courageous. Their presence seems to give the other white men insight into what new behaviors and attitudes are expected of them, as well as models for how they can be different, as men, but not diminished.

So the task of the facilitator is much easier; our job is more to engage the white men in talking to each other, and then let them alone. They nearly always work the issues out themselves.

Once again, however, I must emphasize that there are no magic formulas. There *are* men who are resistant and hostile, and stay that way. I know there are white men (and other people as well) who participate in the training sessions or other aspects of the intervention, sitting quietly and saying as little as possible, and then go back to the workplace and bad-mouth the work—"It's a lot of touchy-feely crap" or "It's a waste of time" or "We're past all this stuff here. None of us are racists (or sexists or whatever)."

But these days, the naysayers have much less influence. They really are outnumbered in most corporations—maybe they always were, but the changing demographics and the increase in general awareness have moved them out of the center. Of course, there are still white men who remain adamantly negative—the Texaco tapes are ample evidence of that—but I firmly believe that they are an increasingly smaller minority.[2]

Some of my best friends are white men—and I'm grateful for their courage, their support and their commitment.

## NOTES

1. J. P. White, "Elsie Cross vs. the Suits: One Black Woman Is Teaching White Corporate America to Do the Right Thing," *Los Angeles Times Magazine*, August 9, 1992.

2. In 1997, a senior white executive at Texaco secretly tape-recorded informal conversations among a small group of other executives, in which they engaged in casual racist slurs. The tapes were eventually used as evidence in a class-action suit against the company.

# 8

## Putting It All Together: The CoreStates Story

By the early 1990s, Elsie Y. Cross Associates, Inc., had become a mature, full-service consulting firm. We were called on by a wide range of companies to consult with them on their diversity concerns, and our expanding network of trainers and consultants (now consisting of more than fifty highly diverse individuals) was kept busy virtually full time. The field of diversity management was growing by leaps and bounds. The changing demographic patterns that we had foreseen more than two decades earlier were beginning to be obvious to everyone. Companies were looking for help, and a whole army of consultants was emerging, eager to cash in on the trend.

But as we talked with executives and managers in many companies, and reviewed the growing body of literature, we found that confusion was growing just as fast. There was no common understanding of what "managing diversity" meant, or agreement on how an organization should set about doing it. Consequently, companies were hiring consultants willy-nilly, with little understanding of what skills these helpers should have or what results they should expect them to achieve. Too often they convinced themselves that paying a lot of money for a one-shot lecture or a few workshops would serve the purpose.

While we did not pretend to have all the answers, we did know that our years of experience and our understanding of how oppression and discrimination operate in organizations provided a solid platform for the work. We could not accept all the offers we received, and of course not all the companies we talked with were willing to ante up the fees we charged—which might represent, over a number of years, several millions of dollars.

But we were concerned that the focus on racism, sexism, heterosexism and other forms of oppression and discrimination was being blurred by consultants and managers who were more interested in personal success and aggrandizement than in solving the problem. A whole language of diversity jargon was springing up, aimed at soothing what was perceived as the "angry white male" by pretending that "diversity is about all kinds of difference" rather than facing the basic problems—the facts of our racist and sexist history and present practice.

We wanted to do what we could to get the message out. My colleague Oron South and I began to talk with others in our network about starting some kind of publication that would reflect our perspective on the field and offer some assistance to people we could not reach directly. We invited Margaret Blackburn White, a friend and former colleague of mine at Goddard College, to work with us, and in the fall of 1992 we published the first issue of our quarterly journal, *The Diversity Factor*, with Oron as editor, Margaret as managing editor, and myself as publisher. The journal quickly became recognized as a serious, high-quality publication and has had, on the whole, the impact we hoped.

During this same period, we were invited by Philadelphia-based CoreStates Financial Corp to consult with them regarding their concerns. The CEO, Terrence A. Larsen, told us that he perceived a general lack of enthusiasm and even unhappiness among his employees. He recognized that this malaise had something to do with race and gender, and he was determined to overcome it—as fast as possible. In December 1990, Larsen had told several hundred of his top officers about his concerns and his plans.[1] He advised them that he wanted to create an organization that had a "sense of family," where people cared about each other and were supportive and respectful, and ready to help. He emphasized the need for mutual trusting, teamwork and team spirit. And he put the officers on notice that he was expecting that the culture of the organization was going to change, and that he would hold them accountable for making that happen.

Terry Larsen is a prime example of the kind of white-male leader I described in the previous chapter. A man with the unusual background (for a bank executive) of a Ph.D. in economics, he had been hired by CoreState's precursor, Philadelphia National Bank, in 1977. He advanced rapidly, having been elected a senior vice-president in 1980 and executive vice-president in 1983. By 1986 he was president of CoreStates, and was appointed chairman and CEO in 1988.

Larsen is a leader who sees the challenge of diversity clearly. He cares about justice and fairness, and he is genuinely pained when he sees what he perceives as a lack of respect and caring in his work force—but he is also completely convinced that doing this work is a business necessity. He seemed to know, from the outset, that no organization could operate at maximum productivity if some of its employees were barred by discrimination, oppression or racist or sexist hatred from making their full contributions. He is also courageous—he has a kind of quiet bravery that is unassuming. He doesn't talk about it, he doesn't brag, he just acts; he says what he thinks; he's uncomplicated.

He's also ambitious. He wanted the company he was leading to be the best that it could be, and that meant removing all the obstacles that got in the way of reaching that goal. During the eight years that we worked together, he was able to keep his focus on the "diversity components" that were obstacles, while still maintaining the focus on financials that would ultimately determine success or failure.

We worked with CoreStates from late 1991 until it was bought out by another major financial organization (which also subsequently selected us as consultants) in 1998. We used the strategies that had become common practice in our work, carefully tailored to the particular circumstances and the specific culture of that organization. Many of these strategies have been described, in brief or in detail, in previous chapters.

In this chapter I focus on those components of our work at CoreStates that were unique to that intervention or that have not been fully explored in previous chapters. The intervention involved many consultants and trainers and dozens—even hundreds—of managers and employees over a period of several years.

Before our arrival on the scene at CoreStates, Larsen had assembled a team of twenty-three senior managers called the People Task Force (PTF) and assigned senior executive Bob Murray (also a white man) to chair the group and lead the culture-change effort. Murray was given the title of assistant to the chairman and reported directly to Larsen, who also made some important changes in his staff. He fired the chief financial officer and the chief operating officer, both white men, and hired a number of new executives, including a white woman who had been CEO of another bank. An opinion survey was administered to all CoreStates employees. At first glance, the data seemed to indicate that people were pretty happy. However, when interpreted along lines of race and gender, the news was bleak—women, who constituted 64 percent of the population, and people of color, at 22 percent, reported a high level of discontent. More bad news was reported by a group of senior women who had been meeting informally for two years. Invited by Larsen to share their perspectives in a written document, they provided a lengthy memo that outlined the frustrations felt by white women and people of color in the organization, and also included a plan of action.

Larsen drew heavily on this information in launching the diversity initiative. He recognized, and told his top executives, that if they were to keep a competitive edge in a period of cut-throat competition in the financial industry, they had to know how to seek out and serve an increasingly diverse customer base. They also had to deal with an investigation under way by federal regulators on the bank's compliance with the Community Reinvestment Act. Getting its diversity ducks in a row, Larsen contended, was not an option; it was a business necessity.

Within months, the People Task Force established a new set of CoreValues ("We value people, performance, diversity, teamwork, communication, and integrity") and announced the creation of the Corey Award—a $1,000 check given to thirty high-performing employees who exemplified adherence to these values.

In the fall of 1991, I was invited by the diversity-consultant search committee to participate in a series of meetings with the committee, Larsen, and the top executives, to explore a possible relationship. I also brought in our top project manager, Delyte Frost, who would eventually be responsible for the management of the contract. As usual, we were upfront about what such a partnership would mean. I told them that our work was aimed at the amelioration of systemic racism, sexism, heterosexism and other forms of discrimination—a phrase that had become our motto. I also told them that our help wouldn't be cheap, and that if they entered into this partnership with us it would take a lot of their time, even more emotional energy, and a long-term commitment. Larsen never blinked. In consultation with Yvette Hyater-Adams, who had been assigned major responsibility for guiding the initiative internally, he accepted our terms and announced to his top management that we would be the consultants for the initiative. So we got started.

In this chapter I review four of the components of the effort: the data collection process; education and awareness; capacity building; and our work with the reengineering effort.

## DATA COLLECTION

In our first weeks with CoreStates, Delyte, using a methodology we call "sponging," went over an enormous body of material—annual reports, industry updates, internal memos, HR newsletters, EEO/AA data, and turnover and retention rates—to assemble a portrait of the company. She also conducted individual and group meetings with dozens of people, in both homogeneous and mixed groups, to get firsthand reports on what life in the organization was really like.

Both of us met with the company's most senior officers, a group which, at CoreStates, as in virtually all other companies, was dominated by white men. While Larsen's strong leadership gave us ready entrée, we were well aware that the actual and ongoing support of this group would be crucial to the intervention's success.

We also recognized—from our experience at Jaraco and many other companies—that we must avoid becoming overidentified with the client. While Delyte was spending virtually all her working time at CoreStates, we knew that it would be counterproductive for her to move into an office and thus be seen as more internal than external. We were determined to help the organization build its own capacity to manage the initiative, and not allow it to become dependent on us—or make us responsible for either success or failure.

Right from the start, we also analyzed the bank's policies, procedures and practices, including factors such as its pay-equity structures, hiring and promotional practices, and work-family programs. We worked with Murray and the PTF to develop a smaller, more flexible group to guide the effort—a twelve-member Diversity Subcommittee that became Delyte's primary partner in developing strategy and creating implementation.

## EDUCATION AND AWARENESS

As in every intervention, we obtained from Larsen and his top reports a commitment to participate in awareness workshops, and then to "cascade" the workshops down through the levels of the organization. Also, as in every intervention, in order to achieve the necessary mixture of race and gender in the workshops for the top executives, we had to "import" white women and people of color from other levels of the organization.

The workshops were powerful, intense and purposeful. Larsen and his direct reports were already aware, from the data collection process, of some of the difficulties that white women and people of color experienced in the company. But the workshops, where they heard the stories, one after another, directly from the lips of people they knew and worked with every day, had a major impact. Our top teams of consultants and trainers worked carefully to facilitate the process, and helped the participants understand how the individual stories they were hearing fit into the larger patterns of racism and sexism that were widespread in the organization.

When the first round of training was completed, Delyte, Murray, Hyater-Adams and Donn Scott, who headed the Diversity Subcommittee, concluded that the next step should be to enable the senior managers to take responsibility for implementing the culture-change process, and they designed another round of workshops to assist them in this task. These three-day sessions challenged representatives of the bank's various business units to explore ways of addressing the diversity concerns in their own divisions.

The workshops involved more than eighty top managers, and resulted in a series of recommendations which were reviewed and prioritized by the Diversity Subcommittee. These recommendations, along with the other data that had been gathered, formed the basis for a comprehensive, step-by-step action plan developed by the subcommittee, which was then formally adopted by the People Task Force and shared with the entire CoreStates community.

## CAPACITY BUILDING

In previous chapters I have discussed the negative impact that a change in top leadership can have on a diversity initiative. At CoreStates we set about from the beginning to create a process that could avoid such results, by creating a critical mass of managers at the middle levels of the organization who would be specifically trained and invited to help senior management carry the initiative forward. In 1993, a large group of trainers from our organization worked with a group of more than one hundred CoreStates personnel to begin to develop this cadre of champions.

Another key factor in the CoreStates effort, though not unique to that organization, was the early development of an office of diversity that was charged with the day-to-day oversight of the initiative. Headed by Yvette Hyater-Adams, this office took on ever-increasing levels of responsibility, and Hyater-Adams herself became a key player, eventually reporting directly to Larsen.

A particularly powerful component of the CoreStates initiative was the development of a group of line managers who were selected to be champions of the effort. Larsen had already made it clear that enthusiastic participation in the diversity process was a career plus in the organization. So selection for what became known as the "diversity trainers and consultants" (DTCs) role was a plum.

While many diversity efforts identify leaders or champions, the CoreStates initiative was unique. The managers who were chosen were high-potential line personnel who were offered the opportunity to leave their jobs for three years to undertake this unusual assignment. Under Delyte's direction, we gave them intensive training—forty days over a ten-month period—helping them learn how to dismantle oppressive behavior and practices, and also gain consultation, group process, training and quality-management skills. After the training, they were appointed to positions throughout the organization to assist the consultants in— and eventually take full responsibility for—facilitating the education and awareness workshops and other components of the effort.

The company's commitment to the initiative was demonstrated in the fact that 60 percent of the managers who participated in this program were later promoted and moved on to higher levels of responsibility.

Eventually, as the initiative evolved into a culture-change process, the office of diversity was phased out and responsibility for leadership was shifted directly to management, particularly to this highly skilled group of middle managers who now became known as change management consultants (CMCs).

## REINING IN REENGINEERING

Sometimes a diversity initiative, like any other organization intervention, proceeds through a smooth process of planning and implementation. In other situations, circumstances overtake the process, and all concerned have to improvise and adjust.

At CoreStates, the deflecting circumstance was a reengineering effort. Even though the firm was a leader among regional banking companies, Larsen and the board knew that there was room for improvement in controlling expenses. In a wildly competitive climate, any vulnerability left them at risk.

So in 1994 a reengineering program was launched, known by the acronym BEST (Building Exceptional Service Together). Diversity training was suspended, and the resources that had been allocated for that purpose were transferred to the BEST process.

Nonetheless, Larsen did not give up his vision. Even while the diversity initiative itself was being put on hold, he pulled together a top group, which included Delyte and Yvette Hyater-Adams, to form a "culture team," and charged them with keeping the reengineering effort consistent with the CoreValues, the quality tools and concepts, and the diversity vision statement.

Trying to combine a reengineering effort with a diversity initiative is like trying to mix oil and water—you can stir them together, but they won't blend. On one hand, diversity—and quality as well—speak of empowerment, of valuing people, of teamwork and integrity. Reengineering, on the other hand, aims at improving performance, removing less-productive employees, and redesigning corporate structures and processes. Diversity and quality also require long-term investments and long-range perspectives, whereas the goals of reengineering are short-range—and often brutal. Reengineering is numbers-driven, not people-driven.

Both quality and diversity are concerned with macro-structures, with the specific interactions between individuals and between groups in organizations, and with the ways in which the interactions between individuals and groups impact on, and are impacted by, both the visible and hidden structures of the organization.

Reengineering tends to focus on micro-structures and relies on traditional methodologies and step-by-step, prepackaged formats. The scheme of change is externally driven, and the details of arriving at the externally defined outcome are broken down into minute segments—sometimes as detailed as hour by hour. The culture team created several strategies to bridge the gaps between the initiatives and to protect the CoreValues:

*Developing a resource pool.* This pool was constituted by members of the internal diversity team—the DTCs—and the organization development department. It developed "triangle-teams," made up of members of the working team, the group leaders and the resource pool. The charge of the triangle-teams was to combine a productivity-and-numbers orientation with a culture-and-process orientation.

*Contracting for change.* Members of the resource pool received training for this role, in which they were assisted in developing contracts with their team members.

*Challenging lapses from the CoreValues.* At the beginning of the reengineering process, the culture team devised a set of criteria to guide the process of selection of employees who would be invited to remain with the company. Senior management referred to the criteria in making appointments, and the culture team gave them feedback on the selections in light of the criteria. The process was highly interactive, not adversarial.

*Maintaining the flow of information.* Resource people served as a conduit for information between the triangle-teams and the culture team. The culture team was then able to apprise the steering committee of incidents and attitudes that would not have risen to their attention otherwise.

*Assisting in the design of the rating and ranking system.* In most organizations, rankings are done behind closed doors, they are carried out by management, they are forced, and they are subjective. The culture team and the HR team together designed a process that proposed that there would be no forced ranking or employee evaluating by managers acting alone. In all evaluation sessions, a resource pool member (DTC) and an HR person would be present. As candidates were presented, the DTCs and HR representatives would challenge slates that were clearly not balanced by race and gender, or ask the manager presenting the slate to defend certain choices. Often the manager would discover that, even though in her or his eyes the choices had been made objectively, other factors had influenced the decisions. In most such situations, managers tend to select on the basis of comfort level, friendship or personal loyalties, rather on merit alone. Because most high-level managers are white men, this tendency—unless monitored and challenged—inevitably results in the selection of a disproportionate number of white men.

To equip them for carrying out their responsibilities in this task, the DTCs and the HR people were given a one-day assessment simulation in which various case scenarios were presented, and they were helped to think about the assessment in terms of diversity values.

In spite of the efforts of top management and the DTCs, the reengineering process was traumatic for the organization. People were routinely asked to work excessively long hours, and to the work force it seemed that CoreStates had returned to its old style of top-down, bully management. Although the process was successful in a financial sense, in reflecting on it later Larsen felt that it focused too much on cost saving. "We needed to have more focus on realignment of the businesses, and better support structures for the people being influenced," he observed. ". . . [W]hile the reengineering did a fair amount of good in some areas, it also did a fair amount of harm in others. I'd do it differently if given the chance."[2]

However, the process did not result in a decimation of the diversity initiative. Only about 8 percent of the work force was let go—about 1,300 altogether, of whom about 900 went out voluntarily. The percentage of white women and people of color in the work force even increased. Further, by using objective criteria and matching actual people and their skills to actual jobs and their needs, the company's managers ended by discovering *more* people they felt they could do without than the reengineering process required.

While the diversity effort was resumed when the reengineering process was concluded, other circumstances intervened and influenced directions. CoreStates had been, for some years, engaging in a process of mergers and acquisitions, and in 1995 it acquired a neighboring financial organization in a marriage that created a $45 billion banking empire that became the dominant player in the area—and eventually led to CoreStates itself being acquired by an even larger, southern-based financial organization.

To help the diversity initiative continue through this volatile period of change, Delyte and Yvette designed and implemented an intensive process called the Learning Lab Initiative. The learning labs challenged intact teams of senior managers to apply diversity and total-quality tools and models to their real business issues, and to create plans of action that would enhance their skills as leaders of the culture-change effort. Twenty of the managers who had been part of the DTC program acted as facilitators, along with the diversity and quality consultants.

The learning-lab process, like the initial education and awareness efforts, was cascaded down the organization, from the CEO and his direct reports, through the senior managerial ranks, and well into the middle-management ranks. While it was not a process that involved line employees directly, it had a ripple effect that engaged many people in a particular business unit in designing and implementing action plans. The learning labs, although they used many of the components of our usual work, were unique to the CoreStates intervention and proved to be extremely useful. They were not a "training design," in the sense of an emphasis on education and awareness, but were opportunities for the leaders of business units to apply their diversity, quality and culture-change skills to the problems identified by the data they had collected.

The labs were especially helpful in integrating the managers from the newly acquired organizations. Where there were participants who came to the work without the long-term exposure and experience that CoreStates' managers had, the lab process was able to slow down and provide opportunities for some basic training, and help the new employees catch up.

By the time CoreStates was absorbed by the other financial organization, it had gone a long way toward the thorough culture change that Larsen had envisioned and that his staff and consultants had worked so hard on for so long. In Larsen's view, CoreStates' successes in the diversity arena, coupled with the financial success that he attributes, in part, to that work, made it an attractive target for acquisition. As he said in an interview in the spring of 1998:

> We were seen as a special franchise—a plum—by a lot of people, because of the combination of financial performance and our marketplace presence; we have achieved a tremendous market position here. And that wasn't just because of our products or anything like that; it came down to the way we do business, the way we interact with our customers. I think the customers really valued what we were creating, and what we were doing in the community as well.[3]

The CoreStates experience was a major step forward for our organization. During the eight-plus years of our involvement, as we took on new clients and continued to provide service to those with whom we had been working on a long-term basis, we kept one eye on what Delyte, the other members of our team, and our CoreStates partners were creating, and many of the strategies we now employ were first designed or refined in the CoreStates effort.

At the time of writing, we are beginning a major, long-term effort with the organization that acquired CoreStates. As I work with and listen to our partners there, I am aware that they have already taken the time to explore with their CoreStates colleagues what the diversity experience meant to them, and that they are entering into this process with more sophistication and clearer expectations than we have seen in other start-ups. Other companies, too, came to CoreStates in the final days of our partnership there, and they were always impressed by the way the employees talked, by their comfort level in speaking candidly to their bosses, by their ability to say to their employer, "I just won't do that; I won't stand for that kind of treatment."

As Yvette and Delyte said at the close of the effort:

Maybe all we can say, overall, is that the process of culture change at CoreStates created a culture in which everyone had the same or similar experiences in the organization. In good times, men and women, members of subordinated groups as well as dominant groups, benefited. In bad times, people of color as well as whites, women as well as men, suffered and complained and resented—but not one group clearly and always more than another.

So we move on to new tasks and new challenges. In the final chapters of this work, I consider what some of those challenges may be.

## NOTES

1. Many articles have been published about the CoreStates initiative, and in this chapter I draw on some of these as well as on my own notes and memory. See, for example, the following: Thomas D. Dretler and Joanne Maher, "Elsie Y. Cross Associates, Inc., and CoreStates Financial Corp," a Harvard Business School case study prepared under the supervision of Professor Rosabeth Moss Kanter in 1997; and articles in *The Diversity Factor*, Summer 1993, Winter 1994, Spring 1994, Winter 1996 and Summer 1998. There were also numerous writeups in internal CoreStates publications.

2. Terrence Larsen, "Moving On: A CEO's Reflections," *The Diversity Factor* 6, no. 4 (Summer 1998): 47–49.

3. Ibid., 48.

# 9

## What We Need to Know to "Manage Diversity"

In the course of this retrospective, I have shared what my colleagues and I have been learning about what is needed to help organizations change their systems and ameliorate the effects of racism, sexism and other forms of oppression. We have developed specific strategies and mechanisms for helping members of our consulting network increase their competencies in this arena.

In this chapter I reflect on the development of the field that is now known as diversity management, comparing what we have learned with other approaches. I review why I feel that some strategies that have been adopted are less valuable—some are even counterproductive—and suggest what I feel are more effective modalities.

### THE ORIGINS OF THE CONCEPT OF MANAGING DIVERSITY

As indicated in earlier chapters, some years ago several of us who had been engaged in this effort began to use the shorthand term "Managing Diversity" to describe it. In our organization, we developed the following definition: "Managing Diversity is the effort to ameliorate racism, sexism and other forms of discrimination in organizations."

After the publication of the Hudson Institute report, *Workforce 2000*, in 1987, many organizations and consultants who had not recognized that these were important issues, or that their importance had increased exponentially as a result of significant changes in national demographics, began to explore the meaning of "managing diversity" and to develop "diversity programs." As the needs of organizations grew, the numbers of consultants and trainers eager to address these needs also increased rapidly. The popular press got wind of some of the less impressive approaches, and began to attack the entire enterprise. By the late 1990s, the idea of managing diversity had become so confused that we often regretted having begun to use the term in the first place.

What are some of the elements of this general confusion? One common theme in some approaches is that "diversity is about all kinds of difference." In my view, this takes us down a dead-end road. Surely the goal of management in general is just that: "managing all kinds of difference." What we need from a field that is called "managing diversity" are theories and practices that help organizations reduce discrimination and enable employees who are increasingly diverse by race, gender, sexual orientation and ability to work together effectively. Managers not only need to be competent in basic management skills, they need to learn how to apply those skills competently and comfortably when the employees in their charge are not like them. They need to know how to apply the organization's policies and practices equitably to all employees.

Since the vast majority of managers in top positions in the United States are still able-bodied, heterosexual white men, the single largest task is to help those white-male managers understand how to work with people of color, white women, gays and lesbians, people with disabilities, and others. Further, we all need to understand that there is enormous diversity *within* each group, far greater than the difference between and across the individual groups.

One approach I often use in talking with managers about these concepts is to ask them to describe to me, in a visual model, how they envision comparisons between white people and African Americans. They always come up with the same picture. The whites in their imaginary scene are upper-class, educated and successful. The African Americans—as they view them—are lower-class, or even "under-class," uneducated and unsuccessful.

When I ask them to look at these stereotypes more carefully, together we come up with a more realistic and productive model. They can see that upper-class African Americans are much like upper-class whites in education, culture, income and so forth. Further, many whites are "lower-class" or "under-class," uneducated and lacking in opportunities.

Because managers in this country have been overwhelmingly white, male, straight (or closeted), and from the middle or upper class, management theory and management practice have not addressed issues of race, gender, sexual orientation, class and so forth. In the past it was realistic (albeit always unfair and later illegal) to expect that people of color and white women would continue to serve in the lower ranks of the organization, and that those people who made their way up through the hierarchy would be other white men. So managing across this one dimension was a very realistic practice.

No longer. Now every organization realizes that it must reach out to people who are not white men—it must recruit them, hire them, train them, develop them, *and promote and retain them*. So white men—and increasingly, everybody else—must learn how *not* to discriminate against, harass, demean and overlook all these "different others." They must learn to recognize that the "differences," although manifested visibly in gender and skin color, are differences in experience—not in innate intellectual, mechanical, spatial or other abilities. Because we are all human, and, in our humanity, more alike than different, those who are in leadership positions must learn how to see the *sameness*, while at the same time not attempting to overlook or downplay the importance of the difference of our experiences.

What happens when people who have no experience and no training in working with people who are different from them—and who have negative feelings and attitudes about their difference—become responsible for managing in a heterogeneous setting? They will behave and manage in predictable ways that have been studied and analyzed.

Here is a typical example from my own practice. One response, when a white man is confronted with the responsibility of managing people of color or white women (or gays and lesbians or people with disabilities), is that he will not want to see the difference, even though every minute he is in the presence of someone different—a black woman, for example—he will be aware of the difference. He will assume that the appropriate behavior in this situation is to pretend that he is "color blind" and that he can treat this woman *in the same way that he treats another white man*. This seems to him like the fair, honorable and logical way to behave.

But taking this attitude—pretending—means that this manager has no way of understanding that there may be dynamics between him and the other person which would create negative feelings in her. He will not understand that he has expectations about that person's behavior—about that person's very being—that he communicates very clearly, even while he is trying to be cool and impartial and fair. If he is working hard to pretend that there is no difference, he is very apt to be patronizing. When he forgets, he is apt to be demeaning. At some level he almost certainly assumes that she is less capable than he is—and less capable than the other white men with whom he is accustomed to working.

Throughout the years I've been working in this field, I've also heard hundreds of stories like the following. A group of workers—peers—are in a meeting. There is one woman in the group. At lunch time, the men will say to each other, "Come on, fellows, let's go and have a beer, let's go have lunch." They don't even think about inviting the woman—they act as though they are totally unaware of her. Or they may assume that she would not like to join them. So she's left standing there, having just two minutes before been their peer, been part of the interaction. She has no way of managing this situation—it's embarrassing and humiliating.

But it's just one small incident, right? Why should she be so "sensitive" to such a tiny slight? The most devastating aspect of discriminatory attitudes and behaviors is that they form accumulations of "mini-aggressions."[1] The single small incidents pile up and pile up and pile up—until, maybe, one such small incident is the one-too-many, and the recipient "blows." "What happened to Margaret?" her white male peers say to one another, in great wonder. "Must be that time of the month."[2]

When I am invited to meet with a CEO and his top executives to discuss how we might work together to solve their problems, the same subjects are always presented. They do not tell me that people in their organization who are in different categories on a personality inventory have trouble getting along. They don't say that people from the Midwest are discriminating against people from the South. They don't even request that we work together to resolve conflicts between people in manufacturing and people in R&D. They say that their work force is increasingly made up of people of color and white women; that their managers are not very comfortable in this new environment; that the retention rates and promotion rates of the new hires are below par; and that people don't seem to be happy. They are asking me, in short, to help them, their managers, and their work force learn to work together across race and gender differences.

What does it take, then, to help an organization accomplish this goal? What do we need to know, and be able to do, to create the harmonious, productive workplaces that we want? I propose that anyone who wishes to lead, manage, consult to or provide training around issues of diversity culture-change needs to approach it from the basis of a particular set of theoretical knowledge and practical experience. The level of knowledge and the particular skills sets required differ, depending on whether the person is an executive, a manager, a consultant or a trainer. But I believe we all need to achieve mastery in the following areas:

- An understanding of the sociopolitical and historical realities of discrimination and oppression.
- A knowledge of how organizations and systems work, and how they can change.
- Competence and experience in helping adults learn.
- Personal understanding of oneself, and of one's self in relation to others, especially across differences of race, gender, sexual orientation and ability.

It is important to stress that all of these are subjects that can be learned. Books, academic courses and majors, training programs, and all the other modes of learning are available to anyone who wishes to learn more about, and be more competent in, any subject. It's neither easy nor quick, but it can be done.

## POLITICAL AND HISTORICAL REALITY

Every American is aware, at some level, of our history of oppression. Mention enslavement of blacks, the use and abuse of Chinese workers on our railroads, persistent anti-Semitism, the shameful treatment of the American Indian, the long and ongoing struggle of women for equal rights, and many other struggles for equality, and everyone knows what you are talking about. What we don't know so well—or at all—are the details of that history and how it continues to affect our ongoing life together in society. We are much less aware of the history, for example, of ethnic indentured servitude; of how poor white people have colluded with white elites to keep blacks and other people of color in subordinated positions; or of the racist and sexist history of our labor unions. I contend that it is impossible to begin to ameliorate—let alone solve!—the problems of discrimination and oppression that result in workplace disruption without understanding our history. It's as basic as learning the principles of navigation in order to chart a course from one place to another. Unless the manager or the consultant or the trainer really understands the way issues of discrimination, denial of opportunity, hurt and lack of respect pile up and pile up—over centuries, over years, over lifetimes—he or she cannot understand why Margaret blows at a small insult, or why running lots of workshops has not made things better.

We need to remember, too, that being a member of a "minority" group, or a woman, a person with disabilities, and so on, gives one personal knowledge of that experience. But it does not somehow magically provide one with a broad historical perspective or a solid understanding of sociopolitical realities. Anyone can learn these things. White men are just as competent as scholars, learners and trainees as anyone else. White women and men of color can draw on their own experience of discrimination to understand the impact of racism or the impact of sexism.

This is an important point in diversity work. Current conventional wisdom emphasizes that it is important to show that "diversity is inclusive of white men." Indeed it is, but not because "white men have problems too." When the work itself is defined as ameliorating oppression, it becomes clear that white men have the same abilities to learn how to confront discrimination and oppression as the rest of us. They may not have quite as much motivation—but they can certainly learn to do it.

Another point to be made about the necessity of learning from history has to do with how people are often selected to lead or manage or consult to diversity initiatives. Attend any diversity conference and you will see a roomful of black men, white women and black women—with a sprinkling of others. Why were they chosen for this work? Because they are people of color or female, they were available, and—in most cases— they have a genuine desire to make things better in the organization. They were not chosen, usually, because they had demonstrated an unusual awareness of history or political realities, or exceptional skills in organization development or systems change—or, above all, the power in the organization to lead the charge. They can certainly learn—we can all learn—but that knowledge was not the basis of the appointment.

## UNDERSTANDING ORGANIZATIONS

For at least fifty years, people have studied how the modern organization works. The fields of organization development, organization behavior, and systems theory are solid social-science disciplines, and are taught in colleges and graduate schools and in many continuing education and corporate courses. Many companies have whole departments devoted to organization development. Part of the responsibility of these departments is to help the organization identify problems, collect data that pinpoint where the problems are and how significant they are, create strategies to resolve them, implement the strategies, and create measures to track and assess their effectiveness. So when the task is to develop strategies to help the organization change, where better to turn for leadership than to the O.D. professionals? When looking for consultants to assist, wouldn't common sense suggest that the person chosen should know how organizations work in general, and what strategies are most likely to help them function in a different way?

But is this, in fact, how people are chosen to assist in managing diversity? In my experience, the most likely candidate for a position as diversity manager is apt to be (again) a white woman or a person of color, from the human-resources department. She or he is not apt to have direct access to power and authority—thus no ability to influence the white male leadership. Whether or not he or she has any academic or experiential knowledge of organizational behavior or organizational development is, furthermore, coincidental. It should also be obvious, it seems to me, that the person who leads or consults to this effort should understand what the business goals of the organization are. Why is it important to this company that it resolve its problems around racism, sexism, heterosexism and so forth? The person from human resources will not know the answer to this question in the same immediate, hands-on way that someone from a line position—someone who has been responsible for helping the company make money, or a nonprofit organization be successful—will.

So—we're looking for someone with a good education that includes a solid understanding of the historical and sociopolitical facts of oppression and discrimination. Someone who understands how organizations work. And someone who understands the functions of this organization and its goals.

## HELPING ADULTS LEARN

Having identified some of the areas of theoretical knowledge that are important in the diversity arena, we now need to consider how to turn this knowledge into action. One primary task is to help the entire work force understand what the issues are. At this point there is a parting of the ways between what the organization's executives and managers need to know and be able to do, and what the internal and external consultants and trainers require. It is important to remember that key to the success of any such enterprise is the commitment and leadership of white men who understand the organization's culture, have an appreciation of the realities of oppression, and have the influence and power to create change. Only with this support can those who are charged with the day-to-day responsibilities of implementing the vision go forward successfully.

Adult education is another well-developed discipline. It goes back at least as far as Socrates. In more recent times, an entire movement formed around the work of John Dewey. Organizations such as the National Training Laboratories pioneered in the application of adult education theory to the organizational setting. It is a field of learning that can be studied, practiced and mastered.

Several aspects of adult-education theory are particularly applicable to the field of diversity culture-change. First, and very basic, adult-education theory recognizes that adults are not blank slates in the learning environment. They bring years of knowledge and experience to it, and learn best when the new knowledge is linked to their prior experience and to the questions they now have. This means that the adult-education methodology must be interactive or experiential. Adults must be treated as equal partners in the learning environment—not as passive recipients of lectures delivered by an authority figure.

Around sensitive issues such as race, gender, abilities and sexual orientation it is also vital that the learning process is guided by a highly qualified and experienced trainer who is well versed in principles of group dynamics. Again, these principles and methods constitute a well-developed, learnable field of study. They cannot be acquired by "book-learning" alone, but must be mastered within a group setting and led by an accomplished teacher and guide. It is important to note that learning in this way is not easy or quick. Most of us are comfortable with learning processes that require reason and logic. But learning about how we relate to each other requires that we go deeper, and draw on our emotions and feelings. Nothing effective and positive can be accomplished in this process in a half-day, one-day or even two-day session. And certainly no one can develop the skills required to lead such a process in a hurry. Most of those who are proficient have had academic training, additional training in an experientially oriented course, and further training in an internship or assistant facilitator role. It takes years, not days.

## LEARNING ABOUT RACE, GENDER AND OTHER HOT TOPICS

All of the above could be usefully applied to any management situation. We all need to be well educated in the realities of our society, we need to know how our organizations function, and we need to know how to help the people in our organizations learn new information and acquire additional skills. But when we are trying to resolve organizational problems that are caused by discriminatory and oppressive attitudes and behaviors, we have to take one additional—and very difficult—step.

We have to understand our own attitudes, feelings and behaviors around race, gender, sexual orientation, physical abilities and other visible forms of difference. Coming to terms with these attitudes and feelings requires the ability to deal with shame, guilt, conflict, power and authority. These are deep-seated psychological issues that are more powerful and more disturbing than virtually any other topic that must be addressed in management education. Guiding people through this process of self-exploration requires a trainer or teacher who has already made substantial progress in her or his own journey of self-awareness, and has developed excellent skills in assisting others.

This is by far the hardest kind of education to master—and it is also the most difficult to find. Very few (if any) business schools offer courses or workshops that equip their students with these competencies. Organization-development and organization-behavior programs may offer introductions to group dynamics, but they seldom take the next step—helping people master the intrapersonal and interpersonal awareness needed to apply principles of group dynamics and adult learning to race, gender and other forms of visible difference. If we are right that effective work in the field of diversity culture-change requires the four components listed above, where can an organization find either consultants or managers who have this knowledge and these skills?

In my experience, it is necessary for a professional consulting firm as well as a successful diversity-management function in an organization to "grow its own" staff of people with these skills.[3] People who want to be helpful in resolving these issues need to be assisted in finding opportunities to increase their understanding of the history and socio-political realities of oppression and discrimination; they must be encouraged to study the principles and practice of organization development and change; they must commit themselves to both academic and experiential learning about how adults learn; and they must be assisted in understanding their own attitudes and behaviors toward people who are different by race or gender or sexual orientation or physical ability. Practitioners and consultants must work in partnership to help develop a competent and well-educated corps of professionals to lead and consult to this work.

If we are to succeed in helping our organizations and our society become more equitable, more open, more inclusive and more profitable, we must not fall into power struggles between the various players. None of us has found the magic potion that dissolves the poisons of racial and gender animosity, or the mechanism that reverses the systems that provide advantage to some groups and create barriers for others. We're all in this together—and together we can make real progress.

## NOTES

1. For this very useful term, I am indebted to my friend and colleague Chip Henderson.

2. For an account of how small incidents pile up, see the sidebar in "Gender Integration in the Canadian Military," *The Diversity Factor* 6, no. 2 (Winter 1998): 4–5. In this brief article, "Battle Fatigue in the Gender Wars," Captain Sandra Perron describes the experiences that led her to abruptly resign from the military after an extremely successful twelve-year career. "I can tell you that what hurt me the most is not one particular incident. It's the accumulation of the little things through the years—all the minor abuses, the little tricks, the hundreds of derogatory comments every week, week after week. It all adds up. It's like battle fatigue—after a certain point, I was slowing down and needed to catch my breath. But there was no way to do that."

3. For an informative account of one such program, see Delyte D. Frost, "Grow Your Own: Strategies for Internal Consultation," *The Diversity Factor* 4, no. 1 (Fall 1995): 35–37.

# 10

## Citizens All: Toward the Future

Looking back over more than a half-century of American history, and considering where we are now and where we are heading, I am struck by the truth of the cliché, "The more things change, the more they remain the same."

This is especially true in race relations in the United States, and doubly true in the attitudes and behaviors of dominant groups toward African Americans. Even as the demographics of the country shift, so that today's minority is swiftly becoming tomorrow's majority, black Americans continue to be relegated to the bottom of the economic heap.

Although affluent, educated African Americans are more visible today than ever before, this visibility itself leads to false impressions. Studies show that in 1989 only one of seven black families had incomes in excess of $50,000 a year, in contrast to nearly one in three white families.[1] Further, the "wealth gap"—the accumulation of assets over time—between African Americans and whites persists, and appears to be increasing for younger blacks. The poverty rate among African Americans fell from over half (55 percent) in 1959 to 32.2 percent in 1969, but has remained virtually stagnant ever since, standing at approximately 30.7 percent in 1989. It has been roughly three times the rate for whites over the past two decades.

Even when African Americans are able to improve their educational attainment, the gap is still great. Graduating from high school cuts the poverty rate for blacks by half—but for whites, it reduces it by at least two-thirds in most areas. And poor blacks are poorer than poor whites, with incomes averaging $5,100 below the poverty line, compared to $4,000 below that line for poor white families. This income deficit actually *increased* by 23 percent for black families between 1979 and 1989.

When I put these facts up against the realities of corporate America today, the picture is gloomy. The top of every organization is still almost entirely white and male. White women predominate in staff positions in human resources and organizational effectiveness, and increasingly in accounting and other non-profit-generating functions; white men continue to predominate in the profit-making areas, where true opportunity lies. So while there is a very real shift in demographics of the employee population, the phenomenon of who's in charge hasn't changed very much.

In this final chapter, I review briefly some of the aspects of the current scene, as we are finding it in our ongoing work, and hazard a few guesses about what may be coming next.

## THE SHAPE OF CHANGE

As our work proceeds, helping corporate America sort out its issues around race, gender, sexual orientation and other foci of discrimination and oppression, we find that we continue to address the same issues that we dealt with ten, twenty and thirty years ago. White people continue to be unaware of their privilege. Men continue to harass women and to be surprised when women protest or sue. Gays and lesbians continue to face the dilemma of whether to be true to themselves or to hide their sexual orientation in the interest of advancing in their careers. And so on.

Nevertheless, there are some differences. People in organizations are more sophisticated now than they were in the past. Many managers and executives, particularly managers in organizational development and human resources, read a great deal. Those who have read the "good stuff" (such as our own publication, *The Diversity Factor*) are more interested in hiring us, and more able to work with us as partners if we do come to an agreement. We're finding that there are many whites and men who had a vision of justice during the 1960s and 1970s who have now come into positions where they have power and influence, and who welcome the opportunity to take on this difficult and frustrating but meaningful challenge. There are others who read what I consider "schlock stuff"— the ones who promote the concept of diversity as being about "all kinds of difference" and feel that success depends on retaining the good will of white men, at whatever cost. These are of course not likely to recommend us to their organizations. Nor would we be apt to be successful in that environment.

Here's an example, from my own experience in late 1998, of the kind of interaction that gives me hope. I was talking with the top leaders of a major insurance firm. One of the men, a southerner, began to share his life experiences.

"I'm a Mississippi boy," he said, "and I know I have a lot to learn. More than a decade ago I hired a black woman to work with me as senior vice-president in a line position. I hired her because I knew she was good and also because I knew she could help me learn some of the things I have to know. I like what you've been saying, Elsie, and I want to work with you. I want to start now, immediately. I want to show this whole company how important this work is."

I asked him why he felt so strongly about it.

"I know all the reasons people are giving—the business case, and all of that," he answered. "And I know it has to be tied to that. But for me it is above all a question of social justice and fairness. It's going to cost a lot of money, I understand that. And making the business case is going to require that we take a much longer-term view than we're used to taking in American business. But there is no way to justify not doing it."

I said, "Well, that's good and I can see that you believe what you're saying. But let me make it clear that I have certain requirements of you."

He smiled, anticipating what was coming. "OK, what are they?"

I just laid it all out. "I have to have access to you any time I want. I want to be able to call you and ask you how things are going and how we are doing. I expect you to give me feedback, directly—from you to me. I don't want any gatekeeper coming between us, to undermine the work."

"Yes, that's likely to happen," he admitted. "But I'm going to make my best effort to prevent it."

This was a very emotional interchange, for both of us. This white southern man, like so many white men I have worked with who are leading our organizations, felt very strongly that connecting with our work and helping his organization overcome its legacy of racism, sexism and other forms of oppression would help him regain some of the idealism and optimism that he had as a young man. Working with us would help him, he believed, fulfill some of the dreams he had had—and it was exciting to him that he could use the power he had achieved in the service of those dreams.

I had challenged him to be wary of gatekeepers coming between us, for very good reasons based on long experience. Even in those organizations where we do find a meeting of minds, we still often encounter people playing the old roles of gatekeepers. There is a growing body of organizational-effectiveness consultants to corporate America, many of whom have academic credentials but few of whom have any experience with issues of race and gender, or any expertise in process consultation. Some of them want to partner with us, and we can work well with them.

Others want to compete with us and expect us to do the work their way. So we have to find a way to manage between them.

My colleague Delyte Frost developed a very promising process for engaging the organizational-effectiveness and human-resources people in the diversity process at the outset. For example, in one new client corporation Delyte put together a three-day workshop for about one hundred people from these functions, in which she helped them understand the theory behind our work, as well as the methodology and the anticipated outcomes. They got to know us—some twenty of our consultants assisted in the process—and we got to know them. So right from the beginning we were all on the same page. They were able to go back to their internal clients and represent our work accurately, and begin the vital process of communicating throughout the organization that is so important to the success of any diversity culture-change process. Another advantage to Delyte's strategy was that other human-resources people came to subsequent workshops already disposed to feel positive about the work. So the tendency for the members of this important group to be defensive, protective of their own turf, and in competition with us has been much reduced.

Another significant new piece is our metrics work. Our colleague Joseph Potts has created a database that is making it possible for organizations to do some real benchmarking around significant information. As the database grows, each new organization is able to compare its stats with those of comparable companies, and also is able to measure its own success and effectiveness over time. Joseph's systems also provide ways for individual managers to learn about their own behavior and to measure their impact on their subordinates and their track record of change. We're looking now for ways to follow the line of cause and effect from improvements in diversity-related areas to improvements in the bottom line.[2]

We are also seeing that our years of investment in understanding and facilitating a culture-change process that begins with race, gender and sexual orientation pays off. Unlike those who "do race" or "do gender" by focusing on "fixing" the people of color or white women, or those who propose that managing diversity should be going "beyond race and gender," we have taken a different tack.

Our strategy shows that if one directly addresses the primary forms of discrimination in an organization—racism, sexism, heterosexism and the like—the organization will be able to take what it learns in this arena and apply it to the overall structure and patterns of the organization. If a manager learns to deal with his or her racism, she or he becomes a better manager—of all employees. If a man understands what it means to respect and work with his female co-workers and subordinates, he understands what it means to respect and work competently with all his co-workers and subordinates. If an organization examines its performance-appraisal processes to determine if they are fair to white women and people of color, it discovers that the performance-appraisal process does not, in fact, appraise performance properly—for anyone. If the executives of the company examine the norms that guide the ongoing work of the organization, they will find that those norms, created in some distant past by white men and in the image of white men, are out of date and ineffective—for everyone.

The immediacy, the reality, the emotionality inherent in addressing the tough issues of race and gender lend urgency and credibility to a culture-change process. Recognizing that differences in an organization operate not only at the individual level—the level of individual differences in values, work styles and temperament—but also at the group level, and at the systemic, organizational level, enables an organization to go beyond window-dressing and get down to the real roots of the problems. This recognition allows us to do solid, concrete strategic planning around diversity-related concerns.

This emphasis on strategy has led us to offer our clients consultation with members of our team whom we call "strategic specialists." Our strategist comes into an organization to soak up as much information from managers and other employees as possible, and then to work very intentionally with a committee, a diversity task force or an executive group to develop a long-term strategic plan. The plan gives the company a road map for the intervention, ways of measuring how the intervention is proceeding, a vision of where it is headed, and a template from which to create new technologies that are specific to that particular company. None of this can be done with off-the-shelf techniques. It must be done in close consultation and partnership with the client.

Another crucial component is our insistence that the client work with us to develop what we call "internal capacity." That is, we make it clear from the outset that we intend to work ourselves out of a job at this particular corporation. While the implementation is different from company to company, the goal is the same for all—we propose to work with managers and executives so that they develop the knowledge and skills to address the company's diversity issues on their own.

We have seen this pay off over and over. At CoreStates, for example, by the time our contract was completed there was a highly skilled cadre of internal consultants, as well as managers who had developed not only excellent skills in working with people who were different from them by race, gender, sexual orientation, physical ability or other specific differences—they had also become highly competent managers, in general.[3]

Overall, the work continues to address the hard issues, ask the hard questions, make the hard demands. And for those companies that have the courage and fortitude to take up the challenge, we, and they, have found that the partnership pays off in developing a more flexible, more productive and more loyal work force.

## WHITE WOMEN AND PEOPLE OF COLOR

Some aspects of demographic change, and changes in organizations, are puzzling or downright discouraging. One of these is the changing status of white women.

There has been a massive shift in American corporations over the past thirty years, due in part to social forces and in part to economics. Almost 60 percent of women age sixteen and over are in the labor force now, as compared to only 38 percent in 1960. They accounted for 46.2 percent of the total labor force in 1997 and are projected to comprise 48 percent by the year 2005. In 1997, 77.4 percent of these women were white, 12.1 percent African-American, 7 percent Hispanic, and 3.6 percent Asian or other.[4]

But this increase in numbers does not mean that women have broken through the glass ceiling, or that white women and women of color have made comparable gains. Women still hold less than 11 percent of total board seats of Fortune 500 companies; only 11 percent of corporate officers are women, and of these, only 20 percent are in profit-making positions. Of the 2.9 million women who hold managerial and administrative jobs in the private sector, 85.7 percent are white, 6.6 percent are African-American, 5.2 percent are Hispanic, and 2.5 percent are Asian or other.[5] Further, most of the women-of-color managers are clustered in three of the lowest-paying industries.

We see the reality of these statistics in our work constantly. For example, the group of one hundred human-resources people I mentioned before—a group that was overwhelmingly female—was also overwhelmingly white. There were only two or three women of color—a very, very small percentage. In such a situation—and it is a situation that is prevalent everywhere—white women are focused on their own advancement, and tend to join the white men with little or no regard to issues of racial fairness or equity.

Some years ago Delyte wrote a paper in which she proposed that white women could not be fully liberated unless they recognized and acknowledged their complicity in racism.[6] As I suggested in an earlier chapter, one of the disappointing aspects of the feminist movement of the 1970s was its failure to address the specific needs and concerns of women of color, or the bias and prejudice of white women.

As an African-American woman, there is no way I could conceive of not being a feminist. It doesn't make sense to be free as a black person and not free as a woman, and vice versa. For a white woman, however, it is more difficult to see that when some women are denied equal access, all women are harmed. This was always a problem, but I see it as an increasingly difficult issue today.

In our work in organizations, I see younger white women who reject the idea of feminism altogether. They are not well educated in the history of sexism and sexist oppression; they have no immediate experience of being denied access to employment or education or advancement. So they believe—just as white men do—that they have attained whatever position they have strictly on their own merits, and that anyone can do so, if they try.

It is truly said that those who ignore history are doomed to repeat it. These young white women managers are overlooking the fact that in this country, in 1998, a white woman manager earned only fifty-nine cents for every dollar earned by white-male managers. Her colleagues who are women managers of color earned even less—about fifty-seven cents on the dollar.[7]

The women we work with are mostly white women in middle management, or the few white women who have managed to break through the glass ceiling and get into the executive suite. They are making good money—even if it is less than their male counterparts receive—and they think they are firmly on the fast track. They aren't thinking about exerting whatever power they have achieved or using their political muscle to change conditions for all women, or about joining forces with other subordinated groups to work for fairness and equity for all.

So in this sense the feminist movement to date has benefited primarily middle-class and upper-middle-class white women, to the exclusion of women of color and women in the lower classes. In our work, we find that we have to deal with the racism of white women more forcefully than we have in the past. When there were only a few women in managerial positions, they more or less dissolved into the white group or in a few cases made alliances with other women. But now we find a larger number of white women who are every bit as racist—and unaware—as white men; and they are not conscious feminists either, so it is harder to make the bridge from sexism to racism.

But there are two persistent ways in which these women are being blindsided, in addition to being shortchanged financially. One is the work and family conflict, and the other is sexual harassment.

In corporate America today, even with all the talk about flextime and work and family policies, the stress on the working parent—and by this we still mean almost entirely the working mother—is unbelievable. Middle and upper managers work ten or twelve hours a day—and working wives and mothers go home and put in another three or four hours meeting the needs of their families. Of course, it is still true that many of the women who have made it into upper management do not have children—and these women may be even less sympathetic than their male counterparts with the dilemmas of the working mother.

The second issue, sexual harassment in the workplace, is no different today than it was thirty years ago. It may be more recognized; there is more public information about it and less tolerance; but it continues to go on. And it continues to be what it always was—a power issue.

It is certainly true that not all men are guilty—only a few. But in any climate where race and gender discrimination takes place, sexual harassment is never far behind. And we have to keep remembering that sexual harassment is not about sex, it's about power. It doesn't matter how many women there are or how many men; what matters is the degree of power the two groups have within the organization.

## SEXUAL ORIENTATION

One issue where we do see more change is in regard to sexual orientation. While there is still plenty of heterosexism and homophobia in corporations and in society, we are beginning to see more open discussion of the issues as gay, lesbian and bisexual people are becoming more active and more assertive about their rights in society. When we ask, in our workshops, how many people have family members or close friends or colleagues who are gay, lesbian or bisexual, we have seen that more and more people respond positively. In some groups, as many as 80 percent indicate that they have personal acquaintance with gays and lesbians—and the remaining 20 percent are apt to be embarrassed to admit that they don't.

That's a dramatic shift. Fifteen years ago we would never have asked the question, for one thing. And had we asked, I think we would have gotten exactly the reverse reaction.

This increased familiarity has made it more possible for participants to address their own homophobia—and this helps them make the connection among heterosexism, sexism and racism. In other words, participants are becoming more able to address *oppression*, as it impacts on many excluded groups.

Another factor that makes addressing gay and lesbian concerns a bit easier is that in the workshops, resistance based on religion seems to have gone underground. I'm sure it's still there, but with the increasing general acceptance, those who hold strongly intolerant views are less willing to expose them openly. This is also affected by the fact that in many situations there are two or three senior men who are "out" as gay. This helps set the tone toward tolerance and acceptance and away from any tendency toward gay-bashing.

I don't want to suggest that corporate America is now totally open and accepting of gays and lesbians. And I know that the anti-gay jokes and slurs continue, just as sexist and racist jokes and behaviors continue. Progress has been made, but, as always, the price of liberty is eternal vigilance.

## AFFIRMATIVE ACTION REVISITED

Another arena in which we must continue to pay the price of eternal vigilance is in the legal strategies that have been devised to keep the dominant group—whites—from preventing other groups from entering the doors of opportunity. People often forget that what is now known as affirmative action, and is currently being painted as a misguided liberal scheme, was a politically conservative strategy developed under the Nixon administration. It was created as a remedy for long-standing patterns of discrimination that were (and are) stubbornly resistant to change. It was designed to implement the equal employment opportunity laws that were passed in the 1960s and 1970s that aimed at eliminating employment discrimination and discrimination in the awarding of federal contracts and so forth.

The laws were focused on the discriminating organizations—corporations or municipalities or state or federal governments. It was originally a simple matter. The law said, you must stop discriminating. Here are some ways that you can—voluntarily—demonstrate that you have done so. But if you refuse or drag your feet too much, we—the federal enforcement agencies—will "mandate" that you correct the situation. We will sue you, and you will find that the financial damage you incur will outweigh the benefits you obtain from continuing in the old ways. And it worked.

Without those legal measures, the great shifts we have seen over the past few decades would not have taken place. At the beginning of this period—say, fifty years ago—virtually 100 percent of the managerial work force was white and male. This doesn't mean that the work force excluded white women and people of color. To the contrary, many industries, such as textile manufacturing, relied almost exclusively on the labor of women—and children. Poor white women and women of color have always been in the work force—without access to power or to self-determination.

But at the top of every organization, and in positions where advancement and lucrative salaries were possible, were white men. Now, due to the positive impact of equal employment opportunity and affirmative action, white women and people of color constitute increasingly larger percentages of entry-level management and middle-management workers. And corporate America and our governmental agencies have benefited mightily. Just imagine what a pickle we would be in if we came into this time of major demographic shift with the white-male work force we had thirty or forty years ago. We would be absolutely unprepared—we would have no competitive capacity at all.

The important thing to remember about affirmative action is that it did not provide any kind of preference. It did not do anything special for white women or for people of color. It just said, quite logically, that citizens could not be excluded from full participation in the society to which they belonged because they were of a different gender or race from the group which held the reins of power. It also said, again quite logically, that it was wrong for our governmental agencies and the corporations that did business with them to exclude some citizens from participating in the economic life of the nation—all citizens, by the fact of citizenship, had the right to sell their wares and their knowledge in the marketplace in the capitalist system. Further, organizations that operated in the public interest—police, fire and so forth—that had been absolutely closed and locked societies from which all people of color and all women were excluded, were operating in violation of our Constitution.

In order to ensure that these tightly locked organizations did in fact accept their constitutional and civic obligations, the federal government created mechanisms to guarantee that progress would be made—mechanisms such as setting aside a certain number of contracts to be awarded to minority or women vendors, or guaranteeing that certain numbers of new applicants to police forces or fire departments would be minorities or women. Without this pressure, it is clear that no change would have occurred—because no change had occurred prior to it.

And change has occurred, however partial and however slow. Enough change that, evidently, the dominant group feels that its dominance is threatened—and so the systems that have helped us inch forward are now under sharp attack. The fact that some people of color have joined in the attack doesn't mean that the systems haven't worked—some of the most strident attackers have benefited from them. Their attacks are, in my view, just one more example of how those of us who are members of subordinated groups often collude with our oppressors.

Another irony is that the attacks are aimed not at the center of the affirmative-action agenda, which was the effort to open up employment and contracts, but at the periphery—higher education. And in that arena the attack is being launched at the processes by which students are admitted, not at the continuing resistance of the educational establishments to overcome the racist and sexist practices that continue to ensure that most university professorships are still held by white men. The charges of "preferential treatment" that are being used as an excuse to exclude race as a factor in college admissions are never applied to the "preferential treatment" that led to the choke-hold white men have on academic and organizational power within the institutions.[8]

These attacks on affirmative action are just another example of the "two steps forward, one step back" progress that our country has made on racial and gender issues throughout our history. It is a replication of what happened after Reconstruction. When it became clear that the processes that had been set in place to ameliorate racism were actually working, the forces of reaction set about destroying them.

A prime example is the Voting Rights Act of 1965, which aimed to make it possible for African Americans to have representation in government. Whites would not vote for black candidates, and thus made it impossible for candidates of color to be elected. Districts were gerrymandered so that whites were in the majority and could continue to exclude blacks from attaining their legally guaranteed access to electoral office and representation.

Recognizing that such exclusion was unconstitutional and unfair, the Voting Rights Act specified that district lines must be drawn so that these injustices were corrected. Finally, African Americans began to be elected to offices, and the needs and voices of people of color began to be attended to—for the first time, again, since Reconstruction.[9] In the late 1990s, whites are once again attempting to return to the "political correctness" of the past—when it was quite acceptable to take legal measures to ensure that whites remained in control, but considered "favoritism" to take legal measures to allow African Americans full access to their rights as citizens.

The same "logic" holds for affirmative action. When the preferences were all for white men, the pretense was that somehow all these white men merited them. When the bases for selection to prestigious schools included not just grade-point average and Scholastic Aptitude Test (SAT) scores, but also whether or not one was the son of an alumnus, or was from a particular geographic area, or had particular athletic or musical talents—these were not seen as negative examples of preferential treatment, even if they resulted (as they did and do) in a preponderance of admissions going to whites. Only when race is factored in as one among other criteria is "preferential treatment" suddenly seen as off the mark.

The use of SAT scores as an "objective" measure is highly flawed, in many ways. For one, the original idea of the test was that it assessed scholastic *aptitude*—not achievement. If it truly measured aptitude, it would not, one would think, be possible for students to improve their scores by receiving tutorial assistance beyond the classroom—but in fact, an entire industry has grown up that provides such tutoring to middle- and upper-class children, enabling them to achieve higher scores and demonstrate more "aptitude" than those poor children whose parents cannot send them for additional assistance.

Another serious flaw is that study after study has demonstrated that these tests predict success *in the first year of college or university* only. After that, achievement levels out, with many other factors influencing success.

Recent studies have even shown that blacks, once admitted to prestigious universities, actually do better than whites. Whatever their SAT scores may have been on entry, if they are actually admitted they have a higher rate of completion.

Two other aspects of the attack on affirmative action are especially troubling. One is the claim by some—including some colluding people of color—that going through a door that was previously closed is somehow damaging to one's self-esteem. How is it that going through the same door that whites have always been able to pass through is anything other than just plain fair play? Why should that cause anyone to question their merit?

The second is that challenges to affirmative action always focus on people of color—when in actual fact it has been white women who have most benefited. Thirty years ago it was difficult for a woman of any race to be admitted to a doctoral program; it was very difficult indeed if she was married; and it was almost impossible for her to gain entrance if she had children (being thereby judged "not a serious student"). Now those barriers are virtually gone—for white women. And here again, sadly, I don't find white women or the white feminist movement stepping up to the plate and claiming their alliance with women of color, or their allegiance to the cause of advancement for *all* women.

I don't want to imply here that the question of affirmative action is one that pertains only to whites and African Americans. Many Hispanic Americans have many of the same issues and have been—and continue to be—discriminated against in the same ways. But there are others who are considered "Hispanic" but whose background is Portuguese or Spanish, who are assimilated into this culture as white, who have sometimes taken unfair advantage of the laws. They have not actually been historically discriminated against in the United States. A similar kind of complication exists for people of Asian heritage. Many have suffered under persistent and degrading discrimination for centuries. Others have arrived more recently, have come here with the advantages of a middle- or upper-class background in their native land, and do not have the same historic claim for redress.

My hope—my dream—has been and to some degree continues to be that we will be able to create coalitions of people of color who are similarly discriminated against, along with white women, to form a vast majority of workers. White men, too, could join this coalition since it is really only a very small minority of white men who form the power elite—most white men are oppressed along with all the rest of us. If we could get together in such a coalition we could certainly say to the white men who hold the reins of power, "If you continue to discriminate against the 60 to 65 percent of your work force who aren't white men, you aren't going to be very productive." From time to time that has happened in this country.

But what I see happening, and likely to continue to happen, is that the old divide-and-conquer strategies will persist. As I have said, we already see that young white women who have *benefited* from feminism and affirmative action now turn their back on feminism, and delude themselves into thinking that they are achieving on their own merit alone. They do not see the links among sexism, sexual harassment and racism—so they do nothing to work for fairness and equity for others.

The same thing is also happening among young privileged African Americans, who sometimes look at those of us in the older generation and wonder why we care so passionately about things like civil rights and equal opportunity.

My greatest fear is that in the demographic hierarchy of the twenty-first century, most African Americans, because of our unique history and our continuing visibility, will continue to fall to the bottom of the pile. Those who are furthest from the ideal of whiteness and maleness are most discriminated against, now as in previous times. And that discrimination persists in every avenue of life—being relegated to poor urban schools, being huddled together in crime-ridden urban ghettos, being underrepresented in our elected bodies and overrepresented in our prisons. Some have escaped and will continue to escape, and will achieve success not unlike that of their white brothers and sisters. But most will not. Nor will they find that those who should be their natural allies in the quest for justice—other people of color, white women and poor whites—will necessarily put their shoulder to the common wheel.

Even the fact that there is an increasing population of people who define themselves as mixed race does not offer much comfort. While many unions between men and women of different races are evidence of the triumph of individual love and respect over societal patterns of bigotry, very few of these marriages are between African Americans and people of other races. Although about 2 percent of the 53 million married couples in 1991 were of mixed races, only about 7 percent of marriages involving an African American were interracial. One-quarter of those of other races (primarily Asian Americans) were married to someone outside their own race, and one-fourth of married Hispanics had a non-Hispanic spouse in 1991.[10]

My point here is that the changing appearance of American citizens does not take away the necessity for *all Americans* to understand and work to ameliorate the history and patterns of racism. This is a difficult—almost impossible—point to get across. African Americans have a long history of being of "mixed race." As we know, the white slave master had free access to the bodies of his African women slaves. Through rape and incest, generations of children were born who, though firmly identified by society as "black" and thus subject to the odiousness of slavery and the subsequent hideousness of racist oppression, were inescapably "part white." Indeed, the facts were so inescapable that for many years the legal system attempted to quantify the degree of blackness and whiteness in a given individual—establishing categories such as octoroon, quadroon and mulatto, with the specific goal of making sure that even those with one distant black ancestor were subjected to discrimination and oppression.

Today, as more immigrants of color who are not African-American enter this country, and as intermarriage between various groups creates increasing numbers of people whose parents are different races and ethnicities, the old idiocies take on new meaning. Children born of mixed-race marriages are struggling to figure out who they are and where they belong in this society. Immigrants of color find that their lives here involve them in complicated patterns of dominance and subordination.

A book by Kevin Johnson, *How Did You Get to Be Mexican? A White/Brown Man's Search for Identity*, lays out the matter clearly:

> Because of the institution of slavery and its legacy, African Americans have suffered unparalleled disadvantages in U.S. society, but other racial minorities have been subordinated by the majority as well. The people of California terrorized the Chinese population in the mid-and-late nineteenth century. In addition to direct physical violence against Chinese immigrants, the United States Congress passed laws prohibiting Chinese immigrants from coming to our shores. About a century later, another nativist outburst resulted in new laws that more subtly affected immigrant populations largely from Asia and Latin America. People of Mexican ancestry in the Southwest continue to suffer from the vestiges of U.S. conquest.
>
> Many people view race relations as a static hierarchy, with blacks at the bottom, whites at the top, and other groups in between. However, race relations in the multiracial, multicultural United States constantly shift and change, ebb and flow depending on the social, political and economic circumstances of the day. Those who are serious about social change must seek to understand how the complexities operate as a whole in maintaining racial subordination.[11]

Do we as a nation have the fortitude and the patience to understand these complexities? Are our educational institutions prepared to train teachers, change curriculum, educate parents, and then educate our children to deal with the realities of race, gender and other forms of difference? I think not—but we will pay the price, sooner rather than later.

## GLOBAL DIVERSITY, ECONOMIC CHANGES AND MORE

Many years ago our company was invited to do some work in the Puerto Rican division of a major pharmaceutical company. The issues we were asked to address were familiar enough—poor management, racism, sexism and so forth—but the plant's location raised additional concerns. This was our first direct exposure to issues such as relations between expatriate Americans and their local counterparts; the impact of the history of colonization; and the different cultural perspectives of the Puerto Rican workers and their supervisors from the mainland. The company had, of course, opened the plant there specifically because labor was less expensive and the Puerto Rican government was eager to grant them significant tax benefits. So the situation was permeated with racism, sexism, class issues, culture issues and more.

Today that small experience is being repeated in ever-increasing circles around the globe. Only a few years ago multinational companies based in Europe insisted that U.S. ideas about diversity were irrelevant to them. They felt that our concerns about race and gender were peculiar to this culture, and that attempts to bring them into conversations about their own operations were more evidence of U.S. imperialist attitudes.

Multinational companies today, however, are recognizing that the global marketplace means more than finding new ways to sell products to new populations. It means learning enough about other cultures to at least market to them in ways that the native population regards as respectful—not to sell a car named Nova in a Spanish-speaking country where "No-va" means "Doesn't go."

The field of cross-cultural management training has mushroomed, and now includes approaches that take into account patterns of racism, sexism, classism and anti-immigrant sentiment, as well as the more familiar strategies that teach expats from one country to recognize cultural specifics and "peculiarities" in another.

In Europe, the conversation tends to begin with concerns around the integration of different immigrant and ethnic groups, and moves from them to more general concerns around racism—and occasionally around sexism. Now we find that some of the multinationals and some governmental agencies as well—such as those in Sweden, Great Britain, France, the Netherlands and Germany—are beginning to look to U.S. consultants for assistance in managing these issues. Some governments are also looking to the United States for model legislation around which to design their own equal employment and affirmative action laws—an ironic development, since this country seems determined to dismantle its structures just as European countries are creating theirs.[12]

There is another aspect of multinational or global corporations that is daunting in the extreme. Some U.S.-based companies—Levi Strauss being one example—either out of the moral conviction of their leaders or under pressure from U.S. activist organizations, are examining their relationships with offshore partners in terms of human-rights issues. Levi Strauss has actually closed some companies that refused to make the changes in working conditions that it required. Most multinationals, however, have not exercised their enormous economic power in the interest of either civil rights or economic justice.

This creates a difficult moral dilemma for a consulting group like ours.

Do we accept contracts with multinational companies, assisting them in some difficult but narrow aspect of "managing diversity"—while turning a blind eye to their complicity with brutal regimes in other countries? Is it possible for a small firm such as ours to have any influence in this vast global arena? Is it even possible for the multinationals to exert moral pressure when such actions might—almost certainly would—lead to a significant drop in profits and thus in returns to their shareholders? Is such pressure even "moral" in another culture—or is it another example of foreign domination, colonization and exploitation? Should multinationals lend their influence to prop up dictatorial or evil regimes, in the interest of guaranteeing short-term peace and stability in the area—which is of course good for business? Or do they have an obligation in the other direction? These are difficult questions that will, in my view, become inescapable in the very near future—but to which I, at least, don't pretend to have answers.

Closer to home, we are finding a new arena of challenge in the merger and acquisition mania that characterized the 1990s and will continue into the new century. Leaving aside the economic and ethical issues that such mergers raise, they generate sets of concerns that impact directly on diversity work.

Years ago, when we were working in numerous companies of one major pharmaceutical corporation, we found that the corporate culture differed from one group to the next. But because there was an overarching culture that characterized the parent corporation, there was not sufficient disparity to derail a diversity initiative or other culture-change effort. Now, however, in industries such as the financial sector, the big-fish-gobbling-up-the-smaller-fish phenomenon is occurring at such a dizzying rate that marriages are taking place between strangers, and between groups with such widely divergent cultures, and holding such different balances of power, as to create entirely new sets of problems. They still have to do with the familiar patterns of dominance and subordination, but now the patterns affect the entire enterprise. The dominant culture—the acquiring organization—insists on having its own way. The subordinated culture either has to conform or undermine and resist or leave. It can become a very punitive process and can destroy the financial advantage that led to the acquisition at the outset.

Some of our clients are beginning to realize that they must pay careful attention to these dynamics. After all, Company Number One acquired Company Number Two in the first place because they needed their expertise. In one case in which we are involved, Company Number Two's expertise in diversity issues was part of what made it attractive for acquisition. And yet managers in Company Number One are exhibiting the most extraordinary kinds of envy and animosity toward managers in Company Number Two—specifically because they are more competent in these areas! From the outside, looking on, it's quite humorous. But from the inside, where the situation has to be managed, it is very difficult indeed. This particular case may be peculiar to us, since we have been retained as consultants by Company Number One, after a long track record with Company Number Two. But the overall challenges of managing the dynamics of merging cultures in the midst of mergers and acquisitions are increasingly difficult, in general.

Finally, there is one other new component in our work today, and that is the role corporations are beginning to play in relation to the communities where they are based or to which their products are marketed. Concerns for community relations are not, of course, altogether a recent phenomenon. In our earliest work, some of our major clients made important contributions to the well-being of the communities where their corporate headquarters were based, often in the form of philanthropic contributions to various local charities.

Some mounted more direct initiatives. One company to which we consulted, based in upstate New York, was concerned about the fact that the community was all white and did not provide a supportive environment for its African-American employees—thus making it difficult to attract more blacks to work there. The company became very proactive— they brought in a radio station that played music popular in the African-American community; they encouraged a black barbershop to open up; they intervened when blacks had problems with the police; and they put a fair amount of money into developing a community-relations function in the town. All of this activity resulted from a combination of some managers having the foresight to realize the import of changing demographics, and from pressure from a black managers' group within the corporation. That was in the early 1980s. We helped them with some of these efforts, and also were involved in similar initiatives with other companies.

What is different now, in our experience, is that some companies are taking a more direct and systemic approach to addressing problems in their home communities. In one southern organization to which we are consulting, the president has volunteered to participate personally in a community organization that is addressing serious racism and race-relations problems in that town. I have assisted in this effort, and find that this president is very clear about his motivation and the motivation of his organization. He recognizes that in order for U.S. businesses to survive and thrive, there must be peace in the community. And there cannot be lasting peace if there is systemic oppression by one group of another. In this sense, the citizens-as-customers concept has merged with concepts of civil rights to drive a major social-change effort.

The "business case," however, is not the president's sole motivation. Although he describes himself as politically conservative, he comes to

these matters with convictions that are more often seen as liberal or progressive. He is convinced that overturning patterns of oppression and
discrimination is a moral imperative. He is perfectly clear about that,
and does not hesitate to make his position known in the corporation and
in the community.

Another such effort was mounted by the Levi Strauss Foundation in
four cities where it had factories. Called Project Change, the effort pulled
together coalitions of community groups and community leaders in long-
term, foundation-funded anti-racism projects. My son, Barry Cross,
through his consulting firm, Cross-Cultural Consultants, assisted with
two of these initiatives. In one city, the effort utilized the Community
Reinvestment Act to pressure the local financial community to work with
the anti-racism organization to reduce discrimination in lending and to
open more opportunities for housing to people of color.[13]

Such community and corporation collaborations are beginning to crop
up around the country, but of course not all derive from high motiva-
tions. Many are funded by the marketing function, sending the clear
message that companies now recognize that the people of color who tend
to be the primary residents of the inner cities, where some corporate
headquarters continue to be based, actually do have money and can be
"converted" into paying customers. But others combine this motivation
with a sense of corporate citizenship, in part as a result of President
Clinton's call for a dialogue on race. When this happens, it can lead to
more equitable partnerships between corporations and their communities. It may also enable the business community to interact with community leaders and citizens to shape governmental policies to the
betterment of both business and society. In one community in which we
are consulting, we are seeing solid citizens coming together across all
kinds of differences and disciplines, learning to communicate effectively
with one another, and planning how to create a municipal environment
that is peaceful and respectful of all its citizens. The corporation is providing a hefty piece of the funding—but funding is also coming from
local organizations, individuals, government agencies and other sources.
So it is not just another case of corporate lobbying to create business-
friendly policies.

Using a social-justice approach within the corporate structure—especially if it satisfies the yearning of some white male executives to regain
some of their youthful idealism—can have powerful albeit indirect results. As executives begin to explore the possibilities of other, less hierarchical or money-driven ways of working, the organization may become
less oppressive internally. And as employees and executives experience
a different atmosphere in their work lives, they may carry the message
outside the corporation, into their interactions in communities and
schools and religious organizations. As they learn, in their work with us

in culture-change efforts, to identify norms that create barriers for some groups within the corporation, and enablers (advantages) for others, they learn to identify similar barriers and advantages in other arenas of their lives.

These initiatives give me the most hope for the future. Working with a network of consultants and trainers who share a common vision of what it means to be citizens in a democracy, and who have joined with me to try to turn that vision into reality, is rewarding beyond measure. I have no delusion that racism or sexism or heterosexism will be overcome in my lifetime, or the lifetimes of my child or grandchild. But I do continue to believe that we can ameliorate their impact in our lives and in the lives of our communities and our nation.

Within the democratic concept of citizenship, a basic tenet is that we are, indeed, all "created equal." More and more I recognize that the essence of discrimination is not difference—it is the fact that we are, in every sense that matters, the same. We all respond in the same ways to abuse, discrimination, intolerance, injustice. We are all tempted by the prerogatives of power to forget our common humanity, and to look for rationalizations of "difference" to justify our advantages. When we finally recognize that we are actually equal, really the same, we can start recognizing one another as citizens and begin creating a democracy that functions in actuality—not just in imagination.

When our leaders gain the skills and find the courage to begin to manage to this end, we will all be able to hold our heads a little higher, as fellow citizens of the world's most promising democracy.

## NOTES

1. For the statistics cited in this section, see William P. O'Hare et al., "African Americans in the 1990s," *Population Bulletin* 46, no. 1 (July 1991).

2. For an overview of the metrics process, with sample questions, see *The Diversity Factor* Article Collection: Metrics ACC5. Also see Appendix 2 in this text.

3. For a full discussion of this process, see Yvette Hyater-Adams and Delyte D. Frost, "Partnership for Change at CoreStates Financial Corp," *The Diversity Factor* 6, no. 4 (Summer 1998).

4. See "1998 Labor Day Fact Sheet," a press release from the Catalyst organization, citing Bureau of Labor Statistics figures. Numbers do not total 100 percent due to rounding.

5. Ibid.

6. Delyte D. Frost, "A Special Place for White Women Only," unpublished paper prepared for Elsie Y. Cross Associates Inc., Philadelphia, PA, 1973; revised 1976, 1987.

7. See *Women of Color in Corporate Management: A Statistical Picture* (New York: Catalyst, 1998).

8. For a thorough study of how white men use that power not only to exclude others but even to define what is "truth," see Rodolfo Acuña, *Sometimes There Is No Other Side: Chicanos and the Myth of Equality* (Notre Dame, IN: University of Notre Dame Press, 1998). Professor Acuña outlines how, in his battle to gain tenure, he was confronted by the insistence of the tenure committee that only the Western European canon was acceptable as "scientific truth" for tenure purposes.

9. For a chilling account of how blacks were systematically stripped of their newly won rights after Reconstruction, see James W. Loewen, *Lies My Teacher Told Me: Everything Your American History Textbook Got Wrong* (New York: The New Press, 1995). Loewen, calling the years between 1890 and 1920 the "nadir of American race relations," shows how restrictions on voting, segregation in public places, and lynchings were used—especially by southern whites—to maintain white supremacy. Many of the "firsts" that are now presented as such laudatory evidence of progress are not firsts at all. For example, Jackie Robinson was *not* the first black player in major-league baseball—blacks had played in the major leagues in the nineteenth century but were forced out by whites by 1889 (p. 155).

10. See William P. O'Hare, "America's Minorities—The Demographics of Diversity," *Population Bulletin* 47, no. 4 (December 1992).

11. Kevin Johnson, *How Did You Get to Be Mexican? A White/Brown Man's Search for Identity* (Philadelphia: Temple University Press, 1998), 176–177.

12. For more information on European and other global initiatives, see Marthe Vakoufari, "Sweden 2000: A Public-Private Partnership," *The Diversity Factor* 6, no. 1 (Fall 1997); Lian Zhou, "Shanghai Fleetguard: Diversity and the Joint Venture," *The Diversity Factor* 3, no. 4 (Summer 1995); and Graham Shaw, "Gaining from Diversity," *The Diversity Factor* 7, no. 1 (Fall 1998).

13. For more information on Project Change, see Margaret B. White, "Project Change," *The Diversity Factor* 4, no. 3 (Spring 1996), and a follow-up article by Shirley Strong, director of Project Change, and consultant Cynthia A. Chavez, "Project Change in Action," *The Diversity Factor* 7, no. 2 (Winter 1999).

# Appendix 1 ⎯⎯⎯⎯⎯⎯⎯⎯⎯⎯⎯⎯⎯⎯⎯⎯

## The Discourses of Diversity: The Links Between Conversation and Organizational Change

Nancie Zane

The following essay by consultant Nancie Zane is based on research conducted during an Elsie Y. Cross Associates, Inc., workshop. The research formed the basis for her doctoral dissertation in social psychology. In the essay "Essie Tower" is a pseudonym for Elsie Cross.

While discussions within organizations about "becoming more diverse" or "managing diversity" have become more common, the meaning of diversity has become more ambiguous.[1] As is frequently the case with socially charged issues that are reduced to a few buzz words, these phrases are subject to a wide range of interpretations. In an effort to understand how one major financial institution made meaning of its commitment to becoming more diverse, I studied the discourse—the conversational patterns and organizational interventions—that took place over a two-year period. By tracking the discourse used by individuals and groups (white men, white women, men of color, women of color) and the corporation itself (such as public statements by the CEO and public documents), I learned that there were powerful interactive links among the organizational language, structure and culture.[2] In other words, changes in the ways people conversed began to reflect and contribute to changes in the quality of relationships among individuals and groups as well as the range of people (across race, gender and status) being listened to when decisions were being made in the organization.

In turn, as the structure and culture of the organization began to change, new conversational patterns about diversity began to appear.

I first review some of these changes by analyzing the "official communications" between the CEO and the organization. Then I describe the process of change for one key group—the senior white men—and the impact participation in well-facilitated diversity-awareness sessions (diverse by race and gender) had on their understanding of race and gender issues.

## THE CONTEXT

In December 1990, Paul Forelli, the CEO of "Eastern Bank," committed the bank to becoming an "excellent" organization, not only in regard to its ability to "manage the numbers" and use cutting-edge technology, but also in its ability to become more humanistic and family-oriented.[3] A cornerstone of Forelli's vision was "valuing diversity," which he defined in straightforward terms—a desire to value individual difference and encourage a "breadth" of perspectives in an environment of respect.

Forelli believed that for his organization to succeed in the face of fierce competition, it must have a new long-term business strategy. Forelli's understanding of the need for profitability was linked with his recognition that financial success required success on the "people" side of the organization as well. At the time of his announcement, he perceived employee morale as low, and attributed much of the dissatisfaction to an insensitive organizational culture.[4] As a white-male senior manager later framed it, Eastern's corporate structure was "ready to explode" as a consequence of the relentless nature of the "macho" work demands, the perceived glass ceilings, and inadequate pay raises.

## FINDINGS

During the period of my research, from 1990 to 1992, Forelli discussed his vision in each of his annual talks, plotting the organization's direction for the next year and describing the high and low points of the previous year. These talks thus provided a conceptual map of his evolving thinking as he led his organization into a culture-change process. Two particularly salient themes marked the transformational course he was negotiating, one related to diversity, the other to organizational structure.

Forelli's 1990 speech demonstrated his understanding of diversity as focused on the individual—a construct I call a *discourse of the golden rule of diversity*. This humanistic, "color-blind" approach assumes that if each person could treat others with respect and kindness, interpersonal and organizational conflicts would dissipate.[5] Forelli was convinced that the organizational culture could be reshaped by altering interpersonal norms, nurturing professional growth of individuals, and rewarding positive work. The resulting new atmosphere would "radiate out" to customers and shareholders, enabling Eastern to maintain its dominant position within the competitive financial marketplace.

The next year, 1991, Forelli's annual talk reflected a change in his conceptual framework about diversity.[6] In this presentation he stressed the importance of recognizing the various demographic (racial, ethnic, gender, etc.) groups to which employees belonged, thus introducing a *discourse of race and gender differences*. He now saw the challenge to be helping individual managers build a well-functioning, caring organization based on the collective strengths of a more heterogeneous work force. To support this venture, he publicly sanctioned the development of organizational groups (e.g., a women's network, people of color group, etc.) to promote the career interests of white women and people of color in the bank. Further, he authorized the hiring of diversity consultants to work with the bank on its diversity initiative.

By 1992, after Forelli had attended a series of diversity workshops, he saw diversity as being a proactive process of seeking and celebrating differences. Articulating a *discourse of eradicating oppression and valuing differences*, Forelli now described the ways managers would be held accountable for working successfully across demographic differences while rooting out discriminatory policies and practices. Forelli underlined the importance of squashing any forms of institutional bigotry in the bank, and recast racism, sexism and homophobia as a set of multilayered, insidious forces operating at the individual, group and institutional levels. His definition of diversity "management" shifted from an emphasis on the more traditional bureaucratic functions such as providing oversight and correction, or gatekeeping around the information flow, to managers becoming coaches and facilitators, helping all employees increase their competencies in a customer-focused environment.

### Organizational Structure

As Forelli's discourses and practices related to diversity evolved, his vision of the organizational structure shifted as well. Rejecting traditional corporate language, he initially presented a *discourse of bureaucratic reform*. Reflected in his talk was a desire to create an organizational culture that was based on authentic relationships and professional growth rather than the rigid roles and rules inherent in paternalistic, bureaucratic structures. He later articulated a *discourse of post-bureaucratic interdependent partnerships*—reflecting a shift in his vision toward a more participative, less hierarchical organization in which shareholders, customers, employees and the community interacted as partners for their common good.

While the design for change was being formulated and introduced at the organizational level, powerful individual and group dynamics were also being stirred as revealed in the reactions of managers and nonexempt employees across race and gender lines.

As I continued my research, I found that with each articulation of the CEO's vision, new organizational contexts developed that allowed previously submerged conversations, conflicts, desires and possibilities to appear.

For example, much of the initial talk of white women and people of color centered on the pain, anger and frustration they experienced because of their exclusion from what they called the white-male organizational culture. As one African-American man said, "Although it is assumed that we will want to play on the team, we aren't asked out to lunch with the politically attuned." In addition, experiential and perceptual differences among race and gender groups—invisible when white women and all people of color were lumped together in a monolithic "minority" category—began to be expressed. For example, white women were particularly outspoken about their perceptions related to promotional policies and practices. As one middle-level white woman said, "The glass ceiling is the floor my boss walks on."

African Americans and Latinos/Latinas, while sharing those concerns, were also worried about recruitment and development. In the words of one middle-level African-American woman, "A major issue for blacks is just getting in and being able to stay in once you are in." Even white males, who appeared to be more comfortable with the norms, values and expectations of the bureaucracy, believed that they paid a high personal cost for working within the bureaucratic culture of the bank. As one senior white man aptly stated, "We're working in the morning, working at night, working too hard, too hard-driving." It was in this very context—of the struggle between "what is" and "what could be"—that new sets of words emerged that pushed the boundaries of contested meanings, legitimizing new activities and conversations.

## THE CHANGING DISCOURSES OF THE SENIOR WHITE MEN

As I tracked the conversations and actions of five groups distinct by race, gender and/or status across time, I began to see that their understandings of themselves, of the race and gender relationships across the organization, and of the distribution of organizational power shifted.[7] In particular, the changes in the perspectives of the white-male senior managers—who initially had little awareness of the impact of their whiteness or maleness on the decisions they made or the ways others perceived them—were quite striking.

When I explored the dominant viewpoint of the white men prior to the beginning of the initiative, I found two elements. First was a belief I call the *bottom-line discourse*, which reflected their concern that engaging in a diversity initiative would be a distraction from the "real work" of making money.[8] Second, they firmly believed that those who worked hard and could get the job done were given additional opportunities to perform, regardless of race, gender or other factors—the *meritocratic discourse*. Embedded in this critique was also the notion that claims of discrimination were thinly veiled attempts to mask poor performance.[9] As one man put it, "I don't have time to listen to people complain about racism if they're not performing. The company shouldn't prop you up because you haven't had opportunities in life."

What happened that led to the changes in the attitudes and actions of the senior white men? Some white-male managers believed that their participation in a series of diversity workshops and the cross-race and cross-gender conversations was a critical step in the process of "opening their eyes" around issues of race and gender.[10]

During the workshops many white men said that they could not relate to the kinds of experiences that members of different race and gender groups shared. However, they reported—when the workshops were completed—that being forced to compare the realities of these participants' painful work lives with their own relatively comfortable situations was transformative. One executive vice-president, "Marv," who had gone into the session with little patience for the idea that there was real discrimination in the organization, said:

> To me the biggest impact came from the personal stories that we heard in our two-day session. Intellectually, I thought I was aware of some of these issues, but when you actually hear the depth of emotion and general consistency in the stories, it made an impression on me that there is a problem here, and it is not just a couple of malcontents whining and complaining.

In addition, the diversity consultants provided managers with a new and broader framework for processing the data by distinguishing among individual, group and institutional levels of analysis, a learning that for "Evan," another executive vice-president, meant that he, like Marv, could "no longer dismiss individual concerns [as being merely] anecdotal stories that can be rejected." Consequently, these men's vision and understanding of some aspect of the world had been permanently altered.

In the following section I present selections from some of the remarks made by senior white men during the workshops. These passages, I believe, illustrate the shifts that were taking place.


## THE WORKSHOP EXPERIENCE

While every diversity workshop is different, there are structures and patterns that are commonly incorporated. In the workshops discussed here, a frequently used methodology is a combination of large-group and small-group sessions.


*Scene One.* In one session, after talking in small homogeneous groups about the impact of the analyses by race, gender and level of organization-wide data that had been collected at the beginning of the culture-change process, participants came back together to discuss the highlights of their conversations.[11] People of color talked movingly about the pain they experienced trying to "make it" in the organization and the systematic erosion of the psyche that takes place after continuously being exposed to racism. The discussion proceeded as follows:

> Elaine, a Chinese mid-level manager, said: "It makes me sad that I'm always having to change myself . . . to adapt myself to others' expectations so they'll accept me."
> Essie Tower, the lead African-American diversity consultant, responded: "What happens if they don't understand your perspective?"
> Elaine: "You take it in internally and I end up feeling like there's something wrong with me."
> Yvonne, an African-American senior-level officer, joined in as well: "I go home questioning my sanity, my intellect, my judgement . . . we hurt ourselves, put a lot of energy into saying, 'I'm somebody, you can't make me feel like a nobody.' "


After hearing their comments, a number of white men challenged the people of color: "Why do you take it?" "Why are you so docile?" "How come there isn't more activism in the streets?" With some impatience, different people of color talked about their fear of white violence and their fear for their children in the outside world. Flora, an African-American mid-level woman manager, elaborated:

> My son has everything going against him. The only thing he has is two intelligent parents. . . . I pray for him. . . . I know that if he gets an attitude he'll end up with a bullet in his ass . . . he's always suspect . . . he's already been asked by a white cop in our own neighborhood, "Where do you live?"

While her story was quite gut-wrenching, the white men did not seem moved. Yvonne, who was clearly angry about whites' assumption that blacks have choices about venting their rage, said forcefully:

> We put up with it because we have no choice. . . . But you know what racism does to us? It destroys us systematically. . . . even with college degrees we can't find work . . . there are bright black men on street corners because there's no place for them in the system . . . they wait to die.

The white men began to talk about their feelings of guilt and responsibility as well as their sense of powerlessness about changing the situation. Essie asked people to move back into their same-race and-gender groups and identify their reactions to what they heard. On newsprint the white men wrote:

> We often feel powerless or unaware of what to do to make a difference.
>
> We want and need feedback—we will make mistakes.
>
> We have feelings of fear, guilt, anxiety.
>
> We feel a lot of the burden is (appropriately) on us and we want and need to help.

During the next intergroup dialogue, a number of people of color responded with surprise: "I had no idea that white men had feelings of impotence or uncertainty."

*Scene Two.* This session began with two white men acknowledging that they had been operating *only* from an individual perspective and did not understand group-level phenomena: "When I thought I 'had it' on an individual level I was most dangerous since I didn't get it on a group level."

An upper-level Puerto Rican woman manager, Rosa, went into depth about how, when she meets whites in power, they either assume that she is stupid or, if seen as intelligent, different from the "others" of her kind. This puts her in the position, if she wants to fit in and succeed, of having to choose to identify with those in power (whites) or with her family, whom the whites see as inferior. "Every time it's a death that I die to think . . . my cousins are less than me. . . . It's painful putting people behind the doors and making them invisible."

The white men once again appeared distant. One man admitted that it was hard to hear Rosa's story. Others tried to portray it as a common theme, the kind of problem many people have. Donna, a white-woman diversity consultant, challenged this, showing how Rosa's situation was specifically the result of prejudice against her race and gender—a burden that white men do not carry. Essie clarified the underlying issues: "How does it feel, that with the luck of the draw, you have the advantage? You feel like you've earned your spot, but haven't recognized the group advantage."

Slowly, some of the white men began to let in the possibility that they have been privileged in certain ways. Chaz, an executive vice-president, said, "You're saying that we got where we are because of who we are . . . you're putting down a life that's been hard to come by . . . that hurts my self-image." John, a black diversity consultant asked, "Why do you hear her negating your hard work?" Chaz replied, "Well, most of us think we did it through hard work." Reluctantly, however, he admitted, "But hard work or not—we had an advantage."

*Scene Three.* During a large-group session Bill began to discuss his new-found belief about race, gender and self-esteem—that is, that while it takes a lot of energy for anyone to maintain self-esteem, it must take more energy for white women and people of color, given the daily psychic assaults with which they are confronted. Bob, another white man, built on that idea and made the connection between self-esteem and power. "Some of us use our positions of power to feel good. If you don't have self-confidence, you don't want to give up the power . . . and lots of us don't have it [self-confidence]."

The conversation then moved to the question of what would motivate white men to share the prize or power or privilege. "I think it would be decency," said Bob. Tim responded in a matter-of-fact tone, "We know that doesn't work. . . . [W]e've been able to wall off others from getting their hands in the cookie jar . . . the system isn't working."

The white men then began to problem-solve about how they should address these issues. Some suggested that the only approach would be to hire more blacks, even if they were less qualified—an idea Essie quickly challenged. One man linked the nature of the organizational structure to its function: "Structures have become invisible to protect white men's self-image." Donna then connected his comment to the question of change and responsibility: "White men's responsibility is to get people to say that the invisible structures that maintain inequity have to change."

## SPEAKING THE NEW LANGUAGE

When I interviewed a number of the senior white men six months after the workshop, I found that there were a range of organizational issues into which they now believed they had gained new insight, and their conversations had changed as a result.

For example, they now saw that the discourse related to the "bottom line" could be better described as the discourse of "global competition," in which diversity was viewed as a cost-effective strategy for enhancing the human resources of the organization. This reflected their acceptance of the facts of demographic change, and the increasing numbers of white women and people of color in the work force. They recognized that they must understand how to maximize the contributions of the new workers, ensure their ability to be productive members of teams, and in general work with them to maintain the overall competitiveness of the organization. As one senior manager now explained, "The population is going to demand that we acknowledge, encourage and value diversity or fall by the wayside—and whoever thinks they can discount that is going to suffer." Several other senior men indicated their agreement with the following statement: "Diversity is critical from the business standpoint because it allows for more competition and a better pool of people to choose from."

The "meritocratic discourse"—the idea that success was available for anyone who worked hard—was now modified by a "discourse of discrimination," recognizing systemic barriers which limited the possibilities of success for white women and people of color. As Bill said rather forcefully before the middle-level managers, "I'm convinced . . . [Eastern] has real problems and I'm glad we're stepping up to deal with them. Morally it's the right thing to do; there should be no discrimination based on color, gender, fitness, eye color, etc."

Evan summed up his learning: "It is really important that everybody involved understand that most of us, me included, were not supersensitive to this. There is a gap, a giant gap, between the two [senior managers and employees] because we don't acknowledge [employees'] value. We don't encourage participation by these people . . . or our participation with them, and that is really key."

Several managers now identified specific problems that needed to be addressed: the lack of mentoring for white women and people of color; recruitment; and internal promotions in some areas in the bank where blacks and white women were well represented in lower levels but not in administration, and others where blacks in particular were nonexistent. Marv, who at one time believed that charges of discrimination were only "individual belly-aching," now felt strongly that the situation should change. Although he was unsure what change strategies to employ, he pointed to the fact that fifteen or twenty years prior, white women were not hired into customer contact jobs because it was believed that "nobody would want to talk to women about their finances." Now, he pointed out, more than 50 percent of the pre-senior, customer-contact management positions were occupied by women.

Finally, a "post-bureaucratic discourse" emerged in which the senior men began to discuss the ways in which the overall bureaucratic culture was burdensome to all employees—including white men.

While initially focused on tensions between work and home demands as being women's problems, the discussion shifted when a number of men shared similar tensions in their own lives. Some complained that the culture demanded that workers spend too much time on the job in order to be considered "serious." As Evan said, "[T]he price to pay for business success is too high. The corporation must allow people to value their family life."

## WHAT THE STORIES TELL US

As I listened to the conversations that took place during the diversity workshops, and also talked with the senior white men after the event, I concluded that these men had undergone a rather striking metamorphosis. By participating in dialogue in which white women, women of color, and men of color spoke candidly from their personal as well as their group-level experiences within the organization, the senior white men were confronted with collective data about life and work experiences that were categorically different from their own. These exchanges, facilitated by highly skilled diversity consultants, convinced them that expressions of concern over discrimination were not statements from whiny individuals, or belly-aching by undeserving members of minority groups. The men were forced to recognize that the issues were systemic, and that there were patterns of discrimination throughout the organization that went far beyond individual experience.[12]

From this research, I saw that as the white men began to perceive themselves not only as individual players within the organization but also as members of a specific identity group in relation with members of other identity groups, they constructed new, more complex critiques about others, about themselves as a group, and about their relationships to the organization. In acknowledging the gaps between their reality and others' realities, many of the white men were able to hold previous assumptions at bay and hear old information in new ways. They not only shifted their beliefs about how white women and people of color are treated within an organization, they changed their analytic lenses. They no longer saw "flawed individuals." Now they were able to perceive the complex intergroup relationships and structural barriers that surrounded them.

In addition, they gained a perspective on the nature of white-male privilege and their relationship to it. In other words, as senior white men engaged in "public talk" with other race and gender groups, they were able to construct a new set of organizational discourses in which there was an embracing, rather than a negating, of race and gender differences, as well as a rejection of discriminatory policies and practices.

## NOTES

1. See M. Limaye, "Responding to Work Force Diversity: Conceptualizations and Search for Paradigms," *Journal for Business and Technical Communication* 3, no. 3 (1994): 353–371; Taylor Cox, Jr., *Cultural Diversity in Organizations: Theory, Research and Practice* (San Francisco: Berrett-Koehler, 1993); and Ann Morrison, *The New Leaders: Guidelines on Leadership Diversity in America* (San Francisco: Jossey-Bass, 1992).

2. I used a process called "grounded theory generation" that demands a close examination of the qualitative data I was gathering and, in particular, the conversational patterns that emerged. (See A. Strauss, *Qualitative Analysis for Social Scientists* [Cambridge, MA: Cambridge Press, 1987].) I employed a range of methods: archival inquiry, participant observations in regard to group meetings and workshop interactions, focus groups, and individual interviews. In addition, concepts of embedded intergroup relations and feminist theories shaped the way I went about my research. (See, for example, C. Alderfer and K. Smith, "Studying Intergroup Relations Embedded in Organizations," *Administrative Science Quarterly* 27 [1982].)

3. The names of the institution and the people employed there have all been changed to maintain anonymity.

4. Although the organization was slightly over 60 percent female, there was an underrepresentation of white women and people of color in the officer-level ranks. Seventy-six percent of the women and 86 percent of the people of color were located at the bottom of the organization. While 33 percent of the total number of women in the organization were in management (compared with 76 percent of men), women made up 43 percent of middle managers and 12 percent of senior managers. For people of color, the statistics were even worse: 11 percent were in middle management, less than 1 percent in senior management.

5. See Morrison, *New Leaders*, 6.

6. During that year, Forelli had authorized the "Eastern Action Committee," a diverse group of top managers, to design and implement the first phases of a culture-change process. One critical activity in which they engaged was an employee satisfaction survey. The results, which were quite dismaying to Forelli, pointed to the ways managerial white women and people of color felt undervalued, underdeveloped and underutilized. In addition, the survey revealed that all employees, except the most senior white men, had negative views of the decision-making process at the bank.

7. I tracked the senior white men; senior white women; middle-level (white and of color) women, including members of the women's network; and both whites and people of color at the branch level.

8. Some worried that the bank was going too far, bringing in race and gender tensions from the larger society, or stirring up issues within the organization that were better left alone. Others, though recognizing the importance of changing race and gender demographics, felt that the energy required for "becoming more diverse" would be too expensive and distracting. Perhaps the real bottom line was expressed by one of the executive vice-presidents when he said, "We have no evidence that diversity is actually economically valuable."

9. They were also convinced of their own color- and gender-blindness: "I don't care who I've got, I just want the best talent."

10. Workshops in the first series, which were two days in length, used a range of teaching methods to familiarize top managers with the dynamics of institutionalized racism and sexism and to help them discover the ways in which these forces were manifested at Eastern. Because the senior-most managers were predominantly white men, the consultant and the action committee decided to invite upper- and middle-level white women and people of color to participate in the workshops to ensure that the senior white men could hear how the other groups' experiences in the corporation differed from their own. The three-day workshops in the second series attempted to build on the learnings of the first in terms of deepening the understanding about patterns of discrimination at the group and organizational level. Upon completion of the workshop series, small heterogeneous "dialogue groups" were established and met regularly as a means of continuing the learning process.

11. There were four small groups: white women, white men, women of color and men of color. The women of color group was not racially homogeneous in that there were Asian-American, Hispanic-American, and African-American women present. The men of color group consisted of African Americans only.

12. The question that remains unexplored, and that is beyond the scope of this work to address, is the cost (and gain) to white women and people of color for their self-disclosures and group-disclosures.

# Appendix 2 ⎯⎯⎯⎯⎯⎯⎯⎯⎯⎯⎯⎯

## Measuring Results

Joseph Potts

When we first began to work in the diversity field, our client corporations were not much interested in measuring results. The CEOs who contracted with us recognized that while the problems they had defined were real, they were somewhat abstract. It would be difficult, they often said, to isolate the impact of a diversity initiative from the numerous other elements that affected the company's business and its culture.

Over time, however, as the field matured, people began to devise ways to track the progress of interventions and to document results both quantitatively and qualitatively. Our colleague, Joseph Potts, a contributing editor to our journal, *The Diversity Factor*, created a system of metrics which uses an extensive data base that allows organizations to benchmark their status against statistics in other companies.

This appendix includes two parts. The first provides Joseph's overview of the system, with a detailed description of the survey instrument. In the second, "Telling the Story," he reviews what often happens when a company is presented with the results of the survey, and suggests how the data may be used to help move the diversity intervention along in a positive direction.

## PART 1: THE DIVERSITY ASSESSMENT SURVEY

Some years ago the management committee of a Fortune 500 company was struggling to understand why it had such a poor track record in retaining "minority" employees. The CEO complained in great frustration, "It seems to me that if everybody in this organization treated everyone else with genuine respect, our diversity problems would go away."

The consultants had heard this many times. It *does* seem that people would get along just fine if we all simply followed the Golden Rule and treated each other respectfully.

But as management committees all over the country are learning, it isn't that simple. Even if we were all "nice enough" to treat others kindly, our differences wouldn't disappear. The Battle of the Sexes is not just an old joke, and conflicts across racial and ethnic lines seem to be part of the human condition.

But American business believes that we can no longer afford to let these conflicts contaminate our business environment. Therefore we must understand why individual change is not enough. We must be able to demonstrate to senior management where the problems lie in each organization, and to point out what remedies are effective for those particular problems in that particular company.

The Diversity Assessment Survey that we have developed is one tool for the task. Part 1 of this appendix describes the survey in brief and gives an overview of some of the comparative findings between two organizations—a major division of a manufacturing organization in the Midwest, which we call "JKLCorp"; and a financial services organization on the West Coast, "InvestCo."

## THEORIES OF CHANGE

The theoretical underpinnings for the Diversity Assessment process lie in the field of systems theory, which states that changes at any level of a complex system will impact and be impacted by other levels of the system.[1] As Kate Kirkham has shown, the management of diversity involves at least three levels of system—individual, group and organization. She further suggests that several types or "layers" of perception— ideas, behaviors, attitudes, beliefs, feelings and values—are required in order to decide what actions are appropriate.[2] Kirkham proposes that to understand the dynamics of race and racism, gender and sexism, or other forms of oppression in organizations, all three levels of system must be analyzed, and all layers of perception must be explored. Kirkham calls the levels of analysis "breadth of awareness" and the layers of perception "depth of insight."

Understanding at one level or even two levels is insufficient. Action taken without understanding all three levels and their interaction is likely to be misguided or inappropriate.

## The Theory Applied to Measurement

Most instruments that have been developed to measure diversity have taken a "multicultural approach" and have focused on the individual level of analysis. Since this approach does not acknowledge that the social system within which the individuals operate is itself biased and oppressive to those who are different from the norm, it does not assist the organization in identifying the systemic bases of difficulties. As Minow has shown, the multicultural approach also fails to acknowledge that there is a norm, that it is unstated, and that this fact is part of the problem.[3]

A few surveys do look beyond the individual level, but the dimensions chosen for measurement tend to lack coherence and are not theoretically based—therefore they are difficult for the client organization to interpret and use.[4] A further limitation is that while many cultural audit or climate surveys include some questions about diversity, few allow analysis by race and gender—thus the differences tend to get "washed out" in the averaging process.[5]

Focus group data collection has been the best available alternative for obtaining comprehensive information about diversity in an organization. Although the focus group is effective for this purpose, it requires skilled consultants who can conduct effective interviews that get at multiple system levels and many layers of perception. Further, the focus group method does not provide quantitative data, thus accurate measurement of progress and comparison with other organizations are not possible.

The Diversity Survey my colleagues and I have developed enables organizations to examine the multiple levels of both system and perception, and provides data that are accessible for quantitative analysis.[6]

## Advantages of Multilevel Analysis

Analysis based on multilevel assessments provides concrete evidence for the development of appropriate change-oriented actions. The analysis also provides the methodological basis for measurement of progress.

Multilevel analysis helps top management understand that white men—themselves included—do not perceive the organization in the same way that white women and people of color do. The data collected in this way give concreteness and legitimacy to the perception of white women and people of color that race and gender affect interactions and consequently have a negative impact on how they are able to do their work. The data demonstrate that the unstated norm of being white and male is a legitimate issue to be dealt with—the norm itself is part of the problem to be solved.

The Diversity Survey also can show how the formal policies and procedures of the organization may provide advantages for white men or disadvantages for people of color and white women. The survey data begin the process of demonstrating how the culture (the informal ways of doing work) is impacted by race and gender identity.

To set the strategic direction for the organization, management must have information that is valid, reliable and comprehensive. Armed with solid evidence, management may charge a task force—which should be diverse by race and gender—to develop tactics and action plans for management's review and authorization. The task force can also use the data to guide analyses and develop mechanisms to measure progress.

Although the survey we have developed is focused on race and gender, its multilevel analysis can be used for other issues. If the client organization is interested in sexual orientation, age, physical disabilities or other differences, these can be added to the Diversity Survey. As few or as many levels and layers can be analyzed as desired or needed by the organization.

## THE DIVERSITY SURVEY

Here I discuss some of the findings for two of the organizations in which the instrument has been used, JKLCorp, which had more than 1,200 survey respondents, and InvestCo, which had more than 500. No group used in any of the comparisons had fewer than forty people. The survey itself was tested for validity and reliability using various standard techniques.[7]

### The Dimensions

The dimensions measured in the Diversity Survey are based on the theory outlined above. The individual, group and organization levels are probed. Behaviors are distinguished from the more deeply held attitudes, beliefs, feelings and values.

The behavior of supervisors and the attitudes of different levels of management are key elements in organization dynamics. These positions have historically been filled by white men. This is, however, no longer always the case. The survey provides analysis of the behavior and attitudes of people in these positions, whatever their race or gender. To gain a comprehensive understanding of organization dynamics, the survey probes the organization's culture and the attitudes about managing diversity.

The Diversity Survey measures nine dimensions:

1. Individual Behaviors—measures the individual's involvement and satisfaction with his or her work.

2. Individual Beliefs, Attitudes, Feelings—measures beliefs, feelings and attitudes that individuals have about the influence of race and gender on themselves and others.

3. Supervisory Behaviors—measures how known supervisors are perceived to deal with tough interpersonal issues and their behavior toward different race and gender groups.

4. Management Attitudes—measures the perception of change required by different levels of management to obtain the full utilization of all employees.

5. Group Behaviors—measures the perception of how membership in a race/gender identity group influences treatment in the organization.

6. Group Beliefs, Attitudes, Values—measures the attitudes and beliefs about the influence of race and gender on acceptance within the work environment.

7. Organization Behavior—measures the perception of the impact of organizational policies and procedures on race/gender identity groups.

8. Managing Diversity—measures the perceptions about the importance of and the commitment to managing diversity in the organization.

9. Organization Culture—measures the climate and norms of the organization regarding race and gender differences and the ability to talk openly about them.

**The Results**

Although each evaluated organization has shown a unique profile, some patterns have emerged. The two cases examined here were chosen because they represent different sectors of business and different geographic areas.

All of the statistical comparisons discussed here are between white men and the other race/gender identity groups. Our earlier work showed us that white men generally are the largest group, the group the organizational norms were developed for, and the group that has the most positive view of the organization.[8] This leads to the conclusion that when organizations are able to create a climate that is as accepting of all race/gender identity groups as it currently is of white men, the problems related to race and gender will be resolved. There will still, no doubt, be management problems—but they will presumably affect all groups equally.

The findings on eight of the nine dimensions are discussed below. One

**Chart 1**
**Percentage Disagreeing that They Have Opportunities for Advancement**

| JKLCorp | | InvestCo | |
|---|---|---|---|
| White Men | 36.1% | White Men | 10.0% |
| White Women | 30.2% | White Women | 21.2%*** |
| Men of Color | 28.4% | Men of Color | 10.2% |
| Women of Color | 28.6% | Women of Color | 25.3%*** |

***Chi Square p < .005, DF = 1
(Chi Square: * = probability less than 5/100 of event occurring by chance; ** = less than 1/100; *** = less than 5/1000. DF = Degree of Freedom)

dimension, Individual Beliefs, did not identity significant differences among the groups.

### Individual Behavior

As noted above, patterns of discrimination within organizations exist independent of the behaviors of individuals. Those behaviors are, however, important and have a cumulative impact on the degree to which members of various groups are able to thrive.

One of the questions we asked along this dimension dealt with perceptions of opportunities for advancement. When the answers were compared for the four groups (white men, white women, men of color and women of color) there were notable differences between JKLCorp and InvestCo. (See Chart 1.)

In JKLCorp nearly one-third of all respondents were skeptical about their opportunities for advancement. In InvestCo, however the percentage of women (both white and women of color) who felt they lacked opportunity was double that for men (both white and of color).

This finding shows that both organizations have serious problems, but the nature of the problems is different. JKLCorp must review its promotion policies and practices overall. This action is especially important to this organization because it is a culture in which "hard work is rewarded" and managers are developed from within. If such a large number of people feel they have little chance to advance, the company is squandering its investment in them.

At InvestCo, the problem resides in gender dynamics. Only about 10 percent of the men feel they have few opportunities for advancement, but the percentage of women who feel that way is more than twice as high. InvestCo therefore must ferret out how it is providing such a discouraging atmosphere for its women employees. This finding is of serious concern because an increasing number of college recruits in financial management and financial services are women.

**Chart 2**
**Percentage Disagreeing that Mentoring Is Practiced in JKL Corp**

**JKLCorp**

| | |
|---|---|
| White Men | 25.5% |
| White Women | 33.0%** |
| Men of Color | 39.4%** |
| Women of Color | 51.2%*** |

**Chi Square p < .01, DF = 1
***Chi Square p < .005, DF = 1
(Chi Square: * = probability less than 5/100 of event occurring by chance; ** = less than 1/100; *** = less than 5/1000. DF = Degree of Freedom)

## Supervisory Behaviors

Since supervisory behavior is a crucial element in the management of diversity, the survey explored twelve different items on this dimension. While there were significant statistical differences on many items, two items—perceptions of the practice of mentoring, and perceptions of the supervisors' encouragement of equality of treatment for all races—provided especially useful data. (See Charts 2 and 3.)

At InvestCo, for example, responses to our questions about whether mentoring is available indicated that fully one-fourth of the white men and over one-half of the women of color feel that it is not. This dramatic finding plainly shows that InvestCo must pay close attention to the need for general supervisory training in the area of mentoring and the need for special attention to the race and gender components of this training.

When participants at the two organizations were asked if their supervisors encouraged equality of treatment for all races, there were strong similarities in the responses received from both companies. In both, for

**Chart 3**
**Percentage Disagreeing that Supervisors Encourage Equality of Treatment for All Races**

| JKLCorp | | InvestCo | |
|---|---|---|---|
| White Men | 6.2% | White Men | 6.6% |
| White Women | 8.0% | White Women | 16.9%*** |
| Men of Color | 21.9%*** | Men of Color | 14.8%* |
| Women of Color | 23.8%*** | Women of Color | 26.3%*** |

*Chi Square p < .05, DF = 1
***Chi Square p < .005, DF = 1
(Chi Square: * = probability less than 5/100 of event occurring by chance; ** = less than 1/100; *** = less than 5/1000. DF = Degree of Freedom)

**Chart 4**
**Percentage Perceiving that Large Change in Attitudes of Senior Management
Is Needed for Full Utilization of Employee Abilities**

| JKLCorp | | InvestCo | |
|---|---|---|---|
| White Men | 23.3% | White Men | 24.9% |
| White Women | 25.9% | White Women | 46.9%*** |
| Men of Color | 33.3% | Men of Color | 34.5% |
| Women of Color | 51.3%*** | Women of Color | 46.8%*** |

***Chi Square p < .005, DF = 1
(Chi Square: * = probability less than 5/100 of event occurring by chance; ** = less than
    1/100; *** = less than 5/1000. DF = Degree of Freedom)

example, most white men felt that supervisors did encourage such equality of treatment, while a significant percentage of men and women of color disagreed. The perceptions of white women at JKLCorp, however, were similar to those of white men; whereas at InvestCo the white women tended to share the perceptions of the people of color.

The findings, when combined with similar data for gender, show that both organizations need to incorporate race and gender dynamics into their supervisory training programs. In addition, they should look at their reward system for supervisors and develop expectations for performance that include specific measures of equal treatment.

### Management Attitudes

A major factor in how well a diverse work force functions is the attitude of senior management. When we asked how much change in senior management attitudes would be necessary to create a productive work environment for all employees, more than 25 percent of all respondents in both organizations responded that "much" to "enormous" change would be required. (See Chart 4.) The breakdown of the answers by race and gender indicates, however, that this overall statistic does not accurately reflect the real situation. At JKLCorp, a far greater percentage of people of color (33 percent of men of color and over 50 percent of women of color) see a need for change in the attitudes of senior management. White women share the views of white men—but the fact that 25 percent of all whites perceive the need for change in senior management attitudes is quite serious.

At InvestCo, differences in perceptions are apparent along both gender and race lines. While the "baseline" of 25 percent of white men perceiving a need for change remains constant, at InvestCo more than 33 percent of men of color and almost 50 percent of all women have negative views of the attitudes of top management.

How can a company succeed in creating a more productive, more inclusive, and more cost-effective work force if such large proportions of its employees feel that management must change to fully utilize the people in the work force? Both JKL Corp and InvestCo—if in fact senior management is committed to "managing diversity" successfully—must find more effective ways to present that commitment to their organizations. The ways chosen must be tailored to the particular corporate culture, but might include senior management doing formal presentations, holding open group discussions, making presentations to community groups, writing articles for company newsletters, and the like. They must also sponsor systems-level changes, such as the establishment of diversity task forces, which assure that the skills and talents of employees—regardless of race or gender—are recognized.

### Group Behaviors

A common problem in achieving successful relationships in a diverse work force is difficulty in giving and receiving feedback across race and gender lines. Therefore we queried participants concerning the feedback they receive. (See Chart 5.)

The answers showed that there are different patterns in the two companies. At JKLCorp, more than 20 percent of white men feel they receive "little to no feedback"—and even more women have this view (over 40 percent of women of color). Since an item asking about "fairness of evaluation by managers" does not show similar race or gender dynamics, it is likely that the women's perceptions are influenced by the lack of feedback from peers and associates.

To address this problem, specific training may be required to enable men and women to feel more comfortable in their interactions with each other as peers, and in soliciting and giving feedback across gender differences as colleagues.

---

**Chart 5**
**Percentage Perceiving They Get Little Straight and Honest Feedback**

| JKLCorp | | InvestCo | |
|---|---|---|---|
| White Men | 21.5% | White Men | 9.8% |
| White Women | 28.5%* | White Women | 26.3%*** |
| Men of Color | 15.5% | Men of Color | 17.4% |
| Women of Color | 41.5%*** | Women of Color | 12.0% |

*Chi Square p < .05, DF = 1
***Chi Square p < .005, DF = 1
(Chi Square: * = probability less than 5/100 of event occurring by chance; ** = less than 1/100; *** = less than 5/1000. DF = Degree of Freedom)

---

At InvestCo, a higher percentage of white women than any other group feels it does not receive adequate feedback; this does not seem to be true for women of color. More information—probably through focus groups—is required before a specific action plan is developed.

### Group Beliefs, Attitudes, Values

Sexual harassment is a continuing fact of life in organizations, with estimates that up to 50 percent of women are harassed.[9] Therefore we asked participants if they believed that sexual harassment was a significant problem in their organization. (See Chart 6.)

In this analysis, in both JKLCorp and InvestCo, a lower percentage of white men perceived sexual harassment to be a problem than did the other race/gender identity groups. There was a statistically significant difference in both companies between white men and white women.

There is also an obvious difference between the two organizations. More than 30 percent of all the respondents in InvestCo agree that sexual harassment is a significant problem, while 5 percent to 10 percent of the respondents perceived that to be the case in JKLCorp.

To understand why the perceptions of men and women are so different, the companies must vigorously investigate what is going on. Is this a general problem, or is it confined to a few individuals who are harassing? Why are white men less aware than others of the problem? The investigation could be pursued through focus groups, individual interviews, or perhaps a review of HR records.

In InvestCo, the fact that more than 30 percent of all employees, regardless of race or gender identity group, perceive sexual harassment to be a significant problem is the most immediate concern. A small task force could be formed to conduct interviews to determine the main causes of this widespread perception. The task force must also look at InvestCo's policies and practices and possibly its awareness training to determine where best to attack the problem.

---

**Chart 6**
**Percentage Agreeing that Sexual Harassment Is a Significant Problem**

| JKLCorp | | InvestCo | |
|---|---|---|---|
| White Men | 5.1% | White Men | 30.0% |
| White Women | 10.3%*** | White Women | 46.7%*** |
| Men of Color | 8.5% | Men of Color | 33.0% |
| Women of Color | 9.8% | Women of Color | 30.5% |

***Chi Square p < .005, DF = 1
(Chi Square: * = probability less than 5/100 of event occurring by chance; ** = less than 1/100; *** = less than 5/1000. DF = Degree of Freedom)

Another item we looked at under the "Group Beliefs, Attitudes and Values" dimension was the way the unwritten rules of organizations affect the abilities of employees to do their work effectively. (See Chart 7.)

This item shows that there were very significant differences in the perceptions of white men and the other groups—and startling similarities between InvestCo and JKLCorp: White men do not perceive that their race or gender affects their ability to make a full contribution, whereas all the other groups perceive that their race/gender makes it difficult for them to contribute fully.

Since approximately 40 percent of JKLCorp and 60 percent of InvestCo employees are white women and people of color, this perception reflects an enormous loss of contribution to both organizations.

Clearly, some of the norms of these organizations need to be changed. However, changing the unwritten rules, or norms, of an organization is a difficult task because wholesale change is not what is required. The organization must maintain its core values and precepts and yet eliminate those aspects that create inequities.[10] JKLCorp and InvestCo, like the many other companies whose data would reveal similar disparities, need to use a combination of task force and management effort, and possibly outside consulting help, to create appropriate change. For these efforts to be effective and credible, formal policies and procedures must also be addressed.

### Organization Behavior

The questions on the survey relating to organization behavior elicit information regarding the impact of organizational policies and procedures on such issues as hiring, retention and promotion. In both organizations studied, all groups agreed that their organization did a good job in hiring, retaining and promoting white men. But there were consid-

---

**Chart 7**
**Percentage Agreeing that Unwritten Rules Make It Difficult for Respondent and Others of Respondent's Race and Gender to Make a Full Contribution**

| JKLCorp | | InvestCo | |
|---|---|---|---|
| White Men | 7.2% | White Men | 3.5% |
| White Women | 26.8%*** | White Women | 34.2%*** |
| Men of Color | 26.8%*** | Men of Color | 25.3%*** |
| Women of Color | 38.5%*** | Women of Color | 40.0%*** |

***Chi Square p < .005, DF = 1
(Chi Square: * = probability less than 5/100 of event occurring by chance; ** = less than 1/100; *** = less than 5/1000. DF = Degree of Freedom)

## Chart 8
## Percentage Disagreeing that Organization Does a Good Job Retaining Women of Color, by Race/Gender Group

| JKLCorp | | InvestCo | |
|---|---|---|---|
| White Men | 13.5% | White Men | 45.4% |
| White Women | 25.9%*** | White Women | 56.0% |
| Men of Color | 34.3%*** | Men of Color | 42.0% |
| Women of Color | 57.1%*** | Women of Color | 48.9% |

***Chi Square p < .005, DF = 1
(Chi Square: * = probability less than 5/100 of event occurring by chance; ** = less than 1/100; *** = less than 5/1000. DF = Degree of Freedom)

erable differences when these same factors were explored as applied to the other race/gender identity groups. (See Chart 8.)

For example, one item dealt with how well the organizations handled the responsibility of retaining women of color. At JKLCorp, fewer than 15 percent of the white men perceive a problem in the retention of women of color, but the other groups disagree. More than half of the women of color feel that the organization does not do a good job in supporting or encouraging them to stay with the company. At InvestCo, however, nearly 50 percent of all groups perceive a problem in the retention of women of color.

These differences indicate that the two organizations will need to take different approaches to resolving the problems. In JKLCorp, a communication and education process concerning actual turnover rates must be implemented before white men are asked for a commitment to reverse the trend. Because InvestCo has a management objective of recruiting the best and the brightest, they will need to look at the impact of the low retention rates on their ability to attract the best and brightest women of color. InvestCo will also need to evaluate why the practices that lead to the low retention rates continue to exist when so many employees—including white men—are aware of the problem.

Both organizations will need to quantify the costs of turnover, and include that information in the education process about the problem.

While it is important to learn about the specific issues impacting differential retention, the "fix" for this problem usually lies elsewhere. It is more effective, for example, to look at the mentoring and coaching practices, and the practices that affect an employee's sense of acceptance and opportunity in the organization, than merely to set higher numerical goals for retention.

## Managing Diversity

One important measure of the attitudes about managing diversity is the perception of senior management's beliefs about and commitment to

**Chart 9**
**Percentage Disagreeing that Senior Management Believes that Effectively Managing Diversity Adds to the Organization's Performance, by Race/ Gender Group**

| JKLCorp | | InvestCo | |
|---|---|---|---|
| White Men | 13.7% | White Men | 32.1% |
| White Women | 14.0% | White Women | 41.2% |
| Men of Color | 18.1% | Men of Color | 37.5% |
| Women of Color | 20.0% | Women of Color | 33.7% |

the process. We therefore included questions about management's views of managing diversity in the survey. (See Chart 9.)

Successful change efforts require leadership from top management. The widespread perception in InvestCo that senior management does not see the value in managing diversity will be troublesome for a successful change effort. Senior management must find ways to communicate their interest in this topic. More important, they must take actions that demonstrate their commitment. This might include the establishment of a steering committee that has key senior managers as members.

### Organization Culture

The questions under the organization culture dimension of the survey measure the climate and norms of the organization regarding race and gender differences and the ability to talk openly about them. One of the questions we asked was about the perceptions of double standards for race and gender in the organizations—that is, how often people were aware of the existence of double standards. (See Chart 10.)

In both organizations white women and women of color perceived the application of double standards for race and gender to occur significantly

**Chart 10**
**Percentage Who Perceive that Double Standards for Race/Gender Occur Frequently in the Organization**

| JKLCorp | | InvestCo | |
|---|---|---|---|
| White Men | 23.2% | White Men | 13.2% |
| White Women | 37.0%*** | White Women | 29.3%*** |
| Men of Color | 37.1%* | Men of Color | 15.1% |
| Women of Color | 48.8%*** | Women of Color | 28.7%*** |

*Chi Square p < .05, DF = 1
***Chi Square p < .005, DF = 1
(Chi Square: * = probability less than 5/100 of event occurring by chance; ** = less than 1/100; *** = less than 5/1000. DF = Degree of Freedom)

more than did white men. Men of color in InvestCo also perceived a difference.

The perception that there is a double standard for race and gender is especially important in InvestCo because of the high percentages of all groups responding that it occurs frequently. Although many white men do not feel that there is a double standard, nearly one in four white men do share the perception that a double standard is used very frequently. In InvestCo the percentages are smaller, and there seems to be a gender split.

Although this aspect of the organization's culture could be attacked directly by using focus groups or interviews, it is generally more effective to address more concrete issues first. As the more concrete actions are taken, the organization culture items such as double standards tend to diminish in magnitude and the differences between race/gender identity groups also decrease. If the improvement is not satisfactory following other actions, in-depth analysis of this area is essential.

## IMPLICATIONS

The survey helps break up the complex topic of diversity into manageable chunks. Each organization can study the results to determine which areas need the most attention. When the priorities are set, actions can be taken and progress can be monitored.

The information from the survey permits task forces and management to operate from objective data and thus reduce the impact of their own biases about the organization. Given the tremendous emotional loading on this topic, it is very important for other employees to see that the action-taking groups are working on the basis of solid evidence.

When management understands the data it is possible to set concrete goals and identify measures of success. This permits management to be realistically accountable for bringing about change. The axiom of quality/continuous improvement is "You can't manage what you can't measure." This is also true for diversity. The survey allows that measurement. It allows management to get away from the trap of measuring success only from financial data. It begins to make clear that discrimination has a cost for those who discriminate as well as for those who are discriminated against.[11]

The data from the survey help reduce the resistance to change and get organizations out of the cycle of accusation, guilt and resentment. These data and information from other organizations show that many aspects of the problem are not known to white men or to managers. The data help the organization understand that lack of awareness of the problem is actually part of the problem. Commitment to the change is increased and resentment about the change is minimized. The fact-based revelation that management (mostly white men) is part of the problem discourages strategies aimed only at "fixing the victim."

Data collected through the Diversity Survey demonstrate the many facets of diversity, leaving no doubt that any single approach to solving this complex problem is doomed to fail. The survey is designed to provide multiple levels of analyses. This allows each organization to determine what areas are most important to them. In a sense, the survey data acknowledge the diversity among organizations as well as people.

The survey also permits comparisons to be drawn not only among various organizations, but also among entities within one organization. The analysis of data that we provide does not specifically identify organizations or entities, but we do provide a description of the type of organization ("manufacturing company," for example) or geographic location ("Midwest"). This helps to answer the nagging question of whether "x percent" is "high" or "to be expected."

In the final analysis, the acceptability of a number must be determined within the organization or the entity itself; but the opportunity to make comparisons, anonymously, is helpful.

Success in learning to manage an increasingly diverse work force depends on management's skill at leading the change process. For the skills to be effectively used, the diagnosis of the system must be accurate. The Diversity Survey is, we propose, a very useful instrument in the diagnostic process.

## PART 2: DIVERSITY ASSESSMENT: TELLING THE STORY

An organization that is concerned about its diversity issues faces two challenges at the outset—defining the problems, and telling the organization what the problems are.

Meeting the first challenge is relatively easy. Using an instrument appropriately tailored to the culture of the organization, managers and consultants can gather the necessary data to build the business case for launching a diversity initiative.

Accomplishing the second task is much more difficult. Once the data have been gathered and analyzed, they must be packaged and presented to the organization in a form that is easily understood and not unduly threatening, and that can lead quickly to the development of action plans.

In this part, I review the process of a collaboration between one company's diversity council and its external consultants, which resulted in a brief, accurate and clear presentation of the findings and provided the basis for action planning.

## "JUST THE FACTS" IS NOT ENOUGH

A diversity assessment survey instrument is designed to collect information that will give the fullest possible picture of the current situation.
The report analyzing the results is data-rich—full of facts, figures, graphs
and charts that document the realities of diversity in the organization.

This level of detail provides the evidence that managers and diversity
councils require to make the case for the diversity initiative and to begin
the process of strategy development and action planning. In that format,
however, it is too long and too complicated for widespread use throughout the organization.

The challenge is to capture the essence of the information presented
by the data analysis and translate it into a narrative that communicates
powerfully to the general employee population—to use the facts to tell
the story.

Telling the story effectively requires cooperation between internal
staff—who understand what elements are most meaningful within the
context of the organization's culture—and the external consultants—who
can have an objective view of the specific company and can also put the
information into the broader context of other organizations in the data
base.

## SAVING FACE

Most organizations firmly believe that they treat their employees
fairly, produce high-quality services and products, are good corporate
citizens, and are able to cope with change. At the same time, however,
most managers know that if they look carefully at the company culture,
the data collected may challenge some or all of these assumptions.

So managers are faced with a dilemma. Data about diversity must be
developed in order to address the issues they suspect (or already know)
are present. But the same data are almost certain to tarnish the self-image
that has been carefully constructed and maintained.

It is one thing to entrust a small council or task force with knowing
the information and developing action plans. It is quite another to present the data to employees in a public forum—to air one's dirty linen in
full view.

The process of sharing information around diversity issues is both
similar to and, in important ways, different from sharing data about
quality. To assess quality, an organization collects data from its customers and employees, asking what can be improved—just as it does for
diversity. In both cases, the organization must decide what to do with
the data if they do indeed suggest that improvements are needed. For

both diversity and quality efforts, it is customary for a working group to analyze the information and develop action plans.

But the next step—providing feedback to the organization about the data—is very different. The emotional loading for diversity issues is much higher than for quality. Most people in most organizations do not talk about race, gender or other differences. So the presentation of diversity data breaks an unspoken norm of silence.

For all these reasons, my colleagues and I have found in our work with diversity councils and managers that the task of translating data on race, gender and other dimensions of diversity requires close and careful collaboration and special sensitivity to the organization's concerns. The process followed in "Company Z" resolved many of the concerns and helped us understand what adjustments need to be made in the future.

## THE PROCESS

We began by submitting the complete report from the Diversity Assessment Survey analysis to the diversity council. The council then asked that the report be given to about one hundred key managers to secure their input on which items should be given top priority for action.

The managers agreed to participate in the process but complained that they were being asked to deal with too much information in too little time. They asked that the presentation be shortened and simplified.

The diversity council shared these concerns and expressed their own wish for a more succinct version of the data. At the same time, however, the council requested additional information. The data had already been broken down along racial lines (men and women of color, white men and women), but the council asked to have the responses analyzed by specific groups—African-American men and women, Asian-American men and women, and Hispanic men and women. They also requested a correlational analysis of the survey items.

The second request, which provided insights about areas where change might have effects on several different levels of the organization, helped to simplify the data. The first, however, while leading to very instructive information, made the analysis more complicated!

The diversity council reviewed the new material and was even more perplexed. In the discussions around the problem of trying to use the data to "tell the diversity story," another layer of difficulty arose—ownership of the data. "Whose story is this?" people began to ask. Is it the consultant's perspective, based on the data and his interpretation of the data that should prevail—with the result that the diversity council and the organization itself could distance themselves from the issues? Or should the prevailing view be that of the members of the council, whose understanding of the organization's culture was naturally deeper—though less objective—than that of the consultant?

The discussions led to an agreement that both factors would be taken into account. Drawing on the data, the consultant would write a short report that accurately reflected the findings. The council would then review the report and make sure that it reflected their cultural norms and their own understanding of what the data meant in that context. Further, it was agreed that a professional writer would be used to put the story into a format and style that the organization was familiar with.

The final report from the diversity council was delivered to the employees at the annual meeting. The report incorporated all three elements: the consultant's analysis, the council's modifications reflecting their understanding of the culture, and the writer's translation of the material into a reader-friendly format.

## TRANSLATING THE FINDINGS

Through this process of negotiation, we all gained valuable insights into how complex and highly charged information can be developed into a relatively brief and clear story that can serve as the basis for a report to the organization. By presenting the implications of the data simultaneously with the findings themselves, we were able to reduce the perceived sense of threat to the organization's self-image and provide a firm basis for action planning.

Tables 1–8 show how we presented the material to the diversity council.

**Table 1**
**Individual Satisfaction**

| Results | Implications |
| --- | --- |
| Respondents' general satisfaction with the organization is evident in several cases. Less than 10% of respondents do *not* like working for Organization Z. Less than 25% of respondents perceive they do *not* have opportunities for advancement. In both cases Organization Z respondents have a more favorable perception of these items than in other organizations in our data base. | *The uniformly high level of satisfaction with the organization and the perception by the majority that there are opportunities for advancement is extremely positive. People want to work for an organization with that kind of reputation. It provides a basis for all employees to want to do their best and contribute to their fullest ability.* |

**Table 1** *(continued)*

| Results | Implications |
|---|---|
| However, 45% of African-American women express dissatisfaction with their current job, and about 25% of Hispanic and African-American women perceive that they have little involvement with decisions affecting work. | *These are key elements in long-term retention, and these negative perceptions may contribute to costly turnover in African-American and possibly Hispanic women in the future.* |

**Table 2**
**Supervisor Behavior**

| Results | Implications |
|---|---|
| Women (of color and white) view supervisor behavior more skeptically than do men. A considerably higher percentage of women than of men perceive supervisor behavior to be unfavorable concerning conflict resolution, inclusion, linking diversity with ongoing assignments and responsibilities, providing effective feedback, and challenging racist or sexist jokes. | *Conflict resolution, inclusion, effective feedback and a sense of fair play by supervisors are critical elements of team functioning. Since women are important contributors to team efforts, and about 20% have an unfavorable view of these issues, it is likely that teams are not functioning optimally because of gender dynamics.* |
| About 15% of the white men, contrasted with about 50% of African-American women, perceive that mentoring is *not* practiced. | *The fact that so many African-American women perceive an absence of mentoring will have a long-term, negative impact on the development of potential outstanding contributors.* |

**Table 3**
**Individual Beliefs**

| Results | Implications |
|---|---|
| More than 90% of all respondents at Organization Z perceive that women are as dependable and competent as men, and also that people of color are as dependable and competent as whites. | *This information could provide a positive basis for the diversity effort, since the vast majority of individuals believe that white women, men of color, and women of color are as dependable and competent as white men. It is in everyone's best interests to remove the barriers that white women and people of color believe negatively influence their performance. This action can help the organization perform to its maximum capability.* |

**Table 4**
**Group Beliefs**

**Results**

White men have a much more favorable view than do white women and people of color about the influence of race and gender on acceptance within the organization. Only 5% of white men perceive organizational barriers (e.g., image of success and making a full contribution) for themselves because of their race or gender.

Nearly 60% of African-American women, 30% of African-American men and Hispanic women and 20% of Asian-American women perceive that their race/gender is a barrier to fitting the image of success.

Similarly, 45% of African-American women, 30% of African-American men and 11% to 16% of white women, Asian-American women, Hispanic men, and Hispanic women perceive that their race or gender is a barrier to making a full contribution.

About 15% of white men perceive that women have to work harder than men to succeed and that people of color have to work harder than whites to succeed.

50% or more of *all* women perceive that women have to work harder than men to succeed.

More than 90% of African-American women perceive that people of color have to work harder than whites to succeed. Also, 70% of African-American men, 55% of Asian-American women, 40% of Asian-American men, and 33% of white women perceive that people of color have to work harder than whites to succeed.

**Implications**

*Most white men are not likely to pay conscious attention to race or gender—theirs or others'—as they carry out their daily tasks. This difference in perception between white men and the other groups about the importance of one's race/gender identity creates its own problem—discussion of these issues becomes very difficult.*

*The work force at Organization Z consists of 35% white men, 45% white women, 10% men of color, and 10% women of color. These unfavorable perceptions by a large segment of the work force and the potential loss of productivity are unacceptable in today's marketplace. Organizations that remove the barriers will gain a competitive advantage.*

*Because white women and people of color experience race- and gender-related barriers, they are likely to assign race or gender explanations to some problems they confront daily. If a white woman or a person of color attempts to initiate a conversation with a white male colleague about her/his perception of barriers related to their race or gender identity, the white man is unlikely to understand. He may perceive the initiator as a complainer, oversensitive, a militant, or a poor team player. This dynamic often leads to silence on these issues.*

**Table 5**
**Accessibility to Senior Management**

**Results**

There are significant differences in perception about the advancement of men of color and women of color. White men have the most favorable view (e.g., less than 4% perceive that senior management positions are *not* accessible to men and women of color). *All other groups* have a significantly more unfavorable perception, with more than 50% of African-American respondents perceiving that senior management positions are *not* accessible to men and women of color.

**Implications**

*These perceptual differences are profound because information about promotions is generally public and widely known throughout most organizations. The obvious question then becomes, "Are groups interpreting the same data differently, or do they have different information?"*

**Table 6**
**Management Attitudes**

**Results**

Less than 10% of white men perceive that there is a need for change in the attitudes of any level of management for their abilities to be more fully utilized.

Significantly higher percentages of white women, African-American men and African-American women perceive that *all* levels of management need to change for their abilities to be more fully utilized.

**Implications**

*The difference in perceptions among the race/gender identity groups represents an important opportunity for management to take actions that show interest in and commitment to the full utilization of all employees. Improvement has the potential to increase productivity of a significant portion of the work force.*

**Table 7**
**Organization Culture**

**Results**

White men tend to have the most favorable view of the organization's culture with respect to race and gender issues, while women of color have the least favorable view. Only 6% of white men perceive that double standards for race and gender occur often or daily. Significantly more white women (19%), Hispanic men (25%), Hispanic women (35%), African-American men (30%) and African-American women (55%) perceive that double standards occur often or daily.

Nearly 20% of Hispanic women and African-American men and 45% of African-American women perceive that racist behavior occurs often or daily. Only 3% of white men share that perception.

**Implications**

*White men are either less exposed to the observable negative actions (double standards and racist behavior) or they are less sensitive to their occurrence. This could be put the other way: Perhaps white women and people of color are more sensitive to these issues. Regardless, there is a gap in perception between white men and the other groups regarding the organization's diversity culture. Each group must understand the other race/gender groups' position for progress to take place.*

**Table 8**
**Managing Diversity**

**Results**

Except for African-American men (45%) and African-American women (33%) on the issue of race, approximately 15% to 25% of respondents perceive that it is unacceptable to talk about race or gender issues in the organization. As with any organization issue, discussion is an important first step in defining and solving the problem; and in this instance that discussion is not acceptable to many respondents. Although troubling, these statistics are more positive than those in any of the other organizations in the current data base.

**Implications**

*These results show that Organization Z may have an advantage over other organizations to begin meaningful cross-race and cross-gender discussions. Although a higher percentage of the "subordinated groups" (people of color on issues of race and women on issues of gender) perceive that it is not acceptable to discuss these issues, a substantial majority find it to be either neutral or acceptable.*

*It is the hesitancy of most subordinate groups to discuss these issues that allows many dominant-group members to continue to be uninformed about the race and gender dynamics that affect all employees.*

**Table 8** *(continued)*

**Results**

**Implications**

*It is the assumption by many dominant group members that it is acceptable to talk about these issues that make them believe that if they hear nothing, everything is okay.*

*Unless dominant group members realize that there are dynamics at the group and organizational levels that make it unlikely that subordinated group members will raise issues of race or gender, they will remain uninformed.*

About 20% of white men are skeptical about whether effectively managing diversity adds to the organization's effectiveness. Only about 10% of white women and *no* women of color are skeptical about the effectiveness of managing diversity.

About 25% of white men are skeptical about whether managing diversity should be among the organization's top 5 priorities. Significantly fewer white women (14%), Asian-American women (4%), Hispanic women (0%), African-American men (3%), and African-American women (3%) are skeptical about managing diversity being among the top 5 priorities.

*White men are more doubtful about the value of managing diversity for the same reasons they are more optimistic about organizational barriers: they do not perceive that women or people of color have to work harder to succeed, and see little need for management to change to fully utilize their abilities.* White men do not pay conscious attention to race or gender—theirs or others'—as they carry out their organizational tasks. *Therefore, a higher percentage of white men see no need for managing diversity. Other race/gender identity groups must pay attention to race and gender to survive and prosper and therefore perceive that managing diversity will add value.*

## STRATEGIC LEVERAGE POINTS

From our perspective, the data presented above offer two possible strategic leverage points that can be identified for the diversity council's consideration. First, more than 90 percent of all respondents perceive that women and people of color are as competent and dependable as men and whites, respectively. This finding is among the most favorable results in our current data base and forms a very strong foundation for removing barriers that might keep competent and dependable performers from making their full contribution.

Second, significantly more white men are skeptical about the value of managing diversity than are white women or people of color. Even so, the skeptical white men comprise only 20 percent to 25 percent of the white men respondents. Including their concerns, thoughts and ideas will be essential for any successful change effort.

## POSSIBLE FIRST STEPS

The analysis of the data suggests a series of actions that the diversity council considered. Among these are the following:

- Collect data about the accessibility of senior management positions to men of color and women of color. Are these positions accessible? Does the representation of men and women of color at these levels reflect their representation in the organization? If so, distribute the information to all employees. This information should decrease, to some extent, the unfavorable perceptions of people of color regarding organization barriers. If not, distribute the information to all employees *with* a strategy and plans. In either case the "facts" should be available to employees.

   Ultimately, men and women of color must be promotable *and* promoted to senior management positions if other men of color and women of color employees are to perceive that they fit the image of success, and management is to gain credibility about changing its attitude. Such promotions must be competency-based and must be perceived as such by employees.

- Develop interventions to address supervisory skills. They should provide skill awareness and skill training in conflict resolution, inclusion and team development, giving feedback, and confronting racist and sexist comments/jokes.

- Develop communication strategies about diversity that build on the idea that competency and dependability should be rewarded for all employees if the organization is to prosper and grow. Continually remind employees that removing barriers is a primary aim of the managing diversity intervention and relate all communications about progress/actions to that objective.

- Seek ways to encourage the efforts of white men who are supporters of diversity through mechanisms such as "champions" programs and membership on diversity action teams or councils. Show white men, the greatest source of skepticism, the ways diversity benefits them and encourage the individual skeptics to make their views known.

## CREATING THE IMPETUS FOR CHANGE

At Organization Z, the story was told based on the points made in the presentation to the diversity council and the professional writer. The "strategic leverage points" and the "possible first steps" were not communicated to the employees. Rather, the emphasis was on training, consulting, skill building and policy reviews, because the council wanted to be sure that it could "walk its talk."

Not all the results were positive, and the implications for change are profound. But the story that emerges from the data provides a basis for setting a strategic direction and permits the organization to focus on getting better business results through full utilization of all employees. The story gives all employees a clear idea of what actions will be taken and the basis for those actions—a critical step in minimizing the resistance to change.

## NOTES

1. For an in-depth analysis of systems theory concepts, see Ludwig von Bertalanffy, *General Systems Theory* (New York: George Braziller, 1968).

2. See Kate Kirkham, "Managing a Diverse Work Force: From Incident to 'ism,'" *The Diversity Factor* 1, no. 3 (Spring 1993): 22–26. A discussion of the framework for breadth of awareness and depth of insight is found in Kate Kirkham, "Dimensions of Diversity," paper presented at the Institute for Women and Organizations Conference, Long Beach, California, 1988.

3. Martha Minow, *Making All the Difference* (Ithaca: Cornell University Press, 1990).

4. Seven surveys designed to obtain race and gender dynamics were reviewed. None of them were comprehensive, in the sense of understanding more than two levels of system, and none of them differentiated behavior from attitude. Information from the pilot testing of the Diversity Assessment Survey and our experience in consulting with organizations on race and gender dynamics show both of these to be important areas to understand.

5. For an example of this phenomenon, see Margaret Blackburn White, "Leadership for Workforce 2000: The CoreStates Experience," *The Diversity Factor* 1, no. 4 (Summer 1993): 26–31.

6. For a general introduction to the survey, see Joseph Potts and Carol Brantley, "On Measuring Diversity: Race and Gender Dimensions," *The Diversity Factor* 1, no. 4 (Summer 1993): 26–31.

7. See Pamela Alreck and Robert Settle, *The Survey Research Handbook* (Homewood, IL: Irwin, 1985), for a discussion of techniques used.

8. See Potts and Brantley, "On Measuring Diversity," and Minow, *Making All the Difference.*

9. See Andrea Zintz, "All in the Family: Confronting Sexual Harassment in the New Culture," *The Diversity Factor* 2, no. 3 (Spring 1994): 25–31.

10. See Peter Senge, *The Fifth Discipline* (New York: Doubleday, 1990), for a helpful discussion of this topic.

11. See Barbara Blumenthal and Philippe Haspeslagh, "Toward a Definition of Corporate Transformation," *Sloan Management Review* 35, no. 3 (Spring 1994), for a review of why measuring success only on the basis of financial data is counterproductive; and Gary Becker, *The Economics of Discrimination*, 2nd ed. (Chicago: University of Chicago Press, 1970), on the costs of discriminating.

# Appendix 3

# Suggestions for Further Reading

The 1990s have been a time of renewed interest in issues of race, gender, sexual orientation and culture change. The following texts were reviewed in our quarterly publication, *The Diversity Factor*. The issue in which the review appeared is indicated in each reference.

Aarons, Leroy. *Prayers for Bobby: A Mother's Coming to Terms with the Suicide of Her Gay Son*. New York: HarperCollins, 1995. In Volume 5, Number 3, Spring 1997.

Adams, Maurianne, ed. *Promoting Diversity in College Classrooms: Innovative Responses for the Curriculum, Faculty and Institutions*. New Directions for Teaching and Learning, No. 52. San Francisco: Jossey-Bass, 1992. In Volume 5, Number 1, Fall 1996.

Adler, Nancy J., and Susan Bartholomew. "Managing Globally Competent People." *Academy of Management Executive* 6, no. 3 (1992): 52–65. In Volume 3, Number 1, Fall 1994.

Agrippa, Henricus Cornelius. *Declamation on the Nobility and Preeminence of the Female Sex*. Edited by Albert Rabil Jr. Chicago: University of Chicago Press, 1996. In Volume 6, Number 1, Fall 1997.

Ali, Abbas J., ed. *How to Manage for International Competitiveness*. Binghamton, NY: Haworth Press, 1992. In Volume 1, Number 4, Summer 1993; and Volume 2, Number 4, Summer 1994.

Alia, Valerie, Brian Brennan and Barry Hoffmaster. *Deadlines and Diversity: Journalism Ethics in a Changing World*. Halifax, Nova Scotia: Fernwood Publishing, 1996. In Volume 5, Number 4, Summer 1997.

Altbach, Philip G., and Kofi Lomotey, eds. *The Racial Crisis in American Higher*

*Education*. Albany: State University of New York Press, 1991. In Volume 5, Number 1, Fall 1996.

Alwood, Edward. *Straight News: Gays, Lesbians, and the News Media*. New York: Columbia University Press, 1996. In Volume 5, Number 3, Spring 1997.

"An American Dilemma Revisited." *Daedalus: Journal of the American Academy of Arts and Sciences* 124, no. 1 (Winter 1995). In Volume 3, Number 3, Spring 1995.

American Indian Media Image Task Force. *The American Indian and the Media*. Minneapolis: National Conference of Christians and Jews, Minnesota-Dakotas Region, 1991. In Volume 5, Number 3, Spring 1997.

Anfuso, Dawn. "Diversity Keeps Newspaper Up with the Times." *Personnel Journal* 74, no. 7 (July 1995): 30–38. In Volume 5, Number 3, Spring 1997.

*Asian American Handbook*. N.p.: National Conference of Christians and Jews, Chicago and Northern Illinois Region, and Asian American Journalists Association, Chicago Chapter, 1991. In Volume 5, Number 3, Spring 1997.

Astin, Helen S., and Carole Leland. *Women of Influence, Women of Vision*. San Francisco: Jossey-Bass, 1991. In Volume 3, Number 3, Spring 1995.

Bales, Fred. "Hantavirus and the Media: Double Jeopardy for Native Americans." *American Indian Culture and Research Journal* 18, no. 3 (1994): 251–263. In Volume 5, Number 3, Spring 1997.

Ball, Edward. *Slaves in the Family*. New York: Farrar, Straus and Giroux, 1998. In Volume 6, Number 4, Summer 1998.

Bazile-Jones, Renée, Bernadette Lynn et al. *Measuring the Impact of Diversity*. Management Accounting Issues Paper 12. Hamilton and Toronto: Canadian Institute of Chartered Accountants and Society of Management Accountants of Canada, 1996. In Volume 5, Number 2, Winter 1997.

Bem, Sandra Lipsitz. *The Lenses of Gender: Transforming the Debate on Sexual Inequality*. New Haven: Yale University Press, 1993. In Volume 2, Number 4, Summer 1994.

Berry, Mary Frances. *The Politics of Parenthood: Child Care, Women's Rights, and the Myth of the Good Mother*. New York: Penguin Books, USA, 1994. In Volume 1, Number 4, Summer 1993; and Volume 2, Number 4, Summer 1994.

*Beyond Borders: Ethics in International Business* (video). Irwindale, CA: Ethics Resource Center, 1996. In Volume 4, Number 4, Summer 1996.

Biagi, Shirley, and Marilyn Kern-Foxworth, eds. *Facing Difference: Race, Gender and the Media*. Pacifica, CA: Pine Forge Press, 1997. In Volume 5, Number 3, Spring 1997.

"Black in America." *The New Yorker*, Special Issue, April 29/May 6, 1996. In Volume 4, Number 4, Summer 1996.

Blau, Francine D., and Ronald G. Ehrenberg, eds. *Gender and Family Issues in the Workplace*. New York: Russell Sage Foundation, 1997. In Volume 6, Number 3, Spring 1998.

Border, Laura L.B., and Nancy Van Note Chism, eds. *Teaching for Diversity*. New Directions for Teaching and Learning, No. 49. San Francisco: Jossey-Bass, 1992. In Volume 5, Number 1, Fall 1996.

Bormann, Tammy, Susan Woods et al. *Resources for Workplace Diversity: An Annotated Practitioner Guide to Information*. N.p.: Workplace Diversity Network, a joint project of the National Conference and Cornell University, ILR, Fall 1996. In Volume 5, Number 4, Summer 1997.

Bowser, Benjamin, Gale S. Auletta and Terry Jones. *Confronting Diversity Issues on Campus*. Newbury Park, CA: Sage Publications, 1993. In Volume 5, Number 1, Fall 1996.

Bowser, Benjamin P., and Raymond G. Hunt, eds. *Impacts of Racism on White Americans*. Newbury Park, CA: Sage Publications, 1996. In Volume 6, Number 2, Winter 1998.

Brown, Claire Damken, Charlotte C. Snedeker and Beate D. Sykes. *Conflict and Diversity*. Cresskill, NJ: Hampton Press, 1997. In Volume 6, Number 4, Summer 1998.

Brown, Pam, and Peggy Gillespie, text; Gigi Kaeser, photographs. *Love Makes a Family: Living in Lesbian and Gay Families*, a photograph-text exhibit. Amherst, MA: Family Ties, 1995. In Volume 5, Number 4, Summer 1997.

Bullard, Sara. *Free at Last: A History of the Civil Rights Movement and Those Who Died in the Struggle*. Montgomery, AL: Teaching Tolerance, Southern Poverty Law Center, 1993. In Volume 1, Number 4, Summer 1993; and Volume 2, Number 4, Summer 1994.

Campbell, Christopher. *Race, Myth and the News*. Thousand Oaks, CA: Sage Publications, 1995. In Volume 5, Number 3, Spring 1997.

Campbell, Will D. *The Stem of Jesse: The Costs of Community at a 1960s Southern School*. Macon, GA: Mercer University Press, 1995. In Volume 3, Number 4, Summer 1995.

Carnes, Jim. *Us and Them*. New York: Oxford University Press, 1996. In Volume 5, Number 2, Winter 1997.

Carnevale, Anthony Patrick, and Susan Carol Stone. *The American Mosaic: An In-Depth Report on the Future of Diversity at Work*. New York: McGraw-Hill, 1996. In Volume 4, Number 4, Summer 1996.

Cavalli-Sforza, Luca, Paolo Menozzi and Alberto Piazza. *The History and Geography of Human Genes*. Princeton, NJ: Princeton University Press. In Volume 3, Number 3, Spring 1995.

Chapin, Helen Geracimos. *Shaping History: The Role of Newspapers in Hawai'i*. Honolulu: University of Hawaii Press, 1996. In Volume 5, Number 3, Spring 1997.

Chávez, Lydia. *The Color Bind: California's Battle to End Affirmative Action*. Berkeley: University of California Press, 1998. In Volume 6, Number 4, Summer 1998.

Cheatham, Harold E., ed. *Cultural Pluralism on Campus*. Lanham, MD: University Press of America, 1991. In Volume 5, Number 1, Fall 1996.

Chicago Area Partnerships. *Pathways and Progress: Corporate Best Practices to Shatter the Glass Ceiling*. Chicago: Women Employed, 1998. In Volume 6, Number 2, Winter 1998.

Chideya, Farai. *Don't Believe the Hype: Fighting Cultural Misinformation about African Americans*. New York: Penguin Books USA, 1995. In Volume 5, Number 4, Summer 1997.

Choy, Philip, Lorraine Dong and Marlon K. Hom. *The Coming Man: Nineteenth Century American Perceptions of the Chinese*. Seattle: University of Washington Press, 1994. In Volume 5, Number 3, Spring 1997.

Clayton, Obie, Jr., ed. *An American Dilemma Revisited: Race Relations in a Changing World*. New York: Russell Sage Foundation, 1996. In Volume 4, Number 4, Summer 1996.

Cobble, Dorothy Sue, ed. *Women and Unions: Forging a Partnership*. Ithaca, NY: ILR Press, 1993. In Volume 3, Number 3, Spring 1995.

Cole, Sally. "Beyond Recruitment and Retention: The Stanford Experience." In P. Altbach and K. Lomotey, eds., *The Racial Crisis in American Higher Education*. Albany: State University of New York Press, 1991. In Volume 5, Number 1, Fall 1996.

Cose, Ellis. *The Rage of a Privileged Class*. New York: HarperCollins, 1994. In Volume 2, Number 4, Summer 1994.

Cox, Taylor, Jr. *Cultural Diversity in Organizations: Theory, Research and Practice*. San Francisco: Berrett-Koehler, 1993. In Volume 2, Number 4, Summer 1994.

*Cracking the Glass Ceiling: Strategies for Success*. New York: Catalyst, 1994. In Volume 3, Number 2, Winter 1995.

Cross, Elsie Y., Judith H. Katz, Frederick A. Miller and Edith W. Seashore, eds. *The Promise of Diversity: Over Forty Voices Discuss Strategies for Eliminating Discrimination in Organizations*. Burr Ridge, IL: Irwin Professional Publishing, 1994. In Volume 3, Number 1, Fall 1994.

Dana, Richard H. *Understanding Cultural Identity in Intervention and Assessment: Multicultural Aspects of Counseling*, Series 9. Thousand Oaks, CA: Sage Publications, 1997. In Volume 6, Number 4, Summer 1998.

Dates, Janette, and William Barlow, eds. *Split Image: African Americans in the Mass Media*. Washington, DC: Howard University Press, 1990. In Volume 5, Number 3, Spring 1997.

Dávila, Arlene M. *Sponsored Identities: Cultural Politics in Puerto Rico*. Philadelphia: Temple University Press, 1997. In Volume 6, Number 4, Summer 1998.

Delgado, Richard, ed. *Critical Race Theory*. Philadelphia: Temple University Press, 1995. In Volume 4, Number 1, Fall 1995.

Delgado, Richard, and Jean Stefancic, eds. *Critical White Studies: Looking Behind the Mirror*. Philadelphia: Temple University Press, 1997. In Volume 6, Number 1, Fall 1997.

Dennis, Everette E., ed. "Race—America's Rawest Nerve." *Media Studies Journal* (Summer 1994). In Volume 5, Number 3, Spring 1997.

Dinnerstein, Leonard. *Anti-Semitism in America*. New York: Oxford University Press, 1995. In Volume 3, Number 3, Spring 1995.

Driscoll, Dawn-Marie, and Carol R. Goldberg. *Members of the Club: The Coming of Age of Executive Women*. New York: The Free Press, 1993. In Volume 3, Number 2, Winter 1995.

Dublin, Thomas, ed. *Becoming American, Becoming Ethnic: College Students Explore Their Roots*. Philadelphia: Temple University Press, 1996. In Volume 5, Number 2, Winter 1997.

Ellinor, Linda, and Glenna Gerard. *Dialogue: Rediscover the Transforming Power of Conversation*. New York: John Wiley and Sons, 1998. In Volume 6, Number 4, Summer 1998.

Entman, Robert. "Blacks in the News: Television, Modern Racism and Cultural

Change." *Journalism Quarterly* 69 (Summer 1992): 341–361. In Volume 5, Number 3, Spring 1997.

Ericksen, Charles. "Hispanic Americans and the Press." *Journal of Intergroup Relations* 9, no. 1 (1981): 3–16. In Volume 5, Number 3, Spring 1997.

Espiritu, Yen Le. *Filipino American Lives*. Philadelphia: Temple University Press, 1995. In Volume 3, Number 4, Summer 1995.

Estes, Ralph. *Tyranny of the Bottom Line: Why Corporations Make Good People Do Bad Things*. San Francisco: Berrett-Koehler, 1996. In Volume 4, Number 4, Summer 1996.

Evans, Nancy J., and Vernon A. Wall, eds. *Beyond Tolerance: Gays, Lesbians and Bisexuals on Campus*. Lanham, MD: University Press of America, 1991. In Volume 5, Number 1, Fall 1996.

Ezorsky, Gertrude. *Racism and Justice: The Case for Affirmative Action*. Ithaca, NY: Cornell University Press, 1991. In Volume 3, Number 4, Summer 1995.

Federal Glass Ceiling Commission. *Good for Business: Making Full Use of the Nation's Human Capital*. Washington, DC: U.S. Government Printing Office, 1995. In Volume 3, Number 4, Summer 1995.

———. *A Solid Investment: Making Full Use of the Nation's Human Capital*. Washington, DC: U.S. Government Printing Office, November 1995. In Volume 4, Number 3, Spring 1996.

Frankenberg, Ruth. *White Women, Race Matters: The Social Construction of Whiteness*. Minneapolis: University of Minnesota Press, 1993. In Volume 5, Number 2, Winter 1997.

Gainen, Joanne, and Robert Boice, eds. *Building a Diverse Faculty*. New Directions for Teaching and Learning, No. 53. San Francisco: Jossey-Bass, 1993. In Volume 5, Number 1, Fall 1996.

The Gallup Organization. "Black/White Relations in the United States." Princeton, NJ: The Gallup Organization, June 1997. In Volume 6, Number 1, Fall 1997.

Gonzales, Claire. *The Empty Promise: The EEOC and Hispanics*. Washington, DC: Policy Analysis Center, National Council of La Raza, March 1994. In Volume 3, Number 2, Winter 1995.

Graham, Lawrence Otis. *The Best Companies for Minorities*. New York: Penguin Books, 1993. In Volume 2, Number 4, Summer 1994.

Gray, Herman. *Watching Race: Television and the Struggle for "Blackness."* Minneapolis: University of Minnesota Press, 1997. In Volume 5, Number 4, Summer 1997.

Green, Madeleine F. *Minorities on Campus: A Handbook for Enhancing Diversity*. Washington, DC: American Council on Education, 1989. In Volume 5, Number 1, Fall 1996.

Hackett, Brian. *The Value of Training in the Era of Intellectual Capital: A Research Report*. New York: The Conference Board, 1996. In Volume 6, Number 4, Summer 1998.

Hampden-Turner, Charles. *Charting the Corporate Mind: Graphic Solutions to Business Conflicts*. New York: The Free Press, 1990. In Volume 2, Number 4, Summer 1994.

———. *Creating Corporate Culture: From Discord to Harmony*. Reading, MA: Addison-Wesley, 1992. In Volume 2, Number 4, Summer 1994.

Harding, Sandra, ed. *The Racial Economy of Science: Toward a Democratic Future.* Bloomington: Indiana University Press, 1993. In Volume 2, Number 4, Summer 1994.

Hawkesworth, Mary, ed. "Feminism and Public Policy." *Policy Sciences* 27, nos. 2–3 (May-August 1994). In Volume 3, Number 3, Spring 1995.

Herbst, Philip H. *The Color of Words: An Encyclopaedic Dictionary of Ethnic Bias in the United States.* Yarmouth, ME: Intercultural Press, 1997. In Volume 6, Number 1, Fall 1997.

Herek, Gregory M., Jared B. Jobe and Ralph M. Carney, eds. *Out in Force: Sexual Orientation and the Military.* Chicago: University of Chicago Press, 1996. In Volume 6, Number 1, Fall 1997; and Volume 6, Number 2, Winter 1998.

Heuterman, Thomas. *The Burning Horse: The Japanese-American Experience in the Yakima Valley, 1920–1942.* Cheney, WA: Eastern Washington State University Press, 1995. In Volume 5, Number 3, Spring 1997.

Higginbotham, Elizabeth, and Mary Romero. *Women and Work: Exploring Ethnicity and Class.* Volume 6 in the Women and Work research and policy series. Thousand Oaks, CA: Sage Publications, 1997. In Volume 6, Number 2, Winter 1998.

Hilliard, William. "Stereotypes on the Sports Page." *ASNE Bulletin* (May/June 1992): 20–21. In Volume 5, Number 3, Spring 1997.

Hine, Darlene Clark, ed. *Black Women in America: An Historical Encyclopedia.* Brooklyn, NY: Carlson Publishing, 1994. In Volume 2, Number 4, Summer 1994.

"Hispanic Culture Breaks Out of the Barrio." *Time*, Special Issue, July 11, 1988. In Volume 5, Number 3, Spring 1997.

Hofstede, Geert. "Cultural Constraints in Management Theories." *Academy of Management Executive* 7, no. 1 (1993): 81–94. In Volume 3, Number 1, Fall 1994.

Holzer, Harry J. *What Employers Want: Job Prospects for Less-Educated Workers.* New York: Russell Sage Foundation, 1996. In Volume 4, Number 4, Summer 1996.

Hopkins, Willie E. *Ethical Dimensions of Diversity.* Thousand Oaks, CA: Sage Publications, 1997. In Volume 6, Number 2, Winter 1998.

Horton, John. *The Politics of Diversity: Immigration, Resistance, and Change in Monterey Park, California.* Philadelphia: Temple University Press, 1995. In Volume 4, Number 2, Winter 1996.

*Immigrant Policy Issues for America's Cities: A 78-City Survey.* Washington, DC: United States Conference of Mayors, June 1994. In Volume 4, Number 2, Winter 1996.

Jackman, Mary R. *The Velvet Glove: Paternalism and Conflict in Gender, Class and Race Relations.* Berkeley: University of California Press, 1996. In Volume 4, Number 2, Winter 1996.

Johnson, Kirk. "Black and White in Boston." *Columbia Journalism Review* 26, no. 1 (May/June 1987): 50–52. In Volume 5, Number 3, Spring 1997.

Jordan, Winthrop. *White over Black: American Attitudes Toward the Negro, 1550–1812.* Institute of Early American History and Culture. Chapel Hill, NC: University of North Carolina Press, 1968. In Volume 3, Number 4, Summer 1995.

Judy, Richard W., and Carol D'Amico. *Workforce 2020: Work and Workers in the Twenty-First Century*. Indianapolis: Hudson Institute, Herman Kahn Center, 1997. In Volume 6, Number 2, Winter 1998.

Keever, Beverly, Ann Deepe, Carolyn Martindale and Mary Ann Weston, eds. *U.S. News Coverage of Racial Minorities: A Sourcebook, 1934–1996*. Westport, CT: Greenwood Press, 1997. In Volume 5, Number 3, Spring 1997.

Kinder, Donald R., and Lynn M. Sanders. *Divided by Color: Racial Politics and Democratic Ideals*. Chicago: University of Chicago Press, 1997. In Volume 6, Number 3, Spring 1998.

Kivel, Paul. *Uprooting Racism: How White People Can Work for Racial Justice*. Philadelphia: New Society, 1996. In Volume 5, Number 4, Summer 1997.

Knight, Margy Burns, with illustrations by Anne Sibley O'Brien. *Who Belongs Here? An American Story*. Gardiner, ME: Tilbury House, 1993. In Volume 4, Number 3, Spring 1996.

Kras, Eva S. *Management in Two Cultures: Bridging the Gap Between U.S. and Mexican Managers*. Rev. ed. Yarmouth, ME: Intercultural Press, 1995. In Volume 4, Number 2, Winter 1996.

Landsman, Gail H. "Indian Activism and the Press: Coverage of the Conflict at Ganienkeh." *American Anthropological Quarterly* (July 1987): 101–113. In Volume 5, Number 3, Spring 1997.

Lazarre, Jane. *Beyond the Whiteness of Whiteness: Memoir of a White Mother of Black Sons*. Durham, NC: Duke University Press, 1997. In Volume 6, Number 3, Spring 1998.

Lester, Paul Martin, ed. *Images that Injure: Pictorial Stereotypes in the Media*. Westport, CT: Praeger, 1996. In Volume 5, Number 3, Spring 1997.

Lew, Gena, ed. *Perspectives on Affirmative Action . . . and Its Impact on Asian Pacific Americans*. Los Angeles: LEAP Asian Pacific American Public Policy Institute, 1996. In Volume 4, Number 2, Winter 1996.

Luttrell, Wendy. "Working-Class Women's Ways of Knowing: Effects of Gender, Race and Class." *Sociology of Education* 62, no. 1 (January 1989): 33–46. In Volume 5, Number 1, Fall 1996.

Maggio, Rosalie. *The Bias-Free Word Finder: A Dictionary of Nondiscriminatory Language*. Boston: Beacon Press, 1991. In Volume 2, Number 4, Summer 1994.

Martindale, Carolyn. *The White Press and Black America*. Westport, CT: Greenwood Press, 1986. In Volume 5, Number 3, Spring 1997.

McCaffery, Edward J. *Taxing Women*. Chicago: University of Chicago Press, 1997. In Volume 6, Number 1, Fall 1997.

McLaren, Angus. *The Trials of Masculinity: Policing Sexual Boundaries, 1870–1930*. Chicago: University of Chicago Press, 1997. In Volume 6, Number 1, Fall 1997; and Volume 6, Number 3, Spring 1998.

Mellon, James. "Images of Micronesia on Film and Video." Paper presented at Pacific History Association Conference, Guam, December 1990. Honolulu: Hamilton Library, University of Hawaii, n.d. In Volume 5, Number 3, Spring 1997.

*News Watch: A Critical Look at Coverage of People of Color*. San Francisco: San Francisco State University Center for Integration and Improvement of Journalism, 1994. In Volume 5, Number 3, Spring 1997.

*NLGJA Style Guide*. Washington, DC: National Lesbian and Gay Journalists Association, n.d. In Volume 5, Number 3, Spring 1997.

Nuiry, Octavio Emilio. "Ban the Bandito!" *Hispanic* 9, no. 7 (July 1996): 26–32. In Volume 5, Number 3, Spring 1997.

Odendahl, Teresa, and Michael O'Neill, eds. *Women and Power in the Non-Profit Sector*. San Francisco: Jossey-Bass, 1994. In Volume 3, Number 3, Spring 1995.

O'Hare, William P. "America's Minorities—The Demographics of Diversity." *Population Bulletin* 47, no. 4 (December 1992). In Volume 3, Number 2, Winter 1995.

Oshry, Barry. *Seeing Systems: Unlocking the Mysteries of Organizational Life*. San Francisco: Berrett-Koehler, 1996. In Volume 4, Number 4, Summer 1996.

Pease, Ted, and J. Frazier Smith. *The Newsroom Barometer: Job Satisfaction and the Impact of Racial Diversity at U.S. Daily Newspapers*. Ohio Journalism Monograph Series, No. 1. Athens, OH: Bush Research Center, E. W. Scripps School of Journalism, Ohio University, 1991. In Volume 5, Number 3, Spring 1997.

Pierce, Carol, et al. *A Male/Female Continuum: Paths to Colleagueship*. Laconia, NH: New Dynamics Publications, 1994. In Volume 1, Number 4, Summer 1993; and Volume 2, Number 4, Summer 1994.

Portes, Alejandro, ed. *The New Second Generation*. New York: Russell Sage Foundation, 1996. In Volume 5, Number 4, Summer 1997.

Price, Deb, and Joyce Murdoch. *And Say Hi to Joyce: The Life and Chronicles of a Lesbian Couple*. New York: Doubleday, 1995. In Volume 5, Number 3, Spring 1997.

*Project Zinger: A Critical Look at News Media Coverage of Asian Pacific Americans, 1992–1994*. San Francisco: San Francisco State University Center for Integration and Improvement of Journalism, 1991, 1992, 1993. In Volume 5, Number 3, Spring 1997.

Reichheld, Fred, and Thomas Teal. *The Loyalty Effect: The Hidden Force Behind Growth, Profits, and Lasting Value*. Boston: Harvard Business School Publications, 1996. In Volume 5, Number 4, Summer 1997.

Repak, Terry A. *Waiting on Washington: Central American Workers in the Nation's Capital*. Philadelphia: Temple University Press, 1995. In Volume 4, Number 2, Winter 1996.

*Report of the National Advisory Commission on Civil Disorders*. New York: New York Times Co., 1968. In Volume 5, Number 3, Spring 1997.

*Rethinking Our Classrooms: Teaching for Equity and Justice*. Milwaukee: Rethinking Schools, July 1994. In Volume 3, Number 2, Winter 1995.

Reyes, Maria de la Luz, and John J. Halcon. "Racism in Academia: The Old Wolf Revisited." *Harvard Educational Review* 58 (1988): 299–314. In Volume 5, Number 1, Fall 1996.

Roediger, David R. *The Wages of Whiteness: Race and the Making of the American Working Class*. New York: Verso, 1991. In Volume 2, Number 4, Summer 1994.

Rotundo, E. Anthony. *American Manhood: Transformations in Masculinity from the Revolution to the Modern Era*. New York: Basic Books, 1994. In Volume 2, Number 4, Summer 1994.

Salette, Elizabeth Pathy, and Diane R. Koslow, eds. *Race, Ethnicity and Self: Identity in Multicultural Perspective.* Washington, DC: National Multicultural Institute, 1994. In Volume 3, Number 2, Winter 1995.

Schein, Edgar. *Organizational Culture and Leadership.* San Francisco: Jossey-Bass, 1985. In Volume 1, Number 4, Summer 1993; and Volume 2, Number 4, Summer 1994.

Seitchik, Vickie. *Queer Son: Family Journeys to Understanding and Love* (video). Produced and directed by Vickie Seitchik, Cape May, NJ, 1994. In Volume 3, Number 2, Winter 1995.

Stiehm, Judith Hicks, ed. *It's OUR Military, Too! Women and the U.S. Military.* Philadelphia: Temple University Press, 1996. In Volume 6, Number 2, Winter 1998.

Stone, Lynda, ed. *The Education Feminism Reader.* New York: Routledge, 1993. In Volume 5, Number 1, Fall 1996.

Stummer, Helen M. *No Easy Walk: Newark, 1980–1993.* Philadelphia: Temple University Press, 1994. In Volume 4, Number 3, Spring 1996.

Subervi-Vélez, Federico, et al. "Mass Communication and Hispanics." In Félix Padilla et al., eds., *Sociology* volume of *Handbook of Hispanic Cultures in the United States*, 304–357. Houston: Arte Público Press, 1994. In Volume 5, Number 3, Spring 1997.

Takaki, Ronald. *Strangers from a Different Shore: A History of Asian Americans.* Boston: Little, Brown, 1989. In Volume 5, Number 3, Spring 1997.

Tashlik, Phyllis, ed. *Hispanic, Female and Young* (an anthology of stories, poems, essays and interviews). Houston: Piñata Books, Arte Público Press, 1995. In Volume 5, Number 4, Summer 1997.

Tatum, Beverly Daniel. "Talking about Race, Learning about Racism: The Application of Racial Identity Development Theory in the Classroom." *Harvard Educational Review* 62, no. 1 (Spring 1992): 1–24. In Volume 5, Number 1, Fall 1996.

Terkel, Studs. *Race: How Blacks and Whites Think and Feel about the American Obsession.* New York: Bantam-Doubleday-Dell, 1993. In Volume 1, Number 4, Summer 1993; and Volume 2, Number 4, Summer 1994.

Tierney, William G. *Academic Outlaws: Queer Theory and Cultural Studies in the Academy.* Thousand Oaks, CA: Sage Publications, 1997. In Volume 6, Number 4, Summer 1998.

Torres, Andrés. *Between Melting Pot and Mosaic: African Americans and Puerto Ricans in the New York Political Economy.* Philadelphia: Temple University Press, 1995. In Volume 4, Number 2, Winter 1996.

Trahant, Mark N. *Pictures of Our Nobler Selves.* Nashville, TN: Freedom Forum First Amendment Center, 1995. In Volume 5, Number 3, Spring 1997.

Turner, Ralph, and Samuel Surace. "Zoot-Suiters and Mexicans: Symbols in Crowd Behavior." *American Journal of Sociology* 67 (July 1956): 14–20. In Volume 5, Number 3, Spring 1997.

Turow, Joseph. *Breaking Up America: Advertisers and the New Media World.* Chicago: University of Chicago Press, 1997. In Volume 6, Number 1, Fall 1997.

Valdivieso, Rafael, and Cary Davis. "U.S. Hispanics: Challenging Issues for the 1990s." *Population Trends and Public Policy*, No. 17, December 1998. Washington, DC: Population Reference Bureau. In Volume 3, Number 2, Winter 1995.

Watkins, Mel. *The Real Side: Laughing, Lying and Signifying—The Underground Tradition of African-American Humor that Transformed American Culture, from Slavery to Richard Pryor.* New York: Simon and Schuster, 1995. In Volume 2, Number 4, Summer 1994.

Weglyn, Michi. *Years of Infamy: The Untold Story of America's Concentration Camps.* New York: William Morrow, 1976. In Volume 5, Number 3, Spring 1997.

Weisgall, Jonathan. *Operation Crossroads: The Atomic Tests at Bikini Atoll.* Annapolis, MD: Naval Institute Press, 1994. In Volume 5, Number 3, Spring 1997.

Weisman, Leslie Kanes. *Discrimination by Design: A Feminist Critique of the Man-Made Environment.* Champaign: University of Illinois Press, 1994. In Volume 2, Number 4, Summer 1994.

West, Cornel. *Keeping Faith: Philosophy and Race in America.* New York: Routledge Press, 1994. In Volume 2, Number 4, Summer 1994.

———. *Race Matters.* Boston: Beacon Press, 1993. In Volume 1, Number 4, Summer 1993; and Volume 2, Number 4, Summer 1994.

Weston, Mary Ann. *Native Americans in the News: Images of Indians in the Twentieth Century Press.* Westport, CT: Greenwood Press, 1996. In Volume 5, Number 3, Spring 1997.

Wetherell, Margaret, and Jonathan Potter. *Mapping the Language of Racism: Discourse and the Legitimation of Exploitation.* New York: Columbia University Press, 1992. In Volume 6, Number 1, Fall 1997.

Wheeler, Michael. *Corporate Practices in Diversity Measurement: A Research Report.* New York: The Conference Board, 1996. In Volume 5, Number 4, Summer 1997.

Wilson, Clint C. II, and Félix Gutiérrez. *Race, Multiculturalism and the Media: From Mass to Class Communication.* Thousand Oaks, CA: Sage Publications, 1995. In Volume 5, Number 3, Spring 1997; and Volume 5, Number 4, Summer 1997.

Winfeld, Liz, and Susan Spielman. *Straight Talk about Gays in the Workplace: Creating an Inclusive, Productive Environment for Everyone in Your Organization.* New York: AMACOM, 1995. In Volume 4, Number 4, Summer 1996.

Woodward, C. Vann. *The Strange Career of Jim Crow.* 3rd rev. New York: Oxford University Press, 1974. In Volume 3, Number 4, Summer 1995.

Compiled by Margaret Blackburn White, editor, *The Diversity Factor.*

# Appendix 4

# The Language of Diversity: An Introductory Guide

American English is saturated with language that reflects our history of discriminatory attitudes and practices. As the influence of white women, women and men of color, people with disabilities, gays and lesbians, and white men who refuse to participate in these negative patterns has grown, the most blatant slurs are no longer acceptable.

However, as we all know, the slurs have not disappeared; they have just gone underground. The whole issue of who says what to whom, and where, and when; what is respectful and what is demeaning; and what language use promotes cooperative, productive interpersonal interaction, is an increasingly difficult topic. Organizations, executives and managers who are committing money and time to "managing diversity" will have to understand how unexamined language use operates—both blatantly and subtly—to undermine even the most sincere effort to change the culture.

Since we have all learned the terminology of oppression simultaneously with learning the English language, we cannot unlearn it without making a conscious effort. As Edward Sapir observed, "The 'real world' is to a large extent unconsciously built upon the language habits of the group. . . . We see and hear and otherwise experience very largely as we do because the language habits of our community predispose certain choices of interpretation."[1]

Some general principles inform the work:

1. Language usage is ever evolving. It reflects current thinking about important issues; it can also lead to changes in thinking.

2. All speakers of a language are influenced by its power to determine social status. White women and men and women of color as well as white men; people with disabilities as well as those who are nondisabled; gays and lesbians as well as nongays—all draw from the same well.

3. Negative language used within a given identity group about itself and its own members is very different from the same language used by people outside the group—though such usage is also often objectionable to group members.

4. Humor is a familiar and treacherous trap.

5. Speaking and writing appropriately is, in the main, easy. Consider: "Would I want someone to use a similar expression about me?"

6. The best way to check the appropriateness of a term is to ask a member of the group being referred to—while remembering that no one individual represents the entire group.

7. People often collude in the process of oppression by failing to challenge negative terminology about their own group and by engaging in such terminology about others.

8. Not everyone in a particular group, or everyone at a particular time, will agree on specific expressions. For example, many white people still identify themselves and their group as "Caucasians." Others find this inaccurate.

9. It's better to risk making mistakes than to pretend to have knowledge or positive attitudes that one doesn't have. Hypocrisy always shows.

10. Learning to be competent in this arena is the same as learning to be competent in anything else. It requires a desire to know, motivation to become informed, opportunities to practice, and the willingness to accept correction.

From time to time, a confluence of social forces provides unusual opportunities to create change. It may be that current shifts in demographics, the concern of the U.S. business community with increasing competition from abroad, and the coming into power of people who grew up in the civil-rights era of the 1960s are creating such opportunities.

This guide is offered as an aid in the unlearning process. We do not pretend that it is definitive or even completely consistent. It represents what we have learned to date about talking about race, ethnicity, sexual orientation and disabilities. We have included very few gender issues, since there are several excellent guides in this area.[2] It is very much a work-in-progress. We welcome suggestions for improvement.

Elsie Y. Cross, Publisher
Margaret Blackburn White, Editor
*The Diversity Factor*

**Aboriginal**. Refers to the first inhabitants of a geographical area. In Canada, used to refer to people indigenous to the area, as opposed to people of color who arrived later, who are often referred to as "visible minorities."[3] In Australia, the term, especially in the shortened form "Abo," is often considered abusive and condescending.[4]

**Accents**. The presence or absence of speech accents depends on the perspective of the hearer. Characterizing a speaker as having a "thick accent" may serve as a mechanism for defining that person as "other" and "less than." Often used as a means of stereotyping.

**Advertising**. Advertising, especially visual advertising, is often a "haven for stereotypes" that affect the public's perception of various groups, with dominant groups (whites, men) being presented as the norm, and others as deviations from the norm.[5]

**Affirmative action**. Federal laws aimed at correcting the effects of discrimination in the employment or education of members of certain groups.

**African American**. Currently preferred by many Americans of African origin; "Black" or "black" is also generally acceptable.

**Age, ageism**. Referring to a person's age in a context in which age is not relevant reinforces U.S. society's emphasis on youth as the optimum stage of life. In the work force, "older workers" become another group to be demeaned or protected. In the media, women are often designated as "grandmothers" when their maternal and grandmaternal station is irrelevant (a man in equivalent situations is rarely referred to as "father of four and grandfather of twelve").

**AIDS**. Individuals diagnosed with AIDS prefer to be identified as "people with AIDS" (PWAs) rather than as AIDS victims.

**All men are created equal**. This basic tenet of our democracy meant male persons, deliberately excluding women—not "men" used generically. And it did not include men of color.

**American**. There is more to "America" than the United States of America. Although there is no good adjective with which to replace it ("United Statesian" doesn't do it!), it is often possible to recast the sentence—"U.S. residents" or "citizens of the United States."

**Animals**. A common ploy in subordinating other groups is to depict them as subhuman and brutish. When Africans imported into slavery were depicted as "apes" it was easier to justify transporting them to the colonies like animals. This ugly image hangs on persistently. A recent example was an internal employee newsletter in a Fortune 500 company in which clients all over the world were depicted as humans except for the client in Africa—whom the illustrator—"as a joke"—depicted as a monkey.

**Anti-Semitism**. Discrimination against or persecution of Jews. (See also *Semite*.) There is an ongoing debate about whether the term should be written "anti-semitism" or "anti-Semitism." The Anti-Defamation League prefers the latter, meaning "people who are anti-Jews." Historian Richard S. Levy prefers "anti-semitism," stating that the word "Semite" was adopted in the nineteenth century to describe "a bundle of uniformly negative traits that the various enemies of the Jews insisted were the racial inheritance of every Jew." People who combat anti-Semitism, says Levy, aren't defending "Semitism," they're defending the human rights of Jews.[6]

**Arab**. Any native of the twenty-two Arab countries, or one who is a native speaker of Arabic, or one who traces one's ancestry to the Arab world. Not all Middle Easterners or Middle-Eastern Americans are Arabs. Non-Arab countries in the Middle East include Iran, Israel, Turkey and Cyprus. Not all Arabs are Muslims (many are Christians), and not all Muslims are Arabs. In fact, most Muslims live outside the Middle East—in Asia, Indonesia, Africa and North America.[7]

There are many terms used in the English language that demean Arabs. The 1993 animated Walt Disney production *Aladdin* included lyrics that were derogatory toward Arabs.[8]

**Asian American**. Appropriately used to designate people of Asian origin, when the context requires general usage. A more recent term is "Asian-Pacific American." Better, more specific usage identifies the country of origin.

**Bisexual**. An individual sexually attracted to members of both sexes. Does not presume nonmonogamy.[9]

**Black History Month**. Although special observances such as Black History Month or Year of the Woman may be helpful in calling attention to the contributions of groups of people who are often not fully recognized in our society, they may continue the marginalization process that characterizes discriminatory attitudes in the United States. The history, current concerns and accomplishments of nonwhites and nonmales are as important year-round as are the concerns and accomplishments of white men.

**Boy**. Using terms designating child status when referring to adults is derogatory. "Boy" has a long history in English of meaning someone of low or menial status, and in the United States was commonly used, especially in the South, when addressing black men. The term has presently gone underground, as society generally recognizes it as taboo. "Homeboy," a term meaning someone native to one's hometown or area, does not carry the derogatory load.

**Caucasian**. The term means, literally, "of the Caucasus, its people, or their culture" or the two independent families of languages spoken in the area of the Caucasus. "Caucasoid" (from the erroneous notion that the original home of the hypothetical Indo-Europeans was the Caucasus) once was used to designate one of the major geographical varieties of human beings, including peoples of Europe, Africa, the Near East, India, etc., generally characterized by tall stature, straight or wavy hair, etc.: loosely called the "white race" although it embraced many peoples of dark skin color.[10] Now generally discredited as an anthropological term.

"Caucasian" is not equivalent to "white."

**Chicano/Chicana**. Refers to people of Mexican-American origin. Not universally accepted, but many younger Mexican Americans use the term. For some, the term alludes to a spiritual and cultural link between Mexican Americans and

Mexico's Aztec Indians. Some older Mexican Americans consider it a derogatory term.[11]

**Closeted, in the closet**. A term used for a gay or lesbian person who chooses not to reveal his or her sexual orientation because of fear of negative consequences.

**Denigrate**. This seemingly innocuous word comes from the same Latin root as the slur "nigger." It uses the concept "blacken" to mean "disparage the character or reputation of; defame."[12]

**Discovery of America**. The idea that the continents of the Americas were ever "not discovered" reveals a narrow, Eurocentric point of view. "The implication is that the inhabitants of a 'discovered' region are so inferior or insignificant to the 'discoverers' that they may be considered as virtually non-existent."[13]

**Diversity**. The quality, state, fact or instance of being different or dissimilar. In current usage, often means being different from a straight white male norm. (See also **Managing diversity**.)

**Domestic partner**. Unmarried partners who share living quarters. Typically used in connection with legal and insurance matters related to gay and lesbian couples.[14]

**Dominant**. A term referring to a group of people who influence and control many aspects of a culture or a political system. In the United States, white people, men, heterosexuals and nondisabled people are dominant groups. The term is not synonymous with "majority"—in South Africa, for example, the minority whites held power for many years.

There is no satisfactory antonym. "Subordinate" is the grammatical opposite. However, some members of nondominant groups feel that the term implies inherent inferiority, and suggest that "subordinated" more accurately describes the condition of having been placed in an inferior position.

**Dred Scott decision**. A Supreme Court ruling written by Chief Justice Taney in 1857 that helped institutionalize racism by defining blacks as having no rights as human beings.

**English-only**. A nativist movement which promotes the idea that English should be designated the official language of the United States, and that no other languages should be recognized or used in official documents. "Nativism" is a recurrent phenomenon in the United States, promoting the interests of "natives" (but not Native Americans) over "outsiders" or immigrants. The focus of nativist prejudice shifts in response to economic, social and political trends. In the mid-nineteenth century those disparaged by the movement tended to be Germans, Irish and Catholics; after the Civil War these groups often joined earlier immigrants in resenting more recently arrived groups—Jews from central, eastern and southeastern Europe, Chinese and other Asian Americans. In more recent times, nativists object to the arrival of Spanish-speakers; therein lies the link to the English-only movement.

**Eskimos**. Appropriate for Inupiat Eskimos or Yupik Eskimos. Not relevant for Aleuts or Inuits.[15]

**Ethnic**. "An adjective describing a group of people sharing common cultural elements; also a noun for a member of such a group. . . . Usage is sometimes contradictory and elusive."[16] The most frequent abuse of the term is to connote "foreigners" or "outsiders" as distinct from "mainstream" white Americans. Also often used as a euphemism to avoid talking about discrimination based on race or skin color.

In organizations that are facing increased diversity in the work force, a common strategy is to hold "ethnic fairs" or to celebrate "ethnic holidays." Although frequently well intentioned as a strategy of inclusion, in practice this approach may deflect attention from examining discriminatory policies and practices and lead to confusion and loss of momentum.

**Ethnocentrism**. "Ethnocentrism, according to the *Random House Dictionary of the English Language*, means 'a tendency to view alien groups or cultures in terms of one's own,' and 'the belief in the inherent superiority of one's own group and culture, accompanied by a feeling of contempt for other groups and cultures.'

"All people are people. It is ethnocentric to use a generic term such as 'people' to refer only to white people and then racially label everyone else. This creates and reinforces the assumption that whites are the norm, the real people, and that all others are aberrations, and somehow a bit less than truly human.

" 'Ethnic' refers to nationality or race. Everyone's nationality or race. Margaret Thatcher, Susan B. Anthony and Bach are just as 'ethnic' as Miriam Makeba, Indira Gandhi and Johnny Colon."[17]

**Eurocentric**. Concepts or expressions that place Europe at the center of the world.

**Female** (used as noun). "Female" and "male" are terms that may refer to the biology of human beings, animals or plants, or even to plumbing fixtures. Inappropriately used as a synonym for "woman" or "women," as it tends to be dehumanizing.

**Gangs**. "An electronic database search of newspapers, magazines, wire services, broadcast outlets and newsletters archived by the Lexis/Nexis service reveals thousands of references to Asian, Chinese, Vietnamese, Hispanic, Latino, black or African-American 'gangs' and 'gangsters,' but few instances in which young white American lawbreakers are characterized as 'white' or 'Caucasian' gangsters. . . . In stories about organized young white criminals, race is deemed irrelevant, or is reported as a surprising fact. This despite FBI statistics showing that 40 percent of youths under 18 arrested for murder and intentional manslaughter in 1992 were white, and that whites accounted for 56 percent of juveniles arrested for aggravated assault during the year. . . . In some cities, Latino and African-American leaders have complained that police will label certain clothing as 'gang attire' if worn by minority youths but dismiss it as 'fashion' when donned by white youngsters."[18]

**Gay/lesbian**. The clinical term "homosexual" may be appropriate in certain contexts, but generally the terms "gay men," "lesbians," "gay people" or "gays" are preferable.[19] Gay, lesbian and bisexual people use various terms to describe their commitments. Ask the individual what term he or she prefers, if possible. If not, "partners" is generally acceptable.[20]

**Gender**. Gender refers to the different roles men and women play in society, and to the relative power they wield. According to Nancy Riley in "Gender, Power, and Population Change," there is no society in which men and women perform equal roles or hold equal positions of power. In the United States, this inequality "is reflected by a glass ceiling, which keeps most women from advancing to top levels of management. In some Asian societies, gender inequality can compromise the basic health of women in poor families because they are the last in the household to receive food and medical care.

"Gender equality has gained wide acceptance as an important goal for many countries around the world. The growing support for and attention to gender equality is bolstered by the assumption that it would improve the lives of most people, especially those of women and children."

"Gender" is usually defined as referring to those aspects of life that are shaped by social forces or to the meaning that a society gives to biological differences. "Sex" refers to the biological aspects of women and men (chromosomes, hormones, secondary sex characteristics). Riley says, "In recent years, gender has come to be described as the way that societies are organized rather than just as attributes of individuals. It is viewed as a set of social and cultural practices that influences the lives of women and men in every society."[21]

**Girl**. "As long as adult women are 'chicks,' 'girls,' 'dolls,' 'babes,' and 'ladies,' their status in society will remain inferior; they will go on being treated as subjects in the subject-master relationship."[22] (See also **Boy**.)

**Heterosexism**. The presumption that heterosexuality is superior to homosexuality, and that all individuals in a given context are heterosexual. Also: prejudice, bias or discrimination based on that presumption. Related to "homophobia," the fear, hatred or dislike of homosexuality and persons of homosexual orientation.[23]

**Hispanic**. This term was coined and institutionalized in the 1970s by U.S. government demographers (Department of Education, Office of Management and Budget, and Bureau of the Census) to refer to the growing multiracial, culturally mixed group of U.S. inhabitants with origins in any one of the many Latin-American nations. The term was created to replace previous designations, such as "Spanish" or "Spanish-surnamed," in their processes of gathering and analyzing demographic statistics used to determine public policy.

The term "Hispanic" refers to a significant part of the cultural attributes shared by this diverse group of people; the word itself implies that the most common identifying factor of this group is its Spanish (Castilian) linguistic heritage; it assumes that the main cultural point of reference of this group is that of Spain—a European culture.

Given the racialized nature of human relationships and power dynamics in the United States, the otherwise ethnic or cultural designation "Hispanic" is used instead as a racial classification. Yet because the racial paradigm is defined in terms of "white" and "black," many people seem not to know where "Hispanics" fit. This phenomenon is further complicated by even newer terms, such as "white Hispanic" and "white non-Hispanic."

A term preferred by many long-term U.S. residents is "Latino/a."[24]

When in doubt, ask.[25]

**Historiography**. The writing of history. What is included in the written history of a nation or a society is determined by the dominant group. The following passage, which appeared in the *Bismarck Tribune* in 1927, illustrates how history may be written from a perspective different from the views of the dominant culture: "On December 1st, 1927, the Grand Council Fire of American Indians presented the following remarks to the mayor of Chicago: "You tell the white men 'America First.' We believe in that. We are the only ones, truly, that are 100 percent. We therefore ask you while you are teaching school children about America First, teach them the truth about the First Americans. . . . [School histories] call all white victories 'battles,' and all Indian victories 'massacres.' . . . White men call Indians savages. What is civilization? Its marks are a noble religion and philosophy, original arts, stirring music, rich story and legend. We had all these. We sang songs that carried in their melodies all the sounds of nature, the running of waters, the sighing of winds and the calls of the animals. Teach these to your children that they may come to love nature as we love it. . . . Put in your history books the Indian's part in the [first] world war. Tell how the Indian fought for a country of which he was not a citizen, for a flag to which he had no claim and for a people who have treated him unjustly."[26]

Although many U.S. residents believe that our history books present an "objective" account of events that have taken place in this country, even a cursory examination reveals the contrary. The impact of subjective historiography is even more readily apparent when there is a turnover in power—in contemporary Russia, for example, where the history of the past fifty years is currently being reconstructed.

**Hyphenation**. Current preferred usage is to avoid using hyphens when designating groups: white Americans, black Americans, African Americans, Asian Americans and so forth. For clarity, however, it is appropriate to add a hyphen when the terms are used as adjectives: Native-American music, European-American customs, Polish-American neighborhood.

**Illegal alien**. Immigrants are not from outer space. Whether documented or undocumented, they are immigrants. The use of "alien" has a negative association that may carry over to attitudes about all immigrants or refugees from a given country, and to U.S. citizens of particular racial or ethnic groups. A better term might be "undocumented person or worker."

**Indian problem**. Or "race problem." The "problem" is not Indians or Jews or blacks or Asians or people with disabilities, etc.; the problem is prejudice, bias and hatred encapsulated by the dominant culture into discriminatory and racist systems.

**Integration**. The bringing of different racial or ethnic groups into free and equal association, seeing other people as equals, and changing systems so that all people have equal access to power.[27] While the term has traditionally related specifically to racial and ethnic groups, it is applicable to everyone—women, men, people with disabilities and the nondisabled, gays and lesbians and nongays, and so forth. The appropriate goal of diversity culture-change initiatives.

**Invisibility**. Many women and people of color have had the experience of being in meetings and being totally ignored. Ideas they present are routinely disregarded—often to turn up again in another setting as the new thought of a white man who was present. African Americans are routinely passed by when summoning taxis. Women alone are often disregarded in restaurants. Being invisible to those in power is a major barrier experienced by people in subordinated groups.

**Islam**. A religion that—like Christianity and Judaism—was born in the Middle East and is now a global religion with more than 1 billion adherents. An estimated 5 million Muslims make their homes in the United States. About 40 percent of all U.S. Muslims are African Americans; South-Asian immigrants are the next largest group, representing about 24 percent. Arab Americans comprise only about 6 percent of Muslims in this country. The majority of Muslims in this country and millions around the world have no ethnic ties to the Middle East.

   Nonetheless, media coverage of events such as the World Trade Center bombing promoted the identification of "terrorist" with "Islam" and the Middle East. In contrast, neither the Branch Davidian stand-off in Waco nor the bombing of the federal building in Oklahoma City prompted identification of "terrorists" with "Christianity."[28]

**Jewish problem**. The English language is replete with demeaning anti-Semitic expressions, carrying forward a long history of such terminology that was evident at least from the days of the Roman Empire. For many Jews, the term "anti-Semite" itself carries with it the memories of Nazism. Some offensive terms continue in common use, especially in the southern United States: To "Jew down" is an everyday expression in many places. (See also *Indian problem*.)

**Latino/Latina**. A self-defining term preferred by many long-term U.S. residents that embraces people of different Latin-American nationalities (Mexican, Puerto Rican, Cuban, etc.) and their distinct cultures, while acknowledging a shared reality of the following:

1. Their Latin-American origin, by birth or ancestry—geography.

2. The Spanish language and Spanish customs and traditions as the dominant cultural forces, with strong, albeit secondary, indigenous and African influences—culture.

3. *Mestizaje* or racial mixture: European, indigenous and African, and in some countries also Asian—race.

4. The 500-year history of colonization of Latin America by both Spain and the United States, as well as resistance to colonization—history.

5. A consciousness of a shared experience of "minority" (or subordinate) status within the race-based paradigm that prevails in the United States, in which the ideas, beliefs, values and behaviors of the "white majority" dominate in all spheres (social, political, economic and cultural) of life—institutional power.

   There is no agreement, currently, as to whether to include people from Brazil, Suriname and other South American and Caribbean nations not colonized by Spain, within this definition.[29]

**Lesbian**. An often preferred term for gay women. Some may prefer "gay."

**Macho**. This Spanish-language word for "male," when used as a biological adjective, is neutral in terms of value or power. It is often used in Latino and Latin-American cultures to mean "sexist." However, when used in English as an alternative to the word "sexist," it tends to conjure up negative stereotypes of Latino men, falsely implying that their behavior is somehow more sexist than the behavior of men of any other racial or cultural group.

**Magic words**. Ernst Cassirer pointed out that some words "do not describe things or relations of things; they try to produce effects and to change the course of nature."[30] Propaganda and its ally, scapegoating, serve this function. Nazism is the most widely known example, but there are many others. In the McCarthy era in the United States, for example, "communism" and "anti-Americanism" were used "magically" to create scapegoats. The conservative wing of southern Protestantism has preempted biblical language to exclude women from positions of leadership. Politicians routinely turn to magical language, invoking patriotism and nationalism, to enlist the emotions of the populace against whatever group is being used as scapegoat at the moment (currently, for example, immigrants, gays and lesbians, and women seeking abortions).[31]

**Male (used as noun)**. "Male" and "female" are terms that may refer to the biology of human beings, animals or plants, or even to plumbing fixtures. Inappropriately used as a synonym for "man" or "men," as it tends to be dehumanizing.

**The Man**. A term used to refer to a person in authority; especially used by black people referring to white men or to the white establishment in general.

**Managing diversity**. A term which has become widely used to refer to initiatives aimed at helping U.S. organizations come to terms with the rapidly changing demographics of the work force. The most common, but unacknowledged, connotation of the term is to "manage white women and people of color" since they are an increasingly larger percentage of workers; the underlying attitude is that it is these new and "different others" who are "the problem."

A more appropriate goal is culture change—that is, ameliorating racism, sexism and other forms of discrimination and oppression in order to create organizations and a society in which all people have equal opportunity.

**Minorities**. This term is increasingly inaccurate as well as demeaning. Logically used to connote a group whose membership is fewer in number than the majority group, it also has come to imply that the group is of less value or worth than the majority. "People of color" is a term that is currently used by those who wish to avoid the negative connotations of "minority." This term, however, though useful, is also limited, since it does not appropriately include people from groups that are discriminated against but whose skin color is white (some Latinos/Latinas, Arabs and others).

Groups designated by the U.S. government as minorities and as "socially and economically disadvantaged" are the following: black Americans, Hispanic Americans, Native Americans, Asian-Pacific Americans, or Asian-Indian Americans. ("Native Americans" are American Indians, Eskimos, Aleuts and Native

Hawaiians. "Asian-Pacific Americans" are U.S. citizens whose origins are Japanese, Chinese, Filipino, Vietnamese, Korean, Samoan, Laotian, Kampuchean, Taiwanese, or in the U.S. Trust Territories of the Pacific Islands. "Asian-Indian Americans" are U.S. citizens whose origins are on the Indian subcontinent.)[32]

**Miscegenation**. Marriage or sexual relations between a man and woman of different races. Miscegenation as a concept appeared around the time of the Civil War, and resulted in the passage of laws criminalizing mixed marriages in many states.

The concept of the criminality of sexual relations between people of different races did not appear during the era of slavery, when the practice of rape or concubinage by a white master of his African women slaves was widespread and unremarked by whites.

**Misogyny**. Hatred of women, especially by a man. Sometimes the basis of, or obscured by, religious, political or social conventions that specify "appropriate roles" for men and women.

**Model minority**. Stereotyping description of a particular subordinated group that is being favored at any given time by the dominant group. The group being favored shifts according to political trends. In the 1990s, Asian Americans are the identified target for this unfortunate designation.

The primary function of designating a given group as "model" is to position it as a buffer between the dominant group and other subordinated groups, diverting attention from the ways in which many members of the "model" group are themselves objects of discriminatory attitudes and practices. As a "divide and conquer" strategy, it has been very successful.

**Multicultural**. This term, which is often used (especially in educational settings) as a synonym for diverse, has many layers of meaning. Wetherell and Potter provide a useful discussion of the term in their study of the Maori minority and the Pakeha (white) majority in New Zealand. Their thesis is that the notion of multiculturalism, with its emphasis on being "sensitive," "tolerant," and sufficiently magnanimous and enlightened to "respect difference" and "appreciate" others, does nothing to either recognize or change the balance of power between the dominant "culture" and subordinated "cultures." The subordinated groups, no longer openly disparaged in this paradigm, are now romanticized; their "traditional" lifestyle, or culture, is seen as beautiful and valuable.

Wetherell and Potter continue, "If Maori people have culture, what do Pakeha people have as the contrast? . . . [T]he implication is that Pakeha people simply possess society. The Pakeha have 'civilization,' they have a mundane, technical and practical outlook. They have the attitudes of the modern world. These are presented not as culture, but as simple common sense." This concept "covers over the messy business of domination and uneven development. . . . There is an inevitability and acceptability in the notion of 'culture contact' not found in the rhetoric of annexation, conquest and oppression."[33]

**Multiracial**. A term designating children of interracial parentage. The subject of hot debate in the preparation for Census 2000, the term is proposed by those who assert that it is necessary to prevent forcing people to choose between parts of their heritage. Opponents assert that adding the term is another weapon in the arsenal of those who oppose affirmative action and other antidiscriminatory measures.

The ability to challenge discriminatory policies and practices depends on being able to collect, maintain and utilize information documenting those practices. Adding a multiracial category places the consistency of all the data at risk. It makes it impossible for those who are the objects of discrimination to prove their case, and it also makes it more difficult to build coalitions among the protected groups.

The multiracial category does not protect the person who chooses it from continuing to be treated by the dominant society as a member of a subordinated group. A person who has one white parent and one black parent will be discriminated against as a black; an American-Indian woman who marries a white man will find that her children are considered Indian by the white community.

**Names**. "The power which comes from names and naming is related directly to the power to define others—individuals, races, sexes, ethnic groups."[34] The power of naming is evident when we analyze what groups have been expected or required to change their names: women, on marrying; blacks sold into slavery; immigrants from Eastern Europe and from Asia, whose names are considered by the mainstream "too difficult to pronounce"; American Indians, both as a group and individually.

To use proper names respectfully, it is important both to learn how to pronounce them accurately and to recognize the significance of the order in which a given culture places personal names and surnames. When in doubt, ask! Some people choose, themselves, to anglicize their names; respect their preference.

**Native Americans**. Although this term is not universally accepted, it (or "First People") may be preferred by some to the term "American Indian," which excludes some Alaska Native groups, including Inuit and Aleut peoples who are not Indians. Many Native Americans prefer to be referred to by their specific tribal affiliation or nation.

However, many terms were imposed by others. When in doubt, ask.

The following words and phrases are often misused as well:

- Powwow. Often used as a synonym for a get-together, rather than its proper usage as a Native-American reference to a spiritual and social gathering or celebration.
- Low man on the totem pole. In addition to being sexist, the term misinterprets a religious practice. All figures on a totem pole were and are considered equal.
- Wampum. A word often used synonymously with money. In Native-American tradition, wampum belts were used to record messages, often of a historic or spiritual dimension.
- Squaw. A particularly offensive term of subjection of women.
- Discovery of America (or the "New World"). Better described as "the European invasion."
- Thanksgiving. While European Americans use this feast-day to celebrate their survival in the land they invaded, Native Americans often observe

it as a day of solemnity and sadness. Particularly offensive is the custom of adorning non-Native children with feathered headbands—an affront to many Native Americans who were raised in societies where feathers were bestowed only for exceptional deeds.[35]

To indicate that someone was born in the United States but isn't Native-American, the best term is "native-born."

**New World**. A Eurocentric term. Related inappropriate expressions: Old World, Orient, Occidental, Far East, Middle East, the West, the discovery of America.

**Numbers**. Replacing names with numbers (as in the Holocaust or in prisons) is a negation of individual humanity.

**Oppression.** *Webster's* defines the verb "oppress" as "to keep down by the cruel or unjust use of power or authority." African Americans who are familiar with the history of white oppression of blacks in the United States are apt to be most comfortable with the term as an accurate description of this history. Many white people tend to think of oppression as something that happens elsewhere, in "nondemocratic" countries. People of color who are not African-American, particularly those who are relatively recent immigrants, may not have experienced the full weight of discrimination in the United States, or may have had experiences in their native lands that counter the importance of the U.S. historical situation.

**Oriental**. Generally regarded as a Eurocentric term, identifying Asian countries and peoples as "east" of Europe (the Latin root "oriens" meaning "direction of the rising sun"). Over the years the term has collected a variety of offensive connotations. Better to use Asian American, Asian, East Asian, South Asian, Southeast Asian, or the names of specific countries.

**People with disabilities**. "Put people first, not their disability." The third edition of "Guidelines for Reporting and Writing About People with Disabilities" provides succinct suggestions, including the following:

- Do not focus on a disability unless it is crucial to a story.
- Do not portray successful people with disabilities as superhuman.
- Do not sensationalize by saying "afflicted with," "suffers from" and so on. Instead, say "person who has multiple sclerosis" or "man who had polio."
- Avoid using euphemisms. Say "blind," not "partially sighted"; "people with disabilities," not "the physically challenged."
- Say "nondisabled" rather than "normal" or "able-bodied."
- Show people with disabilities as active participants of society.[36]

**Pink triangle**. The symbol homosexual men were required to wear in Nazi concentration camps. (Lesbians were classified in various groups. Some wore black triangles.) Starting in the late 1970s, the downward-pointing, equilateral pink triangle was adopted as a symbol of gay pride.[37]

**Pluralism**. The existence within a nation or society of groups distinctive in ethnic origin, cultural patterns, religion, or the like; a policy of favoring the preservation of such groups within a given nation or society.[38] Emphasis on the term and the policy does not lead toward the removal of discrimination based on unequal distribution of power. A more democratic goal is integration (see **Integration**).

**Political correctness**. The term those who wish to maintain the status quo (oppression) use to criticize changes in the language. Such resistance usually comes from the oppressor or would-be oppressor (and may include people of color who seek personal gain in joining with members of the dominant group, or white women who cast their lot with white men) and is a tactic in the service of maintaining the power that comes from the ability to define others.

**Primitive**. When an invading or dominating group wishes to establish or maintain power over other groups, a common tactic is to designate those groups as "primitive" or "uncivilized." It is much easier to convince soldiers and settlers to disparage, discount and even kill people if they can be convinced that the "enemies" are in some basic way both "different from" and "less than" the dominating society. The most frequent use of this concept in the United States is in relation to American-Indian societies; the most vicious use is in descriptions of African societies from which slaves were taken.

An equally racist but less obvious use of the concept of primitivism is the romanticization of cultures so designated. In the United States, people who follow "New Age" thought have been particularly prone to hold such views. Native Americans, for example, may be seen as having a "simpler," "more beautiful," or "more spiritual" lifestyle, which non-Indians may attempt to mimic or adopt.

**Queer**. A term once used only pejoratively to describe gay people; now sometimes used by the gay community in a positive sense.

**Race riot**. A more accurate term for uprisings by minority groups is "rebellion." Such protests, especially when they are organized, are often described by the media as being "stirred up by outsiders" or as "agitation by troublemakers." "This type of confrontation makes for great images on the six o'clock news; however, rarely is any time given to explain the historical and cultural reasons for the protest and why the event being protested is seen as objectionable."[39]

**Racism**. The definition adopted by the Episcopal House of Bishops works well: "Prejudice + power = racism."[40] A further description is the designation of certain groups of people as subordinate by reason of skin color, in order to maintain the power of a dominant group. "In order to justify slavery in a courageous new world which was spouting slogans of freedom and equality and brotherhood, the enslavers, through their propagandists, had to create the fiction that the enslaved people were subhuman and undeserving of human rights and sympathies. The first job was to convince the outside world of the inherent inferiority of the enslaved. The second job was to convince the American people. And the third job, which was the cruelest hoax of all, was to convince the slaves themselves that they deserved to be slaves."[41] (See also *Systemic discrimination*.)

**Rainbow flag.** A flag of six equal horizontal stripes (red, orange, yellow, green, blue, and lavender or violet) adopted to signify the diversity of the lesbian and gay communities.[42]

**Religion.** Although the U.S. republic was founded on a firm concept of separation of church and state, throughout its history there has been an ongoing struggle by various groups, primarily Christian, to become the dominant religion and to gain the power to determine the standards by which its citizens should live.

**Savages.** Defining groups of people as "savages," "barbarians" or "uncivilized" allows dominant groups to justify the most brutal of acts against them. As Peter Farb has said, when such terminology is used against a people it "is an indication not so much of their depravity as that their land is up for grabs."[43]

A more subtle form of racism lies behind the term "noble savage," which "usually implies that indigenous people existed to serve Anglo society and were thankful to be 'civilized' by the Anglo Americans. Related to this is the misconception of the 'stoical Indian,' an image that often translates to a perceived lack of humor. . . . [T]he 'unsmiling Indian' was usually a 'set-up' shot composed by the photographer, usually an Anglo American, to conform to a preconceived notion."[44] The appropriation of Native-American culture and spirituality by "New Age" marketers is another example.

**Semite.** A member of any of the peoples speaking a Semitic language, including the Hebrews, Arabs, Assyrians, Phoenicians, etc. The term is derived from Shem, the oldest son of the biblical figure Noah, and dates to the early 1800s. "Anti-Semitic" (or antisemitic), however, is generally used to refer to discrimination against or persecution of Jews. (See the discussion of the appropriateness of this term under **Anti-Semitism.**)

**Sexual orientation.** Most authorities agree that a person's sexuality (gay or non-gay) is determined by a very young age and, as a rule, can be hidden but not changed in later life. "Sexual orientation" is thus a more accurate term than "sexual preference" or "sexual choice."[45] The concept that one's sexual orientation is open to choice is particularly cruel when it is part of a religious or moral system that teaches that homosexuality is immoral or evil.[46]

**Sovereignty.** Relations between Indian nations and the U.S. government are governed by treaties. The rights recognized by the treaties are not "given" to Native communities, which never relinquished these rights in the first place. It is more accurate, therefore, to use phrasing such as "upheld treaty rights" or "recognized the authority of treaty agreements" rather than verbs such as "assigned" or "allowed"—as in "Judge So-and-so's decision will allow Wisconsin Chippewas to spearfish North Wisconsin lakes."[47]

**Spokespeople.** Determining who speaks for a community and on what subjects is one way the dominant group maintains control. The following statement, aimed at assisting in appropriate media coverage of American-Indian communities, illustrates the point: "If someone tells you he or she is Indian and a spokesperson for an organization or a tribe, check it out. Ask them for proof of enrollment in an Indian tribe. It is a simple matter to check their status by calling the enrollment office of the tribe in which they claim membership. . . . Never forget that each Indian tribe has its own official spokesperson."[48]

A typical tactic of the dominant group is to identify and isolate members of subordinated groups and use them as "fronts" for positions which actually maintain the dominant group's hold on power.

**Sports**. The sports world is particularly rife with negative terms referring to various racial and ethnic groups. The most obvious is the use of names such as "Braves" or "Fighting Sioux" for sports teams, accompanied by "tomahawk chops" and descriptors such as "warpath," "warriors," "scalping," "savages," etc., to describe the action. Such language use trivializes Native Americans as human beings and makes it easier to minimize the importance of Indian concerns.[49] Consider a possible parallel: "A sports team called the Christians with a mascot dressed like the Pope, in long robes and miter, brandishing a crucifix and incense."[50]

Another issue is the frequent use of sports metaphors and analogies by men in business meetings and casual conversation. This usage tends to exclude or distance many women and men who are not sports fans.

**Stereotyping**. The process by which a fixed or conventional notion about a specific group is held by another group, allowing for no individuality or critical judgment. Stereotyping is most damaging when used as justification by the dominant group for restricting freedom or access to power for other groups.

Stereotyping is harmful to everyone, but especially to children. As Lucy Ganje says of the impact on Native Americans: "The consequences of stereotyping in both Native and non-Native communities are far-reaching. According to one Native parent, who filed a legal complaint against the use of school mascots, 'By tolerating the use of demeaning stereotypes in our public school systems, we desensitize entire generations of children.' . . . Native children have the right to grow up believing they're more than mascots for products and sports teams. They have the right to attend a football game without standing next to someone yelling, 'Scalp the Indians!' "[51]

Stereotyping is so much a part of the language that efforts to reduce or eliminate it are often perceived as "silly" or "extreme" by members of the dominant community. It is only by repeated and organized protest that the offensiveness of particular stereotypes is registered in the national consciousness. However, progress can be made. In the case of sports mascots, for example, Stanford University changed its team name from the Indians to the Cardinals, and Marquette University dropped the name Warriors.[52]

**Stonewall**. The Stonewall Inn tavern in New York City's Greenwich Village was the site of several nights of raucous protests following a police raid on June 28, 1969. Although not the nation's first gay-rights demonstration, the Stonewall incident is now regarded as the birth of the modern gay-rights movement.[53]

**Straight**. Heterosexual or nongay. Sometimes objected to by members of the gay community as connoting "normal."

**Systemic discrimination**. Patterns of discrimination that are embedded in the policies and practices of an organization and in society in general. It is helpful to think of structures of discrimination as a three-tiered process. At the individual level, one person may feel and exhibit negative attitudes and emotions—biases and prejudices—based on race, gender, sexual orientation, disability or other differences. At the group level, members of a group may hold firm beliefs about the superiority of all members of one group and the inferiority of members of other groups. These beliefs result in discrimination when they are held by a group that has power over other groups. At the system or organizational level, prejudice and bias become the "isms" (racism, sexism, heterosexism, and so forth) that define the entire culture of the organization or society.

When an organizational or societal structure is examined from this point of view, it becomes clear that negative attitudes held by members of dominant groups have a different impact from those held by members of subordinated groups. Prejudice becomes discrimination when the group holding the negative views has *power* over the other group.

**Terrorist**. "Many Middle-Eastern Americans feel that the word 'terrorist' is too often and too easily attached to people from the Middle East. Rather than use a broad over-inclusive phrase such as 'Shi-ite Muslim terrorists,' mention specific acts that qualify a group as 'terrorist.' . . . Using 'Shi-ite Muslim terrorists' to describe a militant fundamentalist religious sect is as inappropriate as using 'born-again Christian terrorists' to describe abortion clinic bombers and protesters."[54]

**Tribe (U.S.)**. "There are over 300 separate and distinct tribes and nations in the United States. Each nation has its own unique language, customs, beliefs and history. Using the term 'American Indian' to identify someone who is Lakota or Chippewa, for example, is like describing someone from Germany or France as European. And by the same token, to say someone speaks 'Indian' would be the same as saying someone speaks 'European.' One of the biggest misconceptions regarding Native people seems to be that they are all alike, that the tribes in the Pacific Northwest are the same as the southwestern nations [or] the Native peoples of the Upper Plains. This misconception fuels the notion that there can be a spokesperson for all Native people, that they all think alike. . . . Often, when Native people or tribes voice opposing views, this is shown as an example of a lack of cooperation."[55]

**White**. Simplest term for people of European origin. Not synonymous with "Caucasian." (See **Caucasian**.) "European American" or "Euro-American" are other possibilities, though some people may prefer terms more specifically identifying their country of origin: "Italian American," "Greek American." In the western United States and in southern Florida, "Anglo" is often used.

"White" has, however, been the designation often adopted by the particularly bigoted members of the dominant group to identify members—for example, "white man's burden" (the "duty" of "white men" to care for subject peoples of other races) or "white supremacy" (a doctrine espousing the cultural, political and "racial" superiority of white people over nonwhite people).

There is a curious reluctance among some white people to accept the term as a description of their group. In many cases, this reluctance, which may extend to a dislike of thinking of themselves as belonging to a group at all, derives from a tendency to think of white people as the "norm" and everyone else as "the different others." When the dominant group has to think of itself as one among many—potentially equal—groups, the reality of power relationships becomes painfully apparent. What could formerly be taken for granted as "the way things are" is then revealed for "the way things have been created and maintained."

Additional copies of this language guide are available from *The Diversity Factor*. For more information, or to order, call 201–833–0011.

## NOTES

1. Quoted in Haig Bosmajian, *The Language of Oppression* (Washington, DC: Public Affairs Press, 1974), 8.

2. See Rosalie Maggio, *The Bias-Free Word Finder: A Dictionary of Nondiscriminatory Language* (Boston: Beacon Press, 1991); and Casey Miller and Kate Swift, *The Handbook of Nonsexist Writing: For Writers, Editors and Speakers* (New York: Harper and Row, 1988). Another general aid is available via the Internet at http://newswatch.sfsu.edu/StyleGuide.html (a project of the Center for Integration and Improvement of Journalism, San Francisco State University Journalism Department).

3. See Johanne Totta, "Advancing Workplace Equality: Bank of Montreal's Integrated System," *The Diversity Factor* 3, no. 1 (Fall 1994): 2–11.

4. Philip H. Herbst, *The Color of Words: An Encyclopaedic Dictionary of Ethnic Bias in the United States* (Yarmouth, ME: Intercultural Press, 1997), s.v. "native/native people; aborigine."

5. See *Asian American Handbook*, published by the Asian American Journalists Association, Chicago Chapter, and the National Conference of Christians and Jews, Chicago and Northern Illinois Region, 1991, for an excellent discussion and illustrations of this topic.

6. Adapted from "Anti-Semitism or antisemitism?" *Copy Editor* (December 1997–January 1998), 1, 7.

7. "A Journalist's Guide to Middle Eastern Americans," a project of the Asian American Journalists Association, Detroit Chapter, n.d.

8. Herbst, *The Color of Words*, s.v. "Arab, arab, ay-rab."

9. "Stylebook Addenda: Gay/lesbian Terminology," N.p., National Lesbian and Gay Journalists Association, April 1997.

10. *Webster's New World Dictionary*, 3rd college ed., s.v. "Caucasian," "Caucasoid."

11. Judy Gerber, "News Watch Project Style Guide," s.v. "Chicano/Chicana." (http://newswatch.sfsu.edu/StyleGuide.html)

12. The negative origins of this term were called to our attention by Mark Chesler in 1998.

13. Herbst, *The Color of Words*, s.v. "discovered, discovery."

14. "Stylebook Addenda: Gay/Lesbian Terminology."

15. Gerber, "News Watch Project," s.v. "Eskimos."

16. Herbst, *The Color of Words*, s.v. "ethnic."

17. Amoja Three Rivers, "Cultural Etiquette: A Guide for the Well-Intentioned" (Auto, WV: Market Wimmin, 1991), distributed by Market Wimmin, Auto, WV 24917–9999.

18. "Gangs: Label Sometimes Applied to Minority Youth Too Quickly," *News Watch: A Critical Look at Coverage of People of Color*, a Unity '94 Project published by the Center for Integration and Improvement of Journalism at San Francisco State University, 1995, 28–29.

19. "Style Guidelines," NY: Gay and Lesbian Alliance Against Defamation, Inc. (GLAAD), n.d.

20. "Stylebook Addenda: Gay/Lesbian Terminology."

21. Nancy E. Riley, "Gender, Power, and Population Change," *Population Bulletin* 52, no. 1 (May 1997): 2.

22. Bosmajian, *Language of Oppression*, 9.

23. "Stylebook Addenda: Gay/Lesbian Terminology."

24. For this discussion, we are indebted to our friend and colleague, Raúl Quiñones-Rosado, co-director of the Institute for Latino Empowerment.

25. Laramie M. Treviño, "Sensitivity in Covering Latinos and Latino Names," prepared for Unity '94 by the National Association of Hispanic Journalists and the National Conference. Also, "Covering Hispanics," Melita Garza, vice-president/print, National Association of Hispanic Journalists, n.p., n.d.

26. Cheryl Red Eagle (Lakota), "I have spoken . . . ," *Native Directions* 4, no. 2 (Winter 1997), a publication of the Native Media Center, University of North Dakota School of Communication.

27. *Webster's New World Dictionary*, s.v. "integration."

28. "Muslims: Stereotypes, Bias Flaw Bombing Case Coverage," *News Watch: A Critical Look at Coverage of People of Color*, a Unity '94 Project published by the Center for Integration and Improvement of Journalism at San Francisco State University, 1995.

29. Adapted from Raúl Quiñones-Rosado, "Hispanic or Latino: Thoughts on the Struggle for Identity in a Race-Based Society," manuscript, 1998.

30. Bosmajian, *Language of Oppression*, 17.

31. Bosmajian's chapter, "The Language of Anti-Semitism," brilliantly traces the Nazi propaganda process, from the initial use of magical words to the "Final Solution"—the attempt to systematically exterminate a whole segment of humanity.
See also the excellent essay, "Ethnic Epithets in Society," in Philip Herbst's *The Color of Words*.

32. "Let's Do Business," United States Postal Service, Publication 5 (Washington, D.C., September 1994), 1.

33. Margaret Wetherell and Jonathan Potter, *Mapping the Language of Racism: Discourse and the Legitimation of Exploitation* (New York: Columbia University Press, 1992), 134–138.

34. Bosmajian, *Language of Oppression*, 5.

35. Quinn Owen and Nancy Butterfield (Ojibwe), "Covering Native Americans," Native American Journalists Association, n.p., n.d.

36. "Guidelines for Reporting and Writing About People with Disabilities," 3rd edition (1990). Published by the Research and Training Center on Independent Living, Media Project, Bureau of Child Research, University of Kansas,

Lawrence, KS 66045. Funded in part by National Institute of Disability and Rehabilitation Research.

37. "Stylebook Addenda: Gay/Lesbian Terminology."

38. *Webster's New World Dictionary*, s.v. "pluralism."

39. Lucy Ganje, "Native American Stereotypes," in Paul M. Lester, *Images that Injure: Pictorial Stereotypes in the Media* (Westport, CT: Greenwood Press, 1996), 37.

40. See the article of that title by Bishops Arthur B. Williams and Edward L. Lee in *The Diversity Factor* 3, no. 3 (Spring 1995): 18–21.

41. Bosmajian, *Language of Oppression*, 35–36, quoting John Oliver Killens.

42. "Stylebook Addenda: Gay/Lesbian Terminology."

43. Quoted in Bosmajian, *Language of Oppression*, 9.

44. Ganje, *Images that Injure*, 36.

45. "Style Guidelines," 3.

46. For an example of the devastating impact such a system of teaching can have on a young gay person, see Leroy Aarons, *Prayers for Bobby: A Mother's Coming to Terms with the Suicide of Her Gay Son* (New York: HarperCollins, 1995).

47. Owen and Butterfield, "Covering Native Americans," 37.

48. Tim Giago (Nanwica Kciji), "Overview on the American Indian," *Nieman Reports* (Summer 1991). Giago is also executive editor of *The American Indian and the Media*, published in 1990 by the National Conference of Christians and Jews, 100 North Sixth Street, #531-B, Minneapolis, MN 55403.

49. Owen and Butterfield, "Covering Native Americans," 37. In regard to the term "scalping," Lucy Ganje says, "Most people don't know that Europeans, not Native people, were the originators of this practice in America. In the 1700s, Massachusetts was offering bounties of 40 pounds for a male Indian scalp, and 20 pounds for scalps of females or of children under twelve years old." *Images that Injure*, 36.

50. Ganje, *Images that Injure*, 37.

51. Ibid., 38.

52. Ibid., 39.

53. "Stylebook Addenda: Gay/Lesbian Terminology."

54. "Journalist's Guide to Middle Eastern Americans," 3.

55. Ganje, *Images that Injure*, 38.

# Bibliography

Acuña, Rodolfo. *Sometimes There Is No Other Side: Chicanos and the Myth of Equality*. Notre Dame, IN: University of Notre Dame Press, 1998.

Alderfer, Clayton. *Existence, Relatedness, and Growth: Human Needs in Organizational Settings*. New York: The Free Press, 1972.

Alderfer, Clayton, with L. Dave Brown. *Learning from Changing: Organizational Diagnosis and Development*. Beverly Hills, CA: Sage Publications, 1975.

Alinsky, Saul. *Reveille for Radicals*. New York: Vintage Books, 1969.

Ball, Edward. *Slaves in the Family*. New York: Farrar, Straus and Giroux, 1998.

Benne, Ken. *The Laboratory Method of Changing and Learning: Theory and Application*. Palo Alto, CA: Science and Behavior Books, 1975.

Benne, Ken, with Leland P. Bradford and Jack R. Gibb. *T-Group Theory and Laboratory Method: Innovation in Re-education*. New York: Wiley, 1964.

Benne, Ken, with Leland P. Bradford and Ronald Lippett. *Group Dynamics and Social Action*. New York: Anti-Defamation League of B'nai B'rith, 1960.

Bennis, Warren G., Kenneth D. Benne and Robert Chin, eds. *The Planning of Change: Readings in the Applied Behavioral Sciences*. New York: Holt, Rinehart and Winston, 1976.

Catalyst. *Labor Day 1998 Fact Sheet*. New York: Catalyst, 1998.

———. *Women of Color in Corporate Management: A Statistical Picture*. New York: Catalyst, 1998.

Chesler, Mark, J. Winter and J. Rabow. *Vital Problems for American Society*. New York: Random House, 1968.

Clark, Kenneth. *Dark Ghetto*. New York: Harper and Row, 1965.

———. "Desegregation: An Appraisal of the Evidence." *The Journal of Social Issues* 9, no. 4 (1953).

———. *Prejudice and Your Child*. Boston: Beacon Press, 1963.

Cross, Elsie Y., et al. eds. *The Promise of Diversity*. New York: Irwin, 1994.

Davis, Angela. *Women, Race and Class*. New York: Random House, 1981.

de Beauvoir, Simone. *The Second Sex*. Translated and edited by H. M. Parshley. New York: Alfred A. Knopf, 1953.

Ezorsky, Gertrude. *Racism and Justice: The Case for Affirmative Action*. Ithaca, NY: Cornell University Press, 1991.

Fanon, Frantz, *Studies in a Dying Colonialism*. Translated by Haakon Chevalier. New York: Monthly Review Press, 1965.

———. *The Wretched of the Earth*. Preface by Jean-Paul Sartre. Translated by Constance Farrington. New York: Grove Press, 1963.

Franklin, John Hope. *Color and Race*. Boston: Houghton Mifflin, 1968.

Franklin, John Hope, with Alfred A. Moss, Jr. *From Slavery to Freedom: A History of African Americans*. New York: Alfred A. Knopf, 1994.

Freire, Paulo. *Pedagogy of the Oppressed*. Translated by Myra Bergman Ramos. New York: Continuum, 1970.

Friedan, Betty. *The Feminine Mystique*. New York: Norton, 1963.

Frost, Delyte. "Grow Your Own: Strategies for Internal Consultation." *The Diversity Factor* 4, no. 1 (Fall 1995): 35–37.

———. "A Special Place for White Women Only." Unpublished paper prepared for Elsie Y. Cross Associates, Inc., Philadelphia; PA, 1973; revised 1976, 1987.

Gibb, Jack R. *Trust: A New View of Personal and Organizational Development*. Los Angeles: Guild of Tutors Press, 1978.

Greco, Rosemarie. "The View from the Top." *The Diversity Factor* 2, no. 3 (Spring 1994): 43–45.

Hine, Darlene Clark, and Kathleen Thompson. *A Shining Thread of Hope: The History of Black Women in America*. New York: Broadway Books, 1998.

hooks, bell. *Ain't I a Woman? Black Women and Feminism*. Boston: South End Press, 1981.

———. *Feminist Theory: From Margin to Center*. Boston: South End Press, 1984.

———. *Outlaw Culture: Resisting Representations*. New York: Routledge, 1994.

———. *Talking Back: Thinking Feminist, Thinking Black*. Boston: South End Press, 1989.

Hyater-Adams, Yvette. "Toe to Toe: Diversity Meets Re-engineering." *The Diversity Factor* 4, no. 2 (Winter 1996): 24–28.

Hyater-Adams, Yvette, and Delyte D. Frost. "Partnership for Change at Core-States Financial Corp." *The Diversity Factor* 6, no. 4 (Summer 1998): 42–47.

Johnson, Kevin. *How Did You Get to Be Mexican? A White/Brown Man's Search for Identity*. Philadelphia: Temple University Press, 1998.

Johnston, William B., et al. *Workforce 2000: Work and Workers for the Twenty-First Century*. Indianapolis: Hudson Institute–U.S. Department of Labor, 1987.

Jung, Carl. *The Archetypes and the Collective Unconscious*. Translated by R.F.C. Hull. Princeton, NJ: Princeton University Press, 1968.

Kanter, Rosabeth Moss. *Men and Women of the Corporation*. New York: Basic Books, 1977.

Kinder, Donald R., and Lynn M. Sanders. *Divided by Color: Racial Politics and Democratic Ideals*. Chicago: University of Chicago Press, 1997.

Kirkham, Kate. "Dimensions of Diversity: A Basic Framework." Unpublished paper prepared for Elsie Y. Cross Associates, Inc., Philadelphia, PA, 1986.
———. "Managing Diversity and the Performance Appraisal Process." Elsie Y. Cross Associates, Inc., Philadelphia, PA, 1983.
Larsen, Terrence. "Moving On: A CEO's Reflections." *The Diversity Factor* 6, no. 4 (Summer 1998): 47–49.
Loewen, James W. *Lies My Teacher Told Me: Everything Your American History Textbook Got Wrong.* New York: The New Press, 1995.
Maslow, Abraham. *Toward a Psychology of Being.* Princeton, NJ: Van Nostrand, 1962.
Miller, Alice. *For Your Own Good: Hidden Cruelty in Child-Rearing and the Roots of Violence.* Translated by Hildegarde Hannum and Hunter Hannum. New York: Farrar, Straus and Giroux, 1983.
———. *Prisoners of Childhood.* Translated by Ruth Ward. New York: Basic Books, 1981.
———. *Thou Shalt Not Be Aware: Society's Betrayal of the Child.* Translated by Hildegarde Hannum and Hunter Hannum. New York: Farrar, Straus and Giroux, 1984.
O'Hare, William P. "America's Minorities—The Demographics of Diversity." *Population Bulletin* 47, no. 4 (December 1992).
O'Hare, William P., et al. "African Americans in the 1990s." *Population Bulletin* 46, no. 1 (July 1991).
O'Reilly, Kenneth. *Nixon's Piano: Presidents and Racial Politics from Washington to Clinton.* New York: The Free Press, 1995.
Oshry, Barry. *Seeing Systems: Unlocking the Mysteries of Organizational Life.* San Francisco: Berrett-Koehler, 1995.
Perls, Frederick, with Ralph E. Hefferline and Paul Goodman. *Gestalt Therapy: Excitement and Growth in the Human Personality.* New York: Dell, 1951.
Quigley, Patricia. "Coming Out: One Woman's Story." *The Diversity Factor* 2, no. 2 (Winter 1994): 34–35.
Rogers, Carl. *On Becoming a Person.* Boston: Houghton Mifflin, 1961.
Sargent, Alice. *The Androgynous Manager.* New York: AMACOM, 1981.
———, ed. *Beyond Sex Roles.* St. Paul: West Publishing, 1985.
Schein, Edgar. *The Art of Managing Human Resources.* New York: Oxford University Press, 1987.
———. *Organizational Culture and Leadership.* San Francisco: Jossey-Bass, 1985.
Schein, Edgar, with Warren Bennis. *Personal and Organizational Change Through Group Method: The Laboratory Approach.* New York: Wiley, 1965.
Shaw, Graham. "Gaining from Diversity." *The Diversity Factor* 7, no. 1 (Fall 1998): 16–18.
Stalvey, Lois Mark. *The Education of a WASP.* New York: William Morrow, 1970.
Strong, Shirley, and Cynthia Chavez. "Project Change." *The Diversity Factor* 7, no. 2 (Winter 1999): 2–7.
Swanger, Clare C. "Perspectives on the History of Ameliorating Oppression and Supporting Diversity in United States Organizations." In *The Promise of Diversity,* edited by Elsie Y. Cross et al. Burr Ridge, IL: Irwin Professional Publishing and NTL Institute, 1994.

Vakoufari, Marthe. "Sweden 2000: A Public-Private Partnership." *The Diversity Factor* 6, no. 1 (Fall 1997): 2–5.

White, J. P. "Elsie Cross vs. the Suits: One Black Woman Is Teaching White Corporate America to Do the Right Thing." *Los Angeles Times Magazine*, August 9, 1992.

White, Margaret Blackburn. "Gender Integration in the Canadian Military." *The Diversity Factor* 6, no. 2 (Winter 1998): 4–5.

———. "Leadership for Workforce 2000: The CoreStates Experience." *The Diversity Factor* 1, no. 4 (Summer 1993): 26–31.

———. "Project Change." *The Diversity Factor* 4, no. 3 (Spring 1996): 41–46.

Zander, Alvin Frederick. *Groups at Work*. San Francisco: Jossey-Bass, 1977.

———. *Motives and Goals in Groups*. New York: Academic Press, 1971.

———. *Organizational Psychology*. New York: Academic Press, 1971.

Zander, Alvin Frederick, and Dorwin Cartwright. *Group Dynamics: Research and Theory*. New York: Harper and Row, 1968.

Zhou, Lian. "Shanghai Fleetguard: Diversity and the Joint Venture." *The Diversity Factor* 3, no. 4 (Summer 1995): 18–22.

# Index

Multilevel analysis, 181–82
Multinational corporations, 160–64
Murray, Bob, 127, 129

Napier, Rodney, 41; and Matti K.
  Gershenfeld, *Groups, Theory and Ex-
  perience* (1973), 46n. 26
National Association for the Advance-
  ment of Colored People (NAACP),
  34
National Organization for Women
  (NOW, 1966), 38
National Training Laboratories (NTL),
  25–26, 28–29, 42, 46n. 29, 143
Native Americans, barred from access
  to rights, 15
New Age, irrelevancy of, 43
*Nixon's Piano: Presidents and Racial
  Politics from Washington to Clinton*
  (1995, O'Reilly), 44n. 1
Norms, 9; identification, 105; list 106;
  perceptions, 107
*No Stone Unturned: The Life and Times
  of Maggie Kuhn* (1991, Kuhn), 46n.
  23

Office of Integration and Intergroup
  Education (Philadelphia), 25–26
O'Hare, William P., Works: "African
  Americans in the 1990s" (1991),
  165n. 1; "America's Minorities—the
  Demographics of Diversity" (1992),
  166n. 10
"Old boy's club," 78; resistance to
  change of, 26
*On Becoming a Person* (1961, Rogers),
  46n. 28
Oppression, 3, 26, 154; amelioration
  of, 4–5; cycles of, 51; continuation
  of, 148; dynamics of, 87; history of
  36, 141–42; and managing diversity,
  36; and "mixed race," 159–60; personal experience of, xi; racism and
  sexism as most pervasive forms of,
  xii, 74; reality of, 13–14, 143; systemic, 19; theories, 32
O'Reilly, Kenneth, *Nixon's Piano*
  (1995), 44n. 1, 45n. 11

Organizational change intervention,
  components of, 87
*Organizational Culture and Leadership*
  (1985, Schein), 46n. 27, 114n. 1
Organizational culture review, com-
  ponent of Managing Diversity In-
  tervention, 8
Organization development, 40–42, 142–
  43, 167–76; early limitations, 41; im-
  pact on managing diversity, 31;
  tools, 3
*Organizational Psychology* (1965,
  Schein), 46n. 27
Oshry, Barry, *Seeing Systems: Unlock-
  ing the Mysteries of Organizational
  Life* (1996), 91n. 4
*Outlaw Culture: Resisting Representa-
  tions* (1994, hooks), 45n. 19
"Owning the work," 53
Organizing, 6, 23–26

Parameters, 8
Parks, Rosa, 32
Partnerships in diversity initiatives,
  90, 114
Passing for white, 16–18
Pay equity policies and diversity, 7
*Pedagogy of the Oppressed* (1970, Freire), 33, 44n. 4
Peer-counseling system, 67
People of color: assignment to lower
  group, 86; as citizens, 14; as collaborators, 9; as gatekeepers, 88; "im-
  porting" (for managing diversity
  workshops), 28; interviews of, 96;
  and money, 164; painful experiences
  of, 6; perceptions of, 4, 105; relation
  of white women to, 152–54; struggles of in mid-twentieth century, 32;
  as subordinated group, x, 5
People Task Force (CoreStates Financial Corp), 127–30
People with disabilities: as citizens, 14;
  as collaborators, 9; as subordinated
  group, x
Performance: appraisal of, 62–68, 104;
  standards, need for change of, 109–
  10

## About the Author

ELSIE Y. CROSS is founder and president of Elsie Y. Cross Associates, Philadelphia, Pa., an organization development consulting firm. A member and former chairperson of the National Training Laboratories of Applied Behavioral Science (NTL) and member of the Organization Development Network, she holds master degrees in business and in psycho-educational processes from Temple University. Ms. Cross has consulted to national, state, and local governments, governmental agencies and educational institutions, and lists among her many corporate clients a number of Fortune 500 companies in petro-chemicals, pharmaceuticals, communications, power, and manufacturing. This is her third book.